A glossary of computing terms

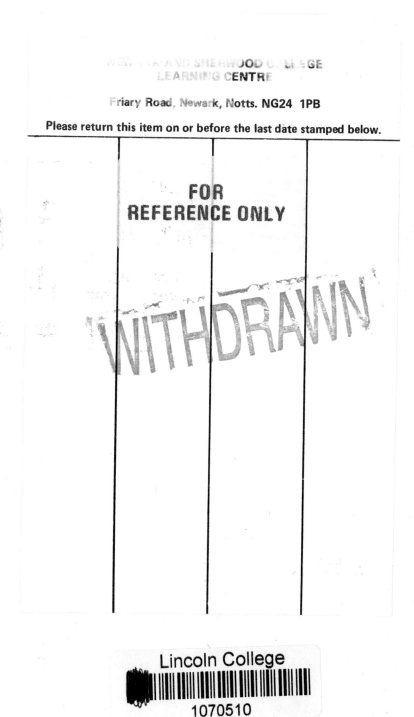

A glossary of computing terms

Ninth edition

Edited by
The British Computer Society Schools Committee
Glossary Working Party

Members of the working party

Arnold Burdett

Diana Burkhardt

John Cushion

Aline Cumming

Alan Hunter

Frank Hurvid

Thomas Ng

Tim Reeve (Chairman)

John Southall

Former members of the working party
(whose work is included in this edition)

Brian Jackson

John Jaworski

Graham Rogers

LONGMAN

on behalf of the British Computer Society

Addison Wesley Longman Limited
Edinburgh Gate, Harlow
Essex CM20 2JE, England
and Associated Companies throughout the world

© British Informatics Society Ltd 1998

First published by the British Computer Society 1977
Fourth, fifth and sixth editions published by Cambridge University Press
Seventh Edition published by Pitman Publishing 1991
Eighth Edition published by Longman Group 1995
Ninth Edition published by Addison Wesley Longman 1998
Second impression 1998

British Library Cataloguing in Publication Data
A catalogue entry for this title is available from the British Library

ISBN 0-582-36967-3

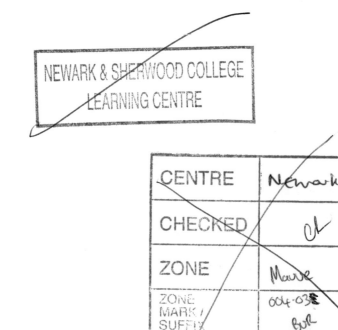

Printed in Singapore (JBW)

Contents

Part C   How Computer Systems Work   *167*

Part D   Appendices   *329*

How to use this glossary

Each term which is defined appears in the comprehensive index, and many users will make this their main method of access to the definitions.

All definitions are preceded by a readily picked out **bold** heading.

Many definitions include associated terms, in these cases the principal definition is immediately followed by an *italic line* which lists terms whose definitions are included in the main term. Terms defined in this embedded way are printed in ***bold italic*** type in the text of the definition. For example, on page 10, the definition of 'Export' reads:

Export
> *including: import*
> is to create a file using one piece of software so that it can be read by a different piece of software. ***Import*** is the corresponding read.........

Where there are alternate terms with the same meaning, the one judged to be least common, is in an *italic line* after its more common synonym. In addition, some definitions contain 'nested definitions' which are set out in the form of sub-paragraphs. In all cases the defined terms have been printed in ***bold italic*** to make them easy to find. For example, on page 28, the definition of 'Graphics tablet' contains the alternative term *graphics pad* and the terms ***Stylus*** and ***Puck*** nested within it:

Graphics tablet
> *also known as: graphics pad*
> *including: stylus, puck*
> is a device ... ...
>
> ***Stylus*** is the name ......
>
> ***Puck*** is a ... ...

Two main forms of cross referencing have been used:

(1) 'see above' or 'see below' – used when the term referred to is to be found on the same page, and

(2) 'see page nn' – used when the term referred to is to be found on another page.

Terms that are being referenced are put in *italics* to draw attention to them, for example, the definition of 'Micro-spacing', on page 11, includes:

'..inserting small amounts of *soft space* (see page 10) in order to...'

Where the reference to an associated term is suggested, it is usually in the form of a separate sentence: 'See also *this term*, page nn.'

All acronyms and abbreviations used in definitions, and many others, are collected together alphabetically in Section D1.

Introduction

The story of the origins of the *Glossary* have been included in the introductions to previous editions. It is still worth reprinting part of the Introduction to the sixth edition.

> *When a conference of the Regional Examining Boards, meeting in 1974, invited the British Computer Society to produce a standardised list of terms for use in computer studies courses and examination syllabi, the Working Party thought in terms of a 'once-off' document containing about 100 terms. There were no O-level courses, only one A-level examination and a small number of CSE syllabi in existence, and those schools involved in computer studies relied on batch processing using punched cards or, for a few fortunates, an on-line terminal connecting them to the local authority computer. Microcomputers were just beginning to appear.*

> *As soon as work on the first edition of the* Glossary *commenced, it was decided to include a simple and concise definition of each term that was unique to computing as well as a list of preferred terms and so the first edition appeared in 1977 containing some 430 terms of which 260 were defined.*

The *Glossary* proved so popular that it was obvious that further editions would be needed to include the new terms appearing almost daily due to the rapid development of the technology and the increasing use of computers in education.

Previous editions found wide acceptance at universities, colleges and industrial training departments as well as in schools and the *Glossary* has been a definitive reference specified in many examination board syllabuses. The continuing process of change in syllabuses for examinations at all levels and the rapid extension of the vocabulary of computing and IT, particularly Internet terminology, made it necessary to update the eighth edition now. The working party has tried to ensure that the *Glossary* meets the needs of students following courses leading to examinations at GCSE, AS and A levels as well as other courses at similar levels.

This ninth edition has a new section on the Internet but retains the same structure and much of the same material as the eighth edition. There is a long-standing vocabulary of communications but there has recently appeared a whole range of new terms, many of which may not survive the life of this edition. We have made decisions about which terms to include and time alone will tell whether we were right. Other terms have been considered but not included since it was judged either that their use in schools and colleges was not yet justified, or that the terms themselves lacked consistent use.

The Working Party is conscious of the need to provide definitions which cover the use of terms in the context of large computer systems as well as the world of microcomputers, even though for many school and college students large computer systems are outside their practical experience.

It must be stressed that it is not intended that the *Glossary* should be used as a textbook. Although many groups of definitions have been expanded to provide more than just a bare definition, in the hope of providing a wider and clearer understanding of the term, these expanded definitions cannot cover all the aspects appropriate to any topic. A standard text should always be consulted for fuller explanations.

The Working Party would welcome offers from teachers willing to involve their students in a review of this edition. Comments on this edition and contributions or suggestions for future editions will be gratefully received and should be sent to the glossary working party:

by post to:	The Registrar, BCS, 1 Sanford Street, Swindon SN1 1HJ
on email:	bcsglossary@hq.bcs.org.uk
BCS WWW page is:	http://www.bcs.org.uk

Alternatively contact any member of the Working Party through BCS.

Part A
How Computer Systems Are Used

This section contains terms which may be met by any computer user working with applications in any of the areas covered. Some sections in Part A are concerned with general issues and others with well defined areas of computer use. Some sections contain terms which might have been placed in Part B or even in Part C, but they were kept with other related terms for completeness; this is particularly true of the sections covering the Internet, sound and user interfaces, which have become more prominent aspects of computer use since the previous edition was published. Some terms have references to terms in Part B or Part C which will provide readers with pointers to other associated terms and concepts.

A1 Data Processing (DP)

Other concepts related to the design and implementation of systems to carry out commercial data processing are found in several later sections, especially C1 Systems Design and Life-Cycle, C2 Systems Documentation and C3 Management and Manipulation of Data.

Data Processing in its broadest – and technically correct – sense covers every task which a computer carries out. Traditionally its meaning has been restricted to those particular computing applications and activities concerned with business and commerce.

The computing needs of business and commerce are very different from scientific computing, where complex mathematical calculations are performed, or indeed the personal computing needs of an individual, where the computer is a tool for use by a single person.

In many business applications, quite simple tasks are carried out but repeated for a very large number of individual transactions. For example, working out one person's pay is not difficult but it has to be done for all employees, each week or month. Typical of such application areas are accounting, payroll, record keeping, route planning, stock control.

A data processing department has to provide a cost-effective and efficient service without expensive errors. The main elements in data processing involve automated data collection, prevention of errors, security of data and procedures to collect, process and use large amounts of information. The terms discussed in this section reflect this focus.

The user organisations typically associated with these traditional data processing applications are banks, government departments and a wide range of businesses. For any particular application type (for example, payroll), there is often a standard package, although there may be many variations of it available. Although all users will need to use a particular type of package to do the same job, they may require a specific version because they have different hardware or operating systems or because they need to use the package in association with another application area.

In addition to its meaning as an operation, 'data processing' is also used as the title for the section of an organisation which carries out this area of work. Most data processing departments will have a Data Processing Manager and a small team of support staff. These will have responsibility for seeing that the system provides a satisfactory service for the users, who may be either individuals or other departments. However, the individual departmental users are responsible for defining those data processing tasks which the system is required to carry out for them. The maintenance of the whole system, both hardware and software, may be done by specialist employees of the organisation or by external contractors.

Data preparation

is the input of large quantities of data into a computer system for further processing. Input may be automatic, for example by scanning optical mark sense forms, or manual, when the data is typed and verified ready for processing. Data preparation is often performed by a smaller computer system to input the data (see *key-to-disk system*, page 117). It is normal for all data to be entered before any is processed.

Direct Data Entry (DDE)

is the input of data directly into a computer system for immediate processing. Unlike a *data preparation* system (see above), where the data is stored for later processing, direct data entry is used when data needs to be available quickly to other users. As each set of data is entered it will be processed.

Data capture

is the action of collecting and inputting data for use in a computer. This may be done automatically, as in the scanning of bar codes in a shop, or manually as in a gas meter reading. See also *data capture* in A10 Control, page 54.

Article number

including: ISBN, UPC, EAN

is the number given to a particular product (e.g. the *International Standard Book Number (ISBN)* found on a book). This is often printed together with its *bar code* representation (see below), so that it can be read both by people and automatically by a *bar code reader* (see page 116/7) or some other *point-of-sale terminal* device (see page 156). The numbers are usually structured, and there are international agreements on how the numbers should be constructed for various types of goods. Two common forms of numbering systems are the *Universal Product Code (UPC)* and the *European Article Number (EAN)*.

Bar code

is a pattern of parallel lines of different thickness used to represent a code number, which can then be read automatically. It is a very cost-effective way of inputting data into a computer. For example, the article number printed on the back cover of this book is given with its bar code version above it.

It is often used by shops to identify a product at the *point-of-sale terminal* (see page 156) so that its price can be found automatically from a computer. This is an alternative to a manual system where prices are marked on goods and the prices are entered through a keypad. See also *article number*, above.

Kimball tag

is a small punched card attached to merchandise, which is detached when goods are sold, to provide machine-readable sales data. The tag is returned to the computer centre where it will be read by the computer to provide sales and stock data. See also *article number*, above. In many cases they have been replaced by bar codes.

Magnetic stripe card

also known as: magnetic card

is a card with a machine-readable *magnetic stripe* (see page 116) which can hold coded information. The initial use of these cards was by banks for credit cards and cash cards. This card format has been adopted for many other uses such as train and car park exit tickets. The information on the magnetic stripe can be used as input data for a computer. See also *keycard* and *PIN number*, page 104.

Smart card

is a plastic card with a microprocessor sealed inside it. The card is the standard size used for cards such as credit cards. The microprocessor has all the components of a computer manufactured as a single *integrated circuit* (see page 298). Special card readers can communicate with the microprocessor on the card allowing data to be securely stored and accessed.

A smart card is much more flexible than a *magnetic stripe* card (see above), in particular it can:

- hold more information and can alter it as required;
- encrypt the data, making it difficult to be understood by unauthorised users (see *encryption*, page 104);
- ensure that a user is authorised to perform a particular action by the use of various security checks.

Electronic money

including: Mondex

is the use of a *smart card* (see above) to replace traditional money such as coins and banknotes. The card would have money transferred to it electronically by a special *automatic teller machine* (see page 51). Money would then be transferred from the card to a shopkeeper's point-of-sale terminal by a special card reader when money is spent. Although credit and debit cards allow a person to buy goods without having to handle large amounts of cash, they really only provide a cheap method of transferring money from one bank account to another, which is otherwise expensive. Electronic money however, is stored on the smart card and can be used as easily and cheaply as traditional money. *Mondex* is currently one of the principal systems of electronic money.

Turnaround document

is printed by a computer and then used to record additional data to be input into a computer later. This has several advantages:

- the data identifies the information accurately (it came from the computer system);
- the printed data only needs altering if wrong;
- errors, for example due to poor handwriting, are reduced;
- the additional data may be simple enough to read automatically, for example using mark sense reading.

Data verification

including: verifier

is the act of checking transferred data – usually at the stage of input to a computer – by comparing copies of the data before and after transfer, for example by repeating the keyboard operations to check that the data has been correctly transferred in a *key-to-disk system* (see page 117). Where a separate device performs verification, it is called a *verifier*. Other methods of verification, such as *control totals* and *hash totals* (see page 192), operate on batches of data.

Transaction

is the data and processes needed to update a computer system to reflect a single change in the information held. A single change in the information can involve several changes, or additions, to the data physically stored in the computer system. There may be other changes such as to indexes used by the computer system. A transaction usually refers to a single piece of financial data or changes to a single *entity* (see page 20) in a database system.

Post a record

is the action to confirm that the *transaction* (see above) being entered is to be stored in the computer system. This usually occurs in finance systems to ensure accuracy and prevent fraud.

Before a record is posted the data can be checked and altered. When it has been posted, a record is added to the datafile and it can no longer be altered. Any change must be made by posting a new record containing the change.

Backup

is making copies of data or programs in case the originals are corrupted or lost. If the system fails it can be rebuilt with accurate data. Backups should be made regularly and provision made for any changes made after the last backup; these backups may be paper records, files in the *grandfather-father-son* method (see page 189) or the use of a *journal file* (see page 169).

A backup of the total software of the system will be stored separately from the computer as a safeguard against physical dangers such as fire or hardware failure. However backups of individual data may simply be additional files stored on the computer system.

Archive

is the storage of information for long periods of time. The data is likely to be compressed to take less space and stored on a cheaper storage medium such as *magnetic tape* (see page 125) or optical disks (see *optical disk storage*, page 121), freeing space on the main computer system. It can be accessed if needed, but is not so easily available as the original information. There are legal requirements on most businesses to keep data for several years and so old data will be archived.

Computer bureau

is an organisation which offers a range of computing services for hire (for example, data preparation, payroll processing). Bureaux usually offer two types of service: they provide computing facilities for organisations which do not have any of their own and they also offer specialist services covering vital common operations (for example, payroll) to organisations which do not have the appropriate piece of applications software.

Management Information Systems (MIS)

are designed to provide small amounts of management-level information – such as summaries of the larger amounts of data which individual user departments might require. This type of information may typically be used by managers as an aid to monitoring budgets, assessing sales targets or making business decisions.

Decision Support Systems (DSS)

are refined *management information systems* (see above) where the emphasis is on providing senior management with key information for strategic decision making. Such systems use sophisticated analysis techniques and may include *expert systems* (see pages 76 and 77).

Information processing

is the organisation, manipulation and distribution of information. As these activities are central to almost every use of computers, the term is in common use to mean almost the same as 'computing'.

Information Technology (IT)

including: ICT (Information and Communications Technology)
is the application of appropriate (enabling) technologies to information processing. The current interest centres on computing, telecommunications and digital electronics. In the UK schools sector the preferred term is *ICT (Information and Communications Technology)*.

Software

including: applications program, applications package, generic software, productivity tool, content free software, framework program
consists of programs, routines and procedures (together with their associated documentation) which can be run on a computer system.

An *applications program* is a computer information system designed to carry out a task (such as keeping accounts, editing text) which would need to be carried out even if computers did not exist.

An *applications package* is a complete set of applications programs together with the associated documentation (see *user documentation*, page 92 and 94). Where the application is appropriate to many areas, it is usual to describe it as *generic software* or as a *productivity tool*. For example, *word processing* (see page 9) can be used in personal correspondence, the production of business 'form letters', academic research, compilation of glossaries, writing books, etc.

Content free software, or *framework program*, can be adapted by a user for a range of unrelated tasks. For example, a program to provide help facilities may also be used to provide an index or may be used independently to provide a simple electronic book. The software does not start with any data, but is a tool to present data to the users requirements.

See also *systems software*, page 271.

Integrated package
also known as: integrated program
is a single piece of software which provides a user with basic information processing functions. It usually provides for word-processing, spreadsheets and small databases and may include additional facilities such as charts, a diary and communications. It is designed so that data can be easily moved between the various parts enabling complex tasks to be performed easily.

File filter
also known as: file loader, file converter, format translator
is software which converts data from one format to another. This allows an application to use data prepared using a different software application. Usually the filter works transparently, without user intervention, as the file is loaded into the application. See also *user transparent*, page 91.

File filters often exist to allow a file to be saved in a format suitable for use in a different application. See also *file*, page 187.

Graphics filter
is a special form of *file filter* (see above) which allows the loading, and sometimes saving, of graphical image files. There are many different formats for graphical image files and appropriate filters are very important in enabling images to be transferred between applications. See also *GIF*, page 44, and *JPEG*, page 311.

Embedded system
is the use of a computer system built into a machine of some sort, usually to provide a means of control. The computer system is generally small, often a single microprocessor with very limited functions. The user does not realise that instructions are being carried out by a computer but simply that there are controls to operate the machine. Examples are electronic washing machines, video recorders, burglar alarms and car engine management systems.

Outsourcing

is the purchase of services from outside contractors rather than employing staff to do the tasks. Traditionally large computer organisations have employed many staff such as *systems analysts* and *programmers* (see section A18 Computer Personnel, page 96). It may be more economic to contract another organisation to provide these services and not have the expense and complication of direct employment of staff.

Facilities management

is the contracting of the computer operations to an outside organisation. The facilities management company employ the staff, run the operation and often own the computer hardware. The contract for this kind of service will specify what the computer system must provide for the fee charged.

A2   Word Processing (WP)

*For details of printing and display devices used in word and
document processing applications, see sections B4 Display Devices
and B5 Printers.*

Word Processing is the application of computing to the editing, formatting and
production of typed letters and documents, including the addition of stored text (for
example, for personalised circulars). A system dedicated to this application is often
referred to as a **word processor**. An alternative to a word processor when only very
limited formatting is needed is a text editor.

   Document Processing is an extension of the formatting functions which have been
common to word-processing packages for some years, in order to allow the integration
of non-textual characters into the layout. Associated with this extension has been the
use of bit-mapping or pixel-mapping to take advantage of the ability of extremely high
definition monitors and of laser-printer techniques to produce fine lines, graduated
density and (where necessary) apparently continuous spectrum colour.

   Typical document production will include diagrams, graphic characters, numeric,
picture representation and symbols as well as text. The software associated with
Document Processing needs to be able to manipulate areas of the document as if it
were a single entity – analogous to alphanumeric character manipulation in text
processing.

   A general requirement of computers which run document processing systems is an
abundance of memory and a fast processor.

Cut & paste
including: clipboard, notepad
is the technique of transferring a section of data (text in a word processor, or diagrams
and text in a page make-up package) from one part of a document to another part of
the same document, or to another document. In some systems the data is held in a
temporary storage area called the *clipboard* or *notepad*. Data held in these storage
areas will normally remain there until overwritten by new data, so allowing one exact
copy of the original to be pasted in more than one place.

Dictionary
is the list of allowable words which can be used in a particular application. Although
most applications contain a standard dictionary, sometimes there is a facility to allow
an individual user to create a separate personal dictionary which is then referred to if a
particular word entered by that user is not found in the standard dictionary.

Desk-top presentation

is the use of graphics, charting and page make-up software, together with high-quality output devices, to produce sophisticated information displays. These will normally be seen on screen or printed out onto paper. However, using specialised devices, the information can also be output directly to overhead projector foil, onto photographic film to provide high-quality slides or even projected directly onto a cinema-style screen, for use in lectures and demonstrations.

Desk-Top Publishing (DTP)

is the use of a *page make-up system* (see page 12) and high-quality output devices to produce material which can be used directly as the first stage in the production process for printed leaflets, manuals, books, magazines, reports, etc.

Export

including: import

is to create a data file using one piece of software so that it can be read by a different piece of software. *Import* is the corresponding read process to accept a file produced by some other software.

Often there is a specific version of a particular package whose file and data formats are chosen by its manufacturer to be the standard version for exporting from and importing into that package. Using these formats reduces the problems of data transfer between different software applications.

Hard space

including: soft space

is intended space that the user has explicitly typed (such as the space between two adjacent words). *Soft space* is inserted by software to even out the look of a line in order to create justified text. Because the user may later alter the formatting of the text, these 'extra' spaces must be remembered by the software, so that they can be removed where necessary. Reformatting justified text does not remove hard spaces.

Mailmerge

is the process of combining a document (often a letter), and a data file (often a list of names and addresses), in such a way that copies of the document for different people are suitably different. In its simplest form, this is merely ensuring that letters have the correct style and title for the addressee and that the address is inserted into the appropriate place. More complex uses can include inserting whole paragraphs into standard letters or documents. The process remains the same for all applications; a document is set up which has marked places within it at which data from other files is inserted.

Justification

including: left justification, right justification, full justification, centring
is the arrangement of characters so that they align with margins. This may occur on
the screen or on a printer, or may be required when setting out data in columns or as
forms.

Left justification is the normal method of aligning
continuous text, with an even left-hand margin. This
often leaves an uneven right-hand margin since each
printed line is likely to contain characters (for
example words, spaces and punctuation marks) which
occupy different lengths of line.

Right justification is normal for columns of numbers,
 although it is sometimes seen in text. Here, an even
right-hand margin is created. This may well result in
a ragged left-hand margin, since each printed line is
   likely to contain characters (for words, spaces and
 punctuation) which occupy different lengths of line.

Full justification (sometimes simply referred to as
justification) has even margins at both left-hand and
right-hand ends of the line. It is created by the
(automatic) insertion of extra spaces (soft spaces)
between words once a line of approximately the
correct length has been entered.

Centring,
which is often used for headings
and
similar displays,
places the characters symmetrically between the
margins.

Figure A2.1: Different justification styles

Line break

is the place where a line of printed text ends. Word processors normally break lines
only between words or, if sufficiently sophisticated, by inserting hyphens at
appropriate places.

Micro-spacing

is a feature available on some printers to print fully justified text by inserting small
amounts of *soft space* (see page 10) in order to spread the total amount of added space
evenly across a line. This ability is particularly necessary when proportional fonts
(where characters occupy different widths of printed space) are being used and fully
justified text is still required.

Non-breaking space

including: pad character

is the type of space (such as that in "Henry IV") which occurs between words that should not appear on separate lines. Many word processors allow the user to type a special combination of keys to insert such a character, sometimes called a *pad character*, which will print as a space, but will not be allowed as a line break.

Overtype

sometimes: overwrite

is to replace text on a screen with other text entered from the keyboard (or possibly read from a file) during the process of entering or editing a document.

Page make-up system

allows on-screen combination of graphics and text. The software allows easy manipulation of the layout to produce a professional-looking result that can be reproduced for leaflets, manuals, magazines, etc.

Spelling checker

is a program which is normally used with a word processor or desk-top publishing system to check the spelling in a document. Each word in the document is checked against the *dictionary* (see page 9). If it does not appear in the dictionary then the user is told this. The word may be correct (but not in the dictionary) or it may be wrongly spelt. Some programs even check the spelling as the document is typed in.

TeX

including: Latex, Metafont

is a specialised text processing system devised by the American mathematician and computer scientist Donald Knuth. It allows much greater control over the display of mathematical and scientific formulas than conventional word processors and is often used by academic authors submitting technical manuscripts to journal or book publishers. The power of TeX makes it a difficult language for beginners, and a number of alternative user interfaces, such as *Latex*, have been designed – this offers the facilities for the production of a number of common types of scientific document without the user needing to write pure TeX. As well as the text-processing features of these languages, there is an associated type-face definition system called *Metafont*.

Text editor

is a program for creating and amending text. It is designed to be used for preparing the source text of programs and for editing text files. It can have similar editing functions to a word processor but requires a more formal approach than is usual in word processing if formatting is to be retained.

Thesaurus

is a dictionary arranged by meaning instead of spelling. A computer-based thesaurus used in conjunction with a word processor allows a user to select a word in the text, and to be offered a range of words with similar or related meanings. Using one of these instead of the original word can enhance the writer's prose style.

Word wrap

is a facility available in many word processing packages which breaks lines automatically between words. When the text being typed on the line reaches beyond the right-hand margin, the whole of the last word is transferred to the beginning of the next line.

WYSIWYG (What You See Is What You Get)

(pronounced 'wizzy-wig') refers to a screen display which matches the eventual printed output in layout, highlighting and underlining, font, etc. Such displays are particularly helpful in applications such as *desk-top publishing* (see page 10) and *spreadsheets* (see A3, page 14).

A3 Spreadsheets

Spreadsheets are an important and powerful use of the computer. A spreadsheet is based on the idea of the computer looking like a large sheet of squared paper with the added advantage of being able to do arithmetic.

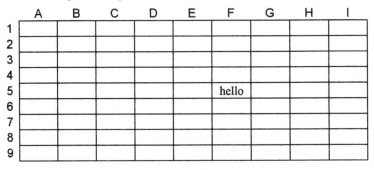

Figure A3.1: A spreadsheet

The squares are usually called cells (sometimes slots) and each is identified by its column label (often a letter or letters) and its row label (often a number). In the example the cell with hello in it has address F5, where F is the column label and 5 is the row label. The contents of a cell may be one of several types:

- a heading or message
  this is just plain text - i.e. a collection of characters.
- a number
  it is important to realise that there is a difference between a number as text and a number that is required for calculation – most spreadsheets allow for the conversion between a number as text and a number in a form suitable for calculation.
- a formula that represents a calculation;
  in this case what is seen in the cell is the result of the calculation rather than the formula itself. An example of a formula may be one that adds the contents of two cells together and multiplies the result by 3:

  3*(A21 + B21)

  (If A21 contains the number 5 and B21 contains the number 6 then the cell containing the formula above will display the number 33. It still contains the formula after the calculation has been done, so that if the contents of A21 or B21 change then a new calculated value will be displayed.)

- an instruction

  an example would be an instruction that takes the contents of a cell (a number) and uses it as a product code. The instruction then causes a table of product codes, prices and descriptions elsewhere in the table (or even possibly a different spreadsheet) to be searched and when the correct product code is found the description is inserted in the current cell which contains the instruction. In another cell would be an instruction to do the same but to insert the price.

Figure A3.2 is an example of a spreadsheet showing how many French francs one would get for different amounts of English money.

	A	B	C	D
1	Exchange Rate			
2	11.50	Pounds	Francs	
3		0	0.00	
4		5	57.50	
5		10	115.00	
6				

NOTE:
Cells C3, C4 and C5 each contain a formula:
in C3 it is B3*A2
in C4 it is B4*A2
in C5 it is B5*A2

Figure A3.2: *A spreadsheet for currency conversion*

In this spreadsheet you can see numbers (for example, in cell B4), labels or headings (for example, in cell C2), and the result of applying a formula (as in cell C4). However, a spreadsheet need not be used for just doing the original calculation, it will also respond to changes in the data. It is this ability to respond to *'what if'* questions that makes a spreadsheet such a powerful business tool.

What if the rate of exchange altered? You can cope with this by simply re-typing the exchange rate in cell A2 and the freshly converted amounts of francs would appear in column C.

What if the amount of pounds that you wanted to exchange was not in the table? Type the amount in place of the zero amount in cell B3 and the converted amount will appear in cell C3.

In the above example the formulas used in column C are all very similar, but not quite identical; they all use A2 but this is multiplied by the appropriate entry in column B. On most spreadsheets there is no need to type each formula in individually: by replication you can repeat them automatically and make the system keep the reference to A2 every time but alter the reference to column B. Many spreadsheets also have a facility to take a set of figures and convert them into some type of graph (such as a pie chart, a line graph, or a bar chart).

The printing out of a spreadsheet can pose problems. Some software will just print out everything that is being used. However, most allow the user to indicate the cells that are to be printed out; many allow the cells to be printed out in a different order from their 'natural' one so that parts of the sheet that are separated by a lot of rows/columns can be printed close together. Some spreadsheets even allow the sheet to be printed sideways to allow for a wide sheet to be printed. A further complication in printing is what should be printed out for some of the cells - should it be a formula or the result of the formula? Again, many spreadsheets allow the user to choose.

The use of spreadsheets has been extended beyond just numbers. Imagine a list of names and addresses; each one might consist of (say) four entries: (a) the name, (b) the house number, (c) the road and (d) the town. Each entry could be put into a different column and each row hold a different name and address, as in Figure A3.3

	A	B	C	D	E
1	Name	No.	Road	Town	
2	Mr Smith	1	Acacia Avenue	Birmingham	
3	Mrs Jones	2	High Street	Luton	
4	Ms Black	77	Sunset Road	Liverpool	
5	Miss Green	12	Hillside	Leicester	
6					
7					

Figure A3.3: A spreadsheet used as a database

So you can use a spreadsheet as a simple database. Further to this, some spreadsheets can be used as word processors (in fact the draft of this text was prepared on such a spreadsheet). Usually this means that the text is set out in one column of the spreadsheet, but the other columns can be used as well. This becomes even more powerful when you wish to include some calculations in your text as there are no calculations for the user to do since the spreadsheet will do them all!

Spreadsheet

is an applications package usually used to display financial or statistical information. It takes its name from the way data is arranged on the screen in rows and columns, as in the traditional layout of figures in account books. The user can specify that numbers displayed in particular positions are to be dependent on entries in other positions, and are to be recalculated automatically when these entries are changed. Hence the effects of changes to one data item on, for example, totals, sub-totals, 'profits' and 'VAT' can be explored.

Cell

also known as: slot
including: address, column, row, block
is the 'square' on a spreadsheet in which only a single entry can be placed, sometimes called a *slot*. The single entry can be either a number, a group of words or a formula. It can be referred to by its *address* in the spreadsheet using the *column* and *row* labels. The column label refers to a vertical group of cells and the row label refers to a horizontal group of cells (see Figure A3.3, above). If we have a rectangular grouping of the cells this is termed a *block*. Usually the block is identified by giving

the addresses of the upper left cell and the lower right cell of the rectangle, for example A3F12 would have 6 columns (A to F) of 10 rows (3 to 12).

Formula

is the way a calculation is represented in a spreadsheet. As well as numbers a formula uses the address of cells to identify other values to be used - the result is then displayed in the cell in which the formula was placed. If any of the cells referenced in the formula change in value then the result of the formula is changed to reflect the altered values.

For example, if the first side of a rectangle is in B3 and you wished to find the second side of the rectangle (in C3, say) whose sides always add up to (say) 12, the formula in C3 might be:

$$(12 - 2*B3)/2$$

Function

is a special type of formula used in a spreadsheet. It has usually been set up to represent a formula that may be too complex or too long to expect an ordinary user to enter, or it may be just very useful. Examples of this might be:

SUM()   a function to calculate the sum (i.e. the total) of a row or
            a column or a block of cells.
MEAN()   a function to calculate the average (mean) of a row or
            a column or a block of cells.
FIND()   a function to find where, in an area of the spreadsheet, a
            particular value is to be found.

Recalculation

is the term used to describe the process whereby the spreadsheet recalculates the values that may have altered because of the last input of data. The process of recalculation can be automatic - done after each and every entry in the spreadsheet - or it can be manual, whereby the user decides when it should be done and presses a particular set of keys to have the recalculation done. The advantage of having it set to manual is that the entry of data is quicker as the user does not have to wait for the updating (which can take an appreciable amount of time if the spreadsheet is large); the disadvantage is that the user has always to indicate when the recalculation should be done. It is sometimes important to know the order of the recalculation - whether it is by row (i.e. the first row, then the second and so on) or by column (i.e. the first column, then the second and so on). With many spreadsheets it is possible to alter the order of calculation.

Replication

including: absolute reference, relative reference

is the process of copying a formula from one cell to another. As a formula usually involves references to cells this means you should be aware of whether you want to keep the exact same reference to the cell (this is termed an *absolute reference*) or whether you want the reference to adjust itself according to either the row or column movement (this is termed a *relative reference*). An example of this is when you have a formula in cell A12 that calculates (say) the sum of a row of figures – something like SUM(A1...A10) – and this is then replicated into cell B12. Generally you will want the result to represent the sum for row B; if you tell it that A1 and A10 are relative then this will happen.

A4 Databases and Information Retrieval

Although a computer can store enormous amounts of data, this data is useless without
appropriate links between individual data items. Imagine, for example, what a
(printed) telephone directory would be like if it was simply two separate listings of
telephone subscribers and their numbers, without the connection that is made by the
printed layout between a particular subscriber and their telephone number. The data is
also useless if it cannot be easily retrieved when required - imagine the telephone
directory in random rather than alphabetic order.

The same applies to computerised collections of data. These are generally referred
to as databases and can vary between a simple name-and-address listing and a massive
collection of structured data that provides information for a large business. It is easy
to be deceived when one is experimenting with techniques for accessing databases. If
a demonstration database can be constructed with tens (rather than millions) of entries,
many of the techniques can seem unnecessarily long-winded. If you were certain that
your data would never extend to more than 100 entries, it would be sensible to store it
in a simple table. When it grew, despite your plans, to millions of entries no table
would be capable of holding it, and your program would need to use sophisticated
methods of data management.

Large databases usually have many potential users. Allowing simultaneous use of
the same data files may lead to operating system problems – the solution to these
problems is usually embedded in a complex piece of software, known as the database
management system (DBMS).

Not all users will be experienced with computers and simple user interfaces are
often provided to access the data. The concepts used in designing and setting up a
large database are complex and require specialist staff, but the data can be accessed
easily without the less experienced user understanding the underlying structure.

Information retrieval
also known as: data retrieval
is extracting useful information from large amounts of stored data, such as a database.
This usually involves specifying some form of *query* (see page 24) and also stating
display and sorting instructions. This enables large amounts of data to be searched
and the results to be output efficiently.

Database
is a (large) collection of data items and links between them, structured in a way that
allows it to be accessed by a number of different applications programs. The term is
also used loosely to describe any collection of data.

Data model

including: entity, attribute, relation

is a diagram of a database. Designers of a large database will normally construct a diagram of the planned database. This will show the things represented in the database (the *entities*) and the information held about them (the *attributes*). The *relations* between entities are shown, and from this model the most efficient arrangement of the data will be worked out. See also *entity-relationship diagram*, page 178.

Database Management System (DBMS)

is software that can find data in a database, add new data and change existing data. The database management system works automatically without users knowing how. It deals with finding the requested data, updates the data and performs other tasks including maintaining indexes.

The database management system may provide its own simple user interface or may just communicate with other programs which request and use the data available to the database.

Large computer systems will have programs written for particular tasks. These programs use the database management system to handle the complexities of managing the database because it is easier than directly accessing the datafiles. Communication between programs and a database management system usually uses commands in *SQL* (see page 247).

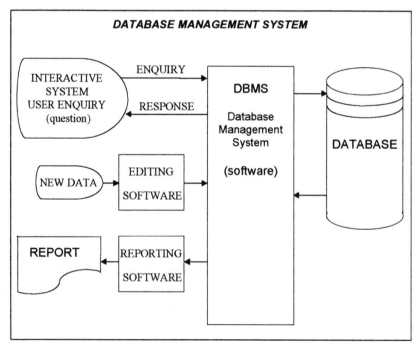

Figure A4.1: How a database management system works

Data dictionary

also known as: data directory

is a file containing descriptions of, and other information about, the structure of the data held in a database. The data dictionary is not usually accessible to users. It is a tool for the managers of the database, for example when they need to alter the way data is stored.

Distributed database

is one where several computers on a network each hold part of the data and co-operate in making it available to the user. If the particular data required is not available at a particular computer it will communicate with the others in the network to obtain it. Often each computer will keep a separate copy of frequently used data. Special methods are needed to ensure that the latest data is used.

Flat file

is a database held as a table and stored in a single file. The data will be structured with a row for each *record* and a column for each *field* (see pages 258 and 259). This allows only very simple structuring of the data, which can only be considered as a two-dimensional table (hence 'flat').

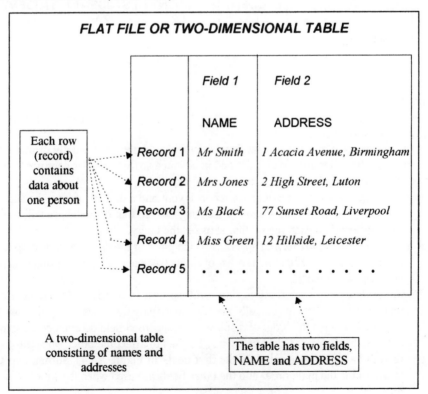

Figure A4.2: A flat file

Hierarchical database

is a database where the data is held in a *tree* structure (see page 254). Each data item can be thought of by users as existing on one of a number of levels. There are links to related data items at the higher level and sometimes at a lower level. The data items at a lower level hold more detail about the item that they are linked to above.

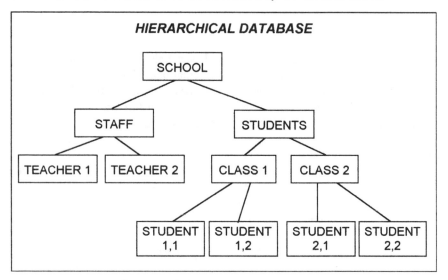

Figure A4.3: Hierarchical database

Report

including: report definition, report format, report layout, display order, sort list, presentation order

is the presentation of selected data from a database. A report is usually printed in the form of a table. Reports may be defined in advance so that the user does not have to set up the report definition each time it is needed.

Report definitions require a query, a report layout and a display order to be defined. Normally the user will set a *query* (see page 24) so that the database will be searched, finding each record that satisfies the query.

Report layout or *report format* specifies which parts of the data are to be output and in what position. Often this is a list of *fields* (see page 259) to be printed as the columns of the report.

Display order, sort list or *presentation order* specifies the order in which records will be output. This is generally done by specifying the fields whose data will be used to determine the order of display. One specified field determines the main order in the display. Other fields may be used to affect the order when the records have the same value for the first field. In Figure A4.4, 'Surname' is used to determine the main order and the other fields are used when the first fields are identical.

Report: Students taking Art				
Forename	Surname	DOB	Class	*header*
Fred	Able	10/02/83	10A	
Jill	Baker	10/10/82	10Y	*data in tabular*
Martin	Baker	17/12/82	10C	*form*
Andrew	Cable	05/08/82	10C	
Total Number: 4				*footer*

Figure A4.4: *A typical report*

Relational database
including: table, view
is a complex database structure to hold a variety of different data. Where data items are related to each other they are linked together by pointers stored in the database.

Table is the name for each group of similar data with rows for each member of the *entity* and columns for each *attribute* (see page 20).

The (relational) database management system provides tools for linking tables together and selecting items from within tables. In this way, each user can be given a different *view* of the data. An example of a view may be a table set up for a particular type of user, such as a receptionist, who would only be able to access data relevant to their job.

Relational databases are especially powerful, because the method of storing data in tables makes no assumptions about how the applications programs will access the data, and hence does not restrict the *queries* (see page 24) in any way.

Schema
including: data description language, subschema
is the precise description of the data items to be stored, and the relationships between them, in a database system.

Managing the large amounts of data of different types stored in a modern database requires that descriptions of the data items are held, as well as the data items themselves. The description, the schema, will be written in a ***data description language***. The *database management system* (see page 20) may re-format the data before presenting it to the user, and will make use of individual ***subschemas*** which describe the data a particular user can access (see *view*, above).

Normal form

is a way of structuring the data in a *relational database* (see page 23) according to theoretical rules, in order to avoid problems of inefficiency in accessing and maintaining the data.

The *schema* (see page 23) is altered using certain mathematical processes to convert it into normal form. If the schema for a database is in normal form errors and inconsistencies will be reduced. For example, data items should not be repeated since there is a risk of error. See also *data protection*, page 100.

Query

including: interrogating, selecting, searching

is a question asked of the data in a database. The query is structured so that the answer is either true or false. To answer a query the computer must check each *record* (see page 258) of the data to see if the answer is true. The result of the query is a list of all the data which satisfies the query. Querying a database is also referred to as *interrogating* the database, *selecting* data or *searching* for data. See also *search*, page 191.

An example of a general request might be

"Which students in Year 11 take French?"

This query is made precise by using words from the *query language* (see page 247) to link the names of the fields, 'year' and 'subject', in the database.

SELECT student WHERE year = 11 AND subject = "French"

Data filter

selects the set of records to be displayed. A data filter is often used in an interactive system to implement a query. Setting a filter, which is easily done but temporary, will involve entering a query. See also *query*, above.

Data warehouse

including: data mining

refers to large amounts of data which are stored together, usually in a single location, for further processing.

Much of the data collected by large businesses with many sites is used immediately for a specific purpose and is stored where it is collected and used. This data, particularly when analysed with other data, can provide useful information for future planning. The data warehouse is where these large quantities of data are collected together from a variety of locations for efficient analysis and also provides a form of archive of the data. Since the data is only being used for further analysis it does not have to be complete or up to date.

Data mining is the analysis of a large amount of data in a data warehouse to provide new information. For example, by using loyalty cards which connect purchases to a particular customer, supermarkets can gather information about the buying habits of individual customers. Combining all the information about customers helps them to establish long-term trends.

A5   Graphics and Design

Other related terms may be found in section B4 Display Devices

The display screen of most computer systems uses the same technology as television. Therefore, it is capable of displaying *pictures* as well as text – indeed, text is simply a specialised form of picture. Because of this technology, there are many computer applications that use computer power to generate graphics.

Sometimes, the graphics may be an end in themselves, with **painting** or **drawing** packages available to illustrators, to enable them to compose and edit high-quality images. Most computer games are now set in a graphical environment, with exciting animated graphics to underline the action.

Other packages use graphics as part of the design process for books and other printed matter – adding illustrations or decorative borders. In some cases, a photograph (or even 'live-action' video) can be 'retouched' electronically, to add, remove or re-colour some elements of the picture. Many TV graphics are nowadays generated purely electronically.

In other applications, the processing power of the computer is used for calculation, as well as for the pure drawing.

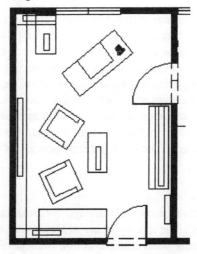

Figure A5.1: *Computer aided architectural design*

Computer aided design packages are used in fields as diverse as architecture and electronics: a builder may design a building on the computer, and call up an itemised list of all the materials to be used in the construction – the length of pipes, cables, amount of masonry and so on. Or the designer of an electronic printed-circuit board may position the main components to his or her liking, and allow the computer to suggest how the connections should be made, to achieve an efficient design.

Clip art

While computer graphics packages allow the user to draw their own illustrations, many publishers offer computer disks full of professionally-drawn pictures that can be edited to suit an individual user's needs. These are popularly known as 'clip art' because of the way in which they are 'clipped' out of the file and 'pasted' into your own drawing.

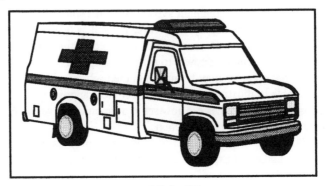

Figure A5.2: Clip art

Computer Aided Design (CAD)

including: drafting

This is the use of a computer system to produce drawings or 'blueprints' as part of the design of some construction project; this might be the civil engineering design of a motorway, the layout of components on a printed-circuit board, or the drafting of furniture positions in an office or a home – to give just three common examples. This computer aided *design* phase is also sometimes known as computer aided *drafting*. Most modern CAD packages also use the design data as the basis for calculations – for example, of costs, mechanical stresses, quantities needed, etc. With the information available from the design stage, it is possible in many cases for the computer system to control the manufacturing process as well. See also *CAD/CAM*, page 53.

Computer animation

is the creation of apparent movement through the presentation of a sequence of slightly different still pictures. The screen display of a computer is re-drawn every 1/25th of a second, at least, whether it has changed or not, because of the television technology used in display devices. With a fast computer, it is possible to generate a new picture in this time, so that an impression of movement can be created, in the same way as a cinema film creates the illusion of movement from still pictures. Computer animation packages are now routinely used in the television and film industry, particularly where they can mix 'live action' with computer-generated images.

Computer graphics

is the use of the computer to display pictorial information. This can be as simple as a line drawing or chart, or as complicated as an animated sequence of pictures. The output might be shown on the computer screen, printed out as hard copy, or transferred directly to videotape.

Drawing package

including: line art

Computer graphics packages with the word 'draw' in their titles tend to be of the sort known as *vector graphics* packages, where the instructions for drawing certain basic shapes, such as lines, rectangles, circles and so forth, are stored, rather than the picture itself. These basic shapes, or 'objects', can easily be moved around the drawing, or laid on top of other objects; because of the way they are constructed, they do not interfere with one another, and can be thought of as existing in separate 'layers'; text in drawings would be stored as shapes – each letter a separate object. Because most 'line art' of this sort tends to have only a few elements, there is a considerable advantage in that less storage is needed, as compared to a *painting package* (see page 28). Scaling the picture up or down in size would not alter the clarity of the drawing. See also *vector graphics,* page 138.

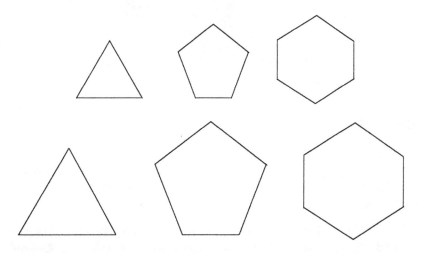

Figure A5.3: *Typical output from a drawing package, at two scalings*

Digitiser

also known as: image scanner

Many graphics images begin life as drawings on paper and must be converted into a form that a computer graphics package can use. A digitiser scans a drawing and turns it into a *bit map* (see page 286); this captures the image, but for CAD packages it is necessary to have information about the precise position of important points and lines. See also *scanner,* page 116.

Digital camera

is a still camera which produces a digital image file of the scene photographed. This colour image can be printed directly or can be downloaded to a computer. The file in the computer can be manipulated for further use. See *download*, page 193.

Painting package

Computer graphics packages with the word 'paint' in their titles tend to be of the sort known as *raster graphics* packages, where a picture is held as a *bit map* (see page 286) – that is, the state of each individual *pixel* (see page 135) is stored. Text in such a picture would be stored as a bit map. Such drawings use a lot of storage space, because even 'blank' portions of the picture contribute to the size. They can also appear jagged when scaled up or down in size. However, for freehand drawings, and areas of tone, such packages are better than *drawing packages* (see page 27). See also *raster graphics*, page 134.

Figure A5.4: Typical output from a painting package

Graphics tablet

also known as: graphics pad
including: stylus, puck
is a device used to input line drawings into a computer. The user draws with a *stylus* on a flat pad or tablet (sometimes called a *graphics pad*), either copying a drawing or working freehand.

Stylus is the name for devices used for drawing on a graphics tablet. The movement of the stylus is detected by the tablet and its software in one of a variety of ways, for example through the use of a wire matrix in the pad or by sensing the angular movement of an arm supporting the stylus. A stylus may be pressure sensitive, producing a darker or more intensely coloured line if pressed firmly.

Puck is a small disk-shaped device, which is moved around on the tablet (or pad) to trace a drawing.

The position of the stylus or puck on the tablet is input to the computer and used to position a cursor on the screen. Subsequent movement causes a drawing on the screen which matches the movements on the tablet. These devices are generally preferred to a mouse for computer drafting packages.

A6 Modelling and Simulation

Imagine having to design and build a new bypass to divert traffic round a town. Before starting on such a venture it would be wise to check on the cost and compare that with the advantages to be gained. Although it is quite possible to produce accurate costings, it is harder to work out how wide the bypass should be (should it be dual or single carriageway, for example) or what route it should take to reduce the traffic flow through the town. By the time the road is built the money will have been spent and the bypass may not be effective. When data on current traffic flow has been collected and likely future traffic requirements have been assessed a model can be produced.

Modelling attempts to show what is happening now and the results of the intended alterations. The model produced is a mathematical description of the rate of traffic flow at all points of interest. The details of this model can be changed, for example by increasing the expected amount of traffic, to see whether this causes any problems. Once the model has been tested with these conditions it can then be judged how good the proposed changes would be. The bypass could then be built, with the likelihood that it would be worthwhile, or it could be abandoned, as not useful enough, having only had the cost of the exploration.

It is when you want to test and use a mathematical model that a computer would be used. The computer can quickly carry out the necessary calculations (many of which are repeated but quite simple) and show the results using tables of numbers or diagrams.

Simulation software uses the model that has been developed, to show the effect of different conditions. To be of any use the model used must be thoroughly tested. It is now possible to buy simulation programs that allow people to solve a range of similar problems. The simulation contains a model which has been developed and tested by the authors. The user may have little control over the model but relies on the work the authors have done to develop and test it. However advanced simulation software may allow the user to build new models.

Weather forecasting uses computer simulation. Data is gathered from many sources at different times and from this the computer predicts what weather we are likely to expect soon or in the future. From experience we know that weather forecasting accuracy can vary from being very good to being dramatically wrong. Economic forecasting is performed in a similar way, but often lacks the accuracy of even a weather forecast. Prediction can only be as good as the model. Any model is limited by human understanding and the need for it to be sufficiently simple to allow results to be calculated in a reasonable time.

Computer simulations are also used in training. A flight simulator is used to prepare pilots to cope with anything from standard flying and landing, to dealing with emergencies without putting anyone's life at risk. A flight simulator can range from a simple screen display to a full-size mock-up of the flight cabin with movement effects.

In education, computer simulation can be used to show a process that would normally be impossible to demonstrate because it would be too dangerous, too expensive or would take too long. In a simulation dealing with a nuclear reactor station, alterations could be made that would not be allowed at a visit to such a station! Similarly, in the field of genetics, alterations could be simulated on a reasonable timescale rather than waiting months or years for even simple processes to be checked.

In silicon chip design, a simulation is used to show how the circuitry would behave. The design is adjusted until the required response is achieved. This saves the expense and time of producing, testing and having to change a series of prototypes. In these circumstances **emulation** software could be used to check computer behaviour for various programs before the new chip becomes available.

Model

is a sequence of ideas that attempt to represent a process realistically. At some stage these ideas are expressed mathematically as a set (or collection) of equations. The accuracy of this model is limited by the knowledge of the process being modelled, the time available to produce the model, the availability of input data and how quickly results are required.

Modelling

is the construction of a *model* (see above) by a mathematical analysis of a situation. The model is refined by testing it in various known situations.

Simulation

is the use of a computer program to predict the likely behaviour of a real-life system. A mathematical *model* (see above) of the system is constructed and tested. The model is usually incorporated into a program that can be used to investigate other situations.

A simple model could be tested mathematically using a program such as a spreadsheet, but the final simulation may produce a graphical display and may react to real time inputs. A more complex situation will require simulation software. By altering the input data for a simulation, the possible results of different actions can be investigated.

Forecasting

is the use of simulations to predict future events, such as forecasting the weather. To be of any value the results of the simulation must be reasonably accurate. The models must be thoroughly tested by comparing predictions with actual events. If the model is accurate it can then be used regularly to aid planning.

Emulation

is a very precise form of *simulation* (see above) which should mimic exactly the behaviour of the circumstances that it is simulating.

An *emulator* (see page 31) may enable one type of computer to operate as if it were a different type of computer.

Emulation may be used by printers to enable them to behave like a different printer. This may enable them to be used with a wide variety of computer software.

Emulator

is a program that allows a computer to behave as if it were a different type of computer. An emulator enables:

- software to be developed which will run on computers not yet built
- software to be used on a type of computer other than the type it was designed for
- software to be tested when it would otherwise use expensive resources
- a computer to be used as a peripheral, appearing to the host computer to have the characteristics expected. This enables microcomputers to act as terminals to larger computer systems.

An emulator is often much slower than the host computer because of the extra processing involved.

A7   Virtual Reality

Virtual reality systems transport the user into an environment created by the computer. Computer-controlled graphics are used to generate realistic scenes with which the user can interact.

To provide realism and to prevent distraction from the immediate environment, the user may wear a headset. The headset incorporates earphones to play the appropriate soundtrack directly into the ears, while small video screens, in goggles covering the eyes, ensure that the only images seen are those generated by the computer.

When the head moves, the simulation changes the image in response to where the user is now 'looking'. This gives the illusion of moving through the scene. The use of the headset provides a powerful psychological effect, giving a strong feeling of realism. An alternative to using a headset is the use of wrap-around displays with stereo sound for group participation.

To increase further the feeling of experiencing the simulated environment, a *data glove* can be worn. This is an input device that enables the position of the fingers and the orientation of the hand to be sensed by the computer. It provides the opportunity for the user to point at or 'touch' objects, which will produce some response from the system.

Full virtual reality is a technology that is still in its infancy; it is very demanding in its requirements for resources. It needs high-quality three-dimensional graphics. The need for immediate and smooth change of scene requires fast processing. There are also enormous storage requirements. However by using **CD-ROM** and accepting lower standards of visual presentation on a screen, low-quality virtual reality can be produced to run on relatively modest computer systems; these products are being sold as virtual reality.

Data glove
is an input device worn on the hand of a user of a virtual reality system. Typically, it enables the position of the fingers and the orientation of the hand to be sensed by the system. In most systems, when the user 'touches' a simulated object, there is no physical sensation returned to the hand. Greater realism is possible in systems which do provide this kind of feedback.

Headset
is an input and output device, like a helmet, worn by a user of a virtual reality system. It gives the wearer the impression of being within the computer-generated scene, with sound provided through headphones and vision through small video screens in goggles worn over the eyes. The headset senses changes of position of the head and inputs this to the computer so that the simulation can be changed appropriately. Since the user is isolated from sounds and visions, other than those provided by the virtual reality system, there is a very strong sense of being within the simulated environment.

Virtual reality system

also known as: VR system

is a computer system that provides a simulated environment by three-dimensional graphical images and an appropriate soundtrack. It gives the user the impression of being within the environment. The graphical images are often of rather poor quality but these are expected to become more realistic as advances in the technology are made.

A8   Internet

This section is concerned with terms likely to be met when using the Internet. Many Internet terms are concerned with the transmission of data between computers within networks. Some of these terms and other related terms may be found in A9 Communications, B6 Networks, B7 Communications Devices and Control Devices or C17 Communications Technology.

The Internet, increasingly referred to as The Net, interconnects a very large number of individual and diverse computer networks. Its name is a diminution of 'interconnected networks'. It uses a wide range of telecommunications media to provide a means of global information interchange which appears to be independent of the power of the user's computer or where in the world other systems or databases are.

Apart from saying that the Internet is very large, it is difficult to give realistic numbers. At the start of 1997, it was estimated that about 250,000 networks and 100 million computers had some means of Internet access and growing awareness of the potential of the Internet means that present figures are much greater.

Each connected network may be of any size, use any hardware or be situated anywhere in the world. These networks include very large and well organised networks, like those of governments, universities or multi-national corporations, and small company networks or individuals using Internet Service Providers (ISPs).

For an individual user to access the Internet, their computer must be connected to a local network which has a connection to the Internet. If the user is using a terminal or personal computer on a company or educational organisation network, there may be a permanent connection to the Internet. If the individual only has a stand-alone computer, then a dial-up connection to a specialist Internet service provider's network will be needed.

The principal requirement of any network which is connected to the Internet is the ability to communicate intelligently with it. To do this, the network must use the protocols – a set of rules in a sort of 'language' – required of all Internet users and have access to telephone, radio or other telecommunications links. Depending upon the types of data that users wish to receive or send, there are also requirements for the capacity of links to the Internet. The Internet has its own protocols, the definition of which is the responsibility of an Internet Committee. The usual protocol is TCP/IP (Transmission Control Protocol/Internet Protocol), although there are others.

There is also a joint Board which coordinates Internet naming procedures and the operation of major communication routes. Making sure that information from any one computer reaches its correct destination is the job of dedicated pieces of equipment, known as routers, located at strategic points around the world. Routers check the destination address for the message and either send it to the appropriate computer if it is on a network connected to the router, or send it on to another router along the path. This process is repeated until the message reaches its destination. Figure A8.1 shows how communication from a computer passes through a number of nodes to reach its destination.

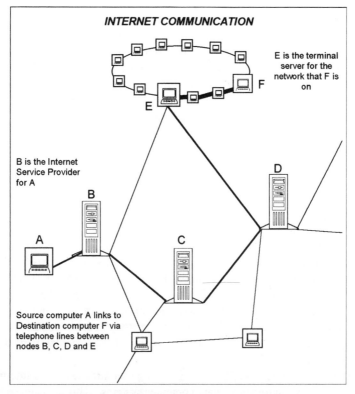

Figure A8.1: An Internet connection

Each machine connected to the Internet has its own unique address, which is a number. There is no central register of machines connected to the Internet nor is there any formal index of either individual users or database addresses.

Essentially the Internet provides three types of service:
- the *World Wide Web*, which gives access to remote databases, through browsing or searching,
- *Electronic mail*, which provides one-to-one communication and exchange of information,
- *File transfer*, which makes it possible to transfer large amounts of information.

Additional services provide Bulletin Boards (broadcast mail), discussion groups and teleconferencing.

Most Internet resources are accessed using the World Wide Web (the Web), which is a multimedia information system. Each information provider makes their information available as a web site, which becomes a part of the Web. In addition to information on the web page, other facilities may be accessed by a user from a web page, such as requesting information using file transfer, completing and returning a questionnaire or making requests for a search engine to locate information about a topic.

When using email, a message has to be prepared and then posted into the email system. Actual transmission may be automatic or the message may be stored on the sender's computer until the email system is next contacted. When the message is received by the email system provider it is prepared for onward transmission. Having passed through the communications system, often provided by the Internet, the message is delivered to and stored on the computer at the addressee's service provider. This message is later collected by the addressee from a mailbox.

All email users must have a unique identifier or address. This ensures that any communication through the Internet finds its target. The identifier contains information to enable return communications to get back to the user. These user identifiers may be numerical or use personal names.

Internet

also known as: The Net

including: ARPAnet, (Advanced Research Projects Agency Network), NSFNET, (National Science Foundation Network), BITNET, JANET, SuperJANET

provides the facility to link computers world-wide, usually using telecommunications systems (such as telephone lines). It allows fast communication between people, the transfer of data between computers, and the distribution of information. Messages and data are passed from the source computer, through other computers, until the destination computer is reached. See *email*, page 38, *file transfer*, page 39, and *World Wide Web*, page 37.

Any computer can be linked to any other computer attached to the Internet, communicating through intermediate computer systems. This is achieved by having common technical standards, a common identification system for computers and a common naming system for data files. See *TCP/IP*, page 45, *domain name*, page 42 and *URL*, page 41. In practice, most users are either part of a local area network, linked to the Internet by a *terminal server* (see page 46), or linked by telephone line to a *host computer* (see page 158), which performs the Internet access.

Much of the initial success of the Internet has been due to the vast amounts of data made available by linking several very large networks to the Internet for academic and research purposes. These networks include:

ARPAnet (Advanced Research Projects Agency Network) is the US Defense Department Network which linked US University Research Centres to the Defense Agency from the late 1960s.

NSFNET (National Science Foundation Network) is the academic network used by US research facilities. It used the concepts from ARPAnet and it was extended to become the basis of the Internet.

BITNET is the academic network used by US Universities. It is based on large IBM computers.

JANET is the UK Joint Academic Network which links British Universities and research centres.

SuperJANET is a development of JANET providing much greater capacity for the 21st century.

Browser

including: kiosk mode browser, line mode browser

is a program which allows Internet users to retrieve information interactively on the Internet. A browser may be used to access the *World Wide Web* (see below) or to provide other facilities such as *file transfer* (see page 39) or *email* (see page 38).

When browsing the World Wide Web, it retrieves web pages from another computer on the Internet and displays them in the multimedia format used by the World Wide Web. Related pages can be easily retrieved by clicking on special links, which are usually shown in a different colour. The browser has facilities to save pages, print pages and move backwards and forward through pages already accessed.

Most browsers are very flexible with many facilities but two specialised browsers are:

Kiosk mode browsers are designed for easy use by the public, allowing limited access to a range of information. They can be operated using robust interfaces such as touch screens.

Line mode browsers are generally character-based and are unable to display graphics. Some may display a message in a box showing where a graphics image should have been. See also *Lynx*, page 48.

See also *HyperText Transfer Protocol (HTTP)*, in *HTML*, page 40.

World Wide Web (WWW)

including: web site, web page, home page, welcome page, personal page, surf

is a collection of information held in multimedia form on the Internet. This information is stored at locations called *Web Sites* in the form of *Web Pages*. A web page is a single document. It may be too large to be displayed as a screen without scrolling.

Web pages are permanently available to any user of the Internet. Each organisation (and many individuals) providing information, organise their information as a web site, often consisting of many pages. Web sites are an effective way of distributing information such as advertisements, technical information, comments and ideas.

Any web page can be accessed directly if its full address is known, but to make locating information easier each web site has a *home page* (*welcome page* or *personal page*) which provides a starting point for a user to search the site. Any web site can provide links to other related web sites.

Since *browsers* (see above) and *search engines* (see page 44) can quickly find pages of interest, users are provided with the tools to *surf* the Internet. Surfing means to search for useful information, following whatever routes may seem interesting.

Web pages are usually prepared using *HyperText Mark-up Language (HTML)*, see page 40.

EUDORA

Is a program which manages the transmitting and receiving of email messages.

Electronic mail

also known as: email

including: snail mail, mailbox, bounce, cross-post, spam

is sending messages from user to user through computer communication. These messages are the equivalent of traditional letters or memos, there is no provision for two-way conversation. Messages are delivered automatically and very quickly through telecommunications networks. In comparison postal delivery is slow and derisively called *snail mail*.

Most email services are provided by organisations linked to the Internet. This allows emails to be sent to anywhere in the world provided the recipient has an email address, a *mailbox*. Many organisations have internal email systems running on their own private, confidential networks.

Since email is relatively cheap, and because the sending and receiving users do not have to be using their computers at the same time, it is a popular way for schools and colleges to communicate with colleagues in other countries.

Email system provider's computers will normally be able to receive mail at any time. If the recipient's mailbox cannot be located, the email will *bounce*. This means that it will be returned to the sender, usually with a suitable message.

line 1	`From:      MX%"fred@rz.uni-jena.de"       26-MAR-1998 17:25:55.00`
line 2	`To: MX%"ngc@austin.ibm.com"`
line 3	`CC: MX%"thomas_ng@greenwood.notts.sch.uk"`
line 4	`Subj: Scotland`
line 5	`Received: from cnve.rz.uni-jena.de by greenwood.notts.sch.uk with SMTP; Thur, 26 Mar 1998 17:25:53 GMT`
line 6	`Received: (from fred@localhost) by fsuj03.rz.uni-jena.de (8.7.1/8.6.10) id SAA16317; Wed, 26 Thur 1998 18:25:48 +0100 (MEZ)`
line 7	`From: Freda Smith <fred@rz.uni-jena.de>`
line 8	`Subject: Scotland`
line 9	`To: ngc@austin.ibm.com (ngc)`
line 10	`Date: Wed, 26 Thur 1998 18:25:46 +0100 (MEZ)`
line 11	`CC: thomas_ng@vax.nott.ac.uk`
line 12	`In-Reply-To: <9703182135.AA20796@ng.austin.ibm.com> from "ngc" at Mar 18, 97 03:35:51 pm`
line 13	`X-Mailer: ELM [version 2.4 PL23]`
line 14	`Content-Type: text`
line 15	Hello......

Figure A8.2: *An email*

There are many kinds of electronic mail package and the mail delivery information they present is not always the same. With the message, many packages provide information about it, the send time, the message arrival time, the name of the mail package used and the computer gateways which the message passed through. Some packages put this information after the message, others put it before the message, as in Figure A8.2.

The convention for an email address is: **user@computer.organisation.country**

MX% (for Message Exchange) **(line 1)** is a piece of software which controls the store-and-forward routing and the delivery of electronic mail messages.
In this example:
User *"fred" from Jena University in Germany* **(lines 1 & 7)**, **sent** a message to **user** *"ngc"* at IBM, Austin, U.S.A. **(lines 2 & 9)**, and **carbon copy** the message to **user** *"thomas_ng"* at Greenwood School Nottingham, UK **(lines 3 & 11)**. The *Subject* of the message is *"Scotland"* **(lines 4 & 8)**. The message was sent on *Thursday 26th March 1998 at 18:25:48 local time* (Middle European Time Zone - 1 hour ahead of Greenwich Mean Time) **(lines 6 & 10)**. The message was sent from a *localhost through fsuj03.rz.uni-jena.de* **(line 6)**, then onwards to *cnve.rz.uni-jena.de* and arrived at *greenwood.notts.sch.uk at 17:25:53 GMT* **(line 5)**. The message took 5 seconds to travel from *Jena University* to *Nottingham*. The name of user *"fred"* is Freda Smith.. The mail package she used was *ELM* **(line 13)**. This message is a reply to an earlier message sent by user *ngc on 18th March* **(line 12)**. The message is made up of text **(line 14)**. **Line 15** is the start of the message.

It is possible to send copies of a message to more than one intended recipient at the same time, this is called *cross-posting* a message. It provides opportunities to send many unwanted emails, such as advertisements. This unwanted material is known as *spam*. See also Multi-purpose Internet Mail Extender, page 40.

File transfer
including: file transfer protocol (ftp), archive, Anonymous FTP (Anonymous File Transfer Protocol)
is a major use of the Internet involving the movement of information about the Internet as copies of files. Information providers store files containing data on computers which can be accessed from the Internet.

A user identifies which file contains the data needed and initiates a file transfer. If a file is copied from one location to another via the Internet, the transfer process has to conform to Internet protocols.

File Transfer Protocol (FTP) allows a user to send a message causing a copy of a file to be transferred between computers. The file can be saved by the user and the data read. The file transfer protocol controls the messages between computers, the sending of the file copy in sections (also called *blocks*, see page 131) and checks the data received for errors. To make the transfer faster, the files provided for file transfer are usually compressed and are referred to as an *archive*.

Anonymous FTP (Anonymous File Transfer Protocol) is a service which offers users the facility to locate and copy files without having to identity themselves as the searcher. See also *Archie*, page 44.

Intranet

including: extranet

is a communication system providing similar services to the Internet solely within a particular company or organisation.

An intranet provides an organisation with services which are only accessible by authorised users and has good security for confidential information. It allows secure email communication and the distribution of information using technology similar to the World Wide Web. It may use the Internet to allow access by its authorised users anywhere in the world. Part of the intranet may allow public access, which gives the organisation an opportunity to advertise itself using the Internet. This Internet access to an intranet is sometimes called an *extranet*.

HyperText Mark-up Language (HTML)

including: tag, link, HyperText Transfer Protocol (HTTP)

is a computer language used to create multimedia pages. It is used for World Wide Web pages. Each page consists of the text to be displayed and *tags*, which are special instructions to the computer, such as to insert a picture or to change text size and style. These tags may also define some text as a *link* to another page, which is the address of that page. When a browser displays a page and a link is clicked on, the browser will retrieve and display the page referred to, from its Internet location.

It is possible to define a web page by adding the tags to the text using a text editor but most page design is done using special editors which save the designed page as an HTML file. HTML files conform to *HTTP* standards (see below).

The process of requesting a particular web page and transferring it is defined by the *HyperText Transfer Protocol* (*HTTP*). If a resource is identified as an http file this indicates that it is a multimedia page constructed using the HTML language.

Multi-purpose Internet Mail Extender (MIME)

is a protocol used to send email messages containing forms of computer data other than text. Some email systems are only designed for textual messages and sending other computer data results in it being corrupted. MIME is a way of coding the data to avoid corruption. On receipt the data will need to be decoded before use.

Usenet

including: emotes, Three Letter Acronym (TLA)

is the use of the Internet for interactive communication between individuals.
Originally this formed a subset of the Internet but now refers to a range of personal communication facilities including *chat* programs, *newsgroups* and *list servers* (see page 41).

Emotes are primitive icons - usually formed by joining together a number of normal characters - used to indicate feelings in email messages. They are often best interpreted at right-angles to the print direction. These icons are often known as 'smilies'. For example   :-)   or   :-(

Three Letter Acronyms (*TLA*) replace frequently used terms to minimise typing and connection time. However many acronyms used have more than three letters!

Chat

including: Internet Relay Chat (IRC)

is a program which allows Internet users to communicate interactively with other users. ***Internet Relay Chat (IRC)*** is one method of allowing many users to chat over the Internet without unreasonable delays in the communication.

Newsgroup

including: flame, Frequently Asked Question (FAQ), moderated newsgroups, lurk, thread

is a message storage area which is dedicated to a particular special-interest subject. Messages are emailed to the newsgroup where they are stored. An interested user can read these messages and perhaps contribute to the group. Newsgroups enable contact and debate between people who do not know each other but have a common interest. See also *bulletin board*, page 50.

The interactive nature of newsgroups has allowed a very specialised vocabulary to develop, including:

Flame is an emailed message, often posted to a newsgroup, attacking another member of the group.

Frequently Asked Question (FAQ) is a list of questions and answers, usually in a mailing list or newsgroup. The purpose is to save time by avoiding the questioner having to send the questions and wait for the replies.

Lurk is to read messages in a newsgroup, but never to post any.

Moderated newsgroups have a person (see *sysop*, page 50) checking all messages before they are made available. This prevents the misuse of the newsgroup by irrelevant or obscene or insulting messages being posted.

Thread is the initial posting and all associated comments linked to it, which is being sent to a particular message area.

List server

is an automated electronic mail distribution system. This is a program which runs on a computer connected to the Internet. The list server can receive requests from people to join (or leave) the mailing list. The requests are processed automatically. A user on a mailing list can send an email to the list server which will copy it to all users currently on the mailing list. This is a useful way of distributing information to a group of users who have a common interest. See *Internet service provider* in *dial-up*, page 42.

Uniform Resource Locator (URL)

is the address for data on the Internet. Each resource, which is usually a file, has a name, its URL, which specifies the file or data and the location where it is stored. The URL includes the transfer protocol to be used, for example *http* (see page 40), the *domain name* (see page 42) where it is stored, and other information such as its individual filename.

For example, http://www.bcs.org.uk/ will load the home page for the British Computer Society's web site.

Dial-up

also known as: dial in

including: service provider, dial-up service, Internet Service Provider (ISP)
is using an ordinary telephone line (and a modem or terminal adapter) to connect a
local computer, or terminal, to a remote computer service such as the Internet.

   In most cases the facility to dial into the computer system is provided by a *service
provider* who runs the *dial-up service*. This may be provided by the IT department of
a company with dial-up facilities for its employees or by a separate company which
provides the service.

   Many people access the Internet using a dial-up service provided by an *Internet
Service Provider (ISP)*. These companies provide a *host computer* (see page 158),
which the user can connect to by dialling in. The host computer manages the
communications and also stores data such as electronic mail, web pages and files for
its subscribers. This host computer is connected to the Internet and subscribers can
communicate with other computers on the Internet. The Internet service provider
charges for these services, and may provide other value-added services. See also
UNIX Internet host, page 44.

Connect time

including: blink, flash session, off-line reader (OLR)
is the length of time a user is connected to the Internet. This is related to the cost of
using the Internet. If there is a telephone connection, it is likely to be charged by the
time used. Some *Internet service providers* (see above) also charge users according to
the time they are connected to the host computer. For a single session these times
ought to be the same.

   To *blink* is to use of an automated process to access the Internet very quickly, to
collect electronic mail and perform file transfers, before processing the data off-line
(see *off-line processing*, page 172). It is also called a *flash session*. One way of
doing this is to use an *Off-Line Reader (OLR)* which is a software package allowing
a user to connect to an on-line system, such as that provided by an Internet service
provider, and automatically download emails and any other addressed messages.
After disconnection from the service provider, the software allows the user to read
and, if wanted, to write replies while off-line. The software then transmits all replies
and any other outgoing messages, at a later time which the user determines. This
makes use of the Internet much cheaper than other methods of access.

Domain name

including: domain name system, domain name server, IP address
is the name for the apparent location, or site, of a resource on the Internet. Each
location has a unique domain name and this is part of the filename of each resource.

   The *domain name system* defines how domain names are structured. Domain
names are allocated and registered in this format by companies contracted to do this.
Domain names, once registered, are stored on a large database and a program called a
domain name server accesses this database to provide the (physical) location of the
data.

Each computer linked to the Internet has a physical address, a number called its IP address. The *IP address (Internet Protocol address)* uniquely identifies the physical computer linked to the Internet. The domain name server converts the domain name into its corresponding IP address.

Usually the domain name refers to the computer where the data is stored but it is possible for the data to be stored elsewhere and, in this case, the domain name is a pseudonym for the real location of the data.

ITU (International Telecommunications Union)

formerly: CCITT (Committée Consultatif International Téléphonique et Télégraphique)

including: Internet Society, Internet Architecture Board (IAB)

is the international organisation which co-ordinates world-wide telecommunications. It is part of the United Nations Organisation. Originally it was based in France and known as the CCITT, an acronym by which it is still widely known. It seeks to obtain agreement on the setting and adherence to international standards for data telecommunications.

Various other organisations work with the ITU.

The *Internet Society* is an organisation representing the major Internet network owners.

The *Internet Architecture Board (IAB)* is a committee of the Internet Society and considers the use of appropriate Internet standards and protocols.

MUG (Multi-User Game)

including: modem play, network play, null-modem

is a networked game where several players take part at the same time. The players may play against each other or act as a group playing against the computer. Traditionally, the program controlling the game is run on a central computer with players dialling in directly or connecting through the Internet. Often the game runs continuously with players leaving and new players joining all the time.

It is possible to link two computers running the same game so that players can compete with each other rather than competing with the computer. This is called, *modem play* or *network play,* and can be played by dialling in to the other computer or using an Internet link. An alternative to a network connection is a *null-modem* connection where two computers are connected directly together to exchange data, usually using the *serial ports* (see page 297). A special null-modem cable is used because the output from one computer must be linked to the input of the other.

Cyberspace

is the complete set of information which can be accessed using the Internet. It can be thought of as a imaginary or virtual world, made up of all the sites and all the files available. This virtual world can be explored electronically in the same way as we may explore a real area of the world by moving around and looking for interesting things.

GIF (Graphics Interchange Format)

including: PNG (Portable Network Graphics)
is a format for storing graphics images as files. These files then have the file type, GIF. The data in these files is compressed making them faster to load and transfer across the Internet. The GIF standard allows interlaced images, which means that a low quality version of the image can be displayed whilst the rest of the data is still being transmitted over the Internet. Simple animations can be stored and transmitted in GIF format. See *interlace*, page 134.

Other graphics formats used for images displayed on *web pages* (see page 37) include *PNG* (*Portable Network Graphics*) and *JPEG* (see page 311).

UNIX Internet host

including: Gopher, Veronica, Archie, WAIS (Wide Area Information Server)
is a computer running the UNIX operating system that provides facilities for Internet users. UNIX is a powerful operating system particularly suited to network operation and many Internet service providers use computers running it. The user operates a simple command line interface or accesses one of the available menu systems. Few users now work with UNIX, preferring a *browser* (see page 37). See also, *Internet service provider*, page 42, *UNIX*, page 273, and *host computer*, page 158

Many programs were developed for UNIX systems including:

Gopher: a menu system that helps the user find resources by searching its comprehensive indexes. There are many different gopher systems and each has slightly different data in its indexes.

Veronica is a *search engine* (see below) that searches all the gopher indexes to produce a list of resources in response to a user's request. See *gopher*, above.

Archie is a *search engine* (see below) that holds indexes of all the files available for *file transfer* (see page 39) on the Internet.

WAIS (Wide Area Information Server) is a *search engine* (see below) that searches some of the databases attached to the Internet. There are several hundred databases including news services, reviews and specialist document archives.

Information Superhighway

is a name given to the Internet now that communication speeds are much higher. This name reflects the fact that large amounts of information can be communicated rapidly between users.

Search Engine

is a computer program which searches a very large database to find data items which match a requested *query* (see page 24).

Search engines are useful for locating resources on the Internet. Search engines collect details of Internet resources and their locations, often automatically, and hold this data in a very large database for the search engine to use. A search engine uses a variety of methods to find the required data, such as finding alternative keywords using a thesaurus.

Virtual Reality Mark-up Language (VRML)

is a computer language used to define 3-dimensional objects for a special type of web page. A special *browser* (see page 37) may be needed to display VRML images.

Internet protocol

including: Transmission Control Protocol/Internet Protocol (TCP/IP), Address Resolution Protocol (ARP), Internet Control Message Protocol (ICMP), Point to Point Protocol (PPP), Serial Line Internet Protocol (SLIP), Simple Mail Transfer Protocol (SMTP), Post Office Protocol 3 (POP3), UNIX to UNIX Copy Protocol (UUCP), User Datagram Protocol (UDP/IP)

is a standard set of rules used to ensure the proper transfer of information between computers on the Internet. Internet protocols define how data is to be structured, and what control signals are to be used and their meaning.

Some protocols primarily deal with how particular types of data are structured, such as *File Transfer Protocol* (*FTP*) and *HyperText Transfer Protocol* (*HTTP*), see pages 39 and 40. Other protocols are essentially technical, governing how the individual data elements are communicated over the Internet. These protocols include:

Transmission Control Protocol/Internet Protocol (TCP/IP) is the set of working practices which allow all Internet users and providers to communicate with each other whatever their equipment is. TCP/IP specifies how individual signals are sent over the Internet.

Address Resolution Protocol (ARP) defines how to identify the technical destination of a message.

Internet Control Message Protocol (ICMP) defines the messages used to report status and errors when communicating with another computer.

Point to Point Protocol (PPP) defines communication between two computers connected directly. It is commonly used between individual users and their *Internet service provider*, see page 42, when using a telephone line. The Internet Service Provider will access the Internet on the user's behalf using the TCP/IP protocol.

Serial Line Internet Protocol (SLIP) is an Internet protocol allowing personal computer users to dial in to a suitable Internet service, using only a telephone line, but using the full TCP/IP protocol. Such a user has full Internet access.

Simple Mail Transfer Protocol (SMTP) is a TCP/IP protocol used in the transfer of email between computer systems. The user's incoming mail is stored on the service provider's computer. SMTP does not automatically download it as soon as the user connects to the server but requires a specific request to do so. See also *POP3*, next.

Post Office Protocol 3 (POP3) defines the transfer of email between computer systems. It provides more facilities than *Simple Mail Transfer Protocol*, see above.

UNIX to UNIX Copy Protocol (UUCP) defines the copying of files between systems running the UNIX operating system.

User Datagram Protocol (UDP/IP) is used by some applications instead of the TCP/IP protocol.

Remote login

including: telnet

is a service which allows a user at one computer to log in to another computer on any connected network as if the user's computer is a terminal of the remote computer. This is achieved by the use of a program such as ***telnet***, which is a terminal emulator program used for remote access to computers linked to the Internet. This enables a user to have the power of the larger computer available for their use.

Point of Presence (PoP)

is an access point to an Internet service provider's network. This is usually the telephone exchange where the transmitted data leaves the public telephone network and enters the Internet service provider's network. See also *Internet service provider* (*ISP*), page 42.

Terminal server

is a computer which is attached to a *local area network* (see page 151) and accesses the Internet on request from any of the terminals attached to the local area network. The network may be permanently connected to the Internet or use a modem connection to dial-in to an *Internet service provider* (see page 42) when required.

Post

is to send a message by email. Where the message is available on a bulletin board, the message is described as posted on the *bulletin board*, see page 50. See also *cross-posting*, in *email*, page 38.

Postmaster

is a system controller with responsibility for email.

White pages

is a database holding a directory of Internet users, their correct Internet site names and email addresses.

Finger

is a program which lists the users on a remote system, often giving information such as physical addresses, telephone numbers, etc. See also *WhoIs*, below

WhoIs

is a program which can find email addresses using only the name of a known Internet user.

Internet Information Systems

are large, and often dispersed, databases which can be accessed from the Internet. There are many such systems but three commonly used ones are *Gopher* and *WAIS*, see page 44, and the *World Wide Web* (*WWW*), page 37.

Site

is any individual computer, or network, which is part of the Internet.

Packet Internet Groper (PING)

is a program which checks whether a computer with a particular address is attached to the Internet. See also *IP address*, page 42/3.

Off-line

refers to a computer, which is normally attached to a network, but operating in stand-alone mode. See also *off-line processing*, page 172.

On-line

refers to a computer, which is normally attached to a network, and available for external connections to be made at all times on demand from users. See also *on-line processing*, page 172.

Netiquette

is the set of social conventions which seek to define good behaviour when using the Internet. These conventions try to encourage behaviour that does not cause inconvenience to other users.

Server (software)

is software which allows one computer to offer a service to another computer. The software running on this other computer may make requests for services from the server. Sometimes the computer with the server-software is itself called the server. See also *server*, page 157.

Robot (software)

is a web-server program which receives a message and then takes some action appropriate to the message. A typical robot action may be to search for HTML documents by reference to links between them, building up a map of the information held on the *WWW*, see page 37. See *server (software)*, above.

Winsock

is a program which allows personal computers to communicate with other computers over the Internet, using the standard *TCP/IP communications protocol* (see page 45). Winsock converts commands from the PC into a correctly formatted message for transmission to a linked computer. Many personal computer communication programs use Winsock to perform the actual communication, although this is transparent to the user.

Freenet

is a service provider which allows free Internet access to a defined group of individual users. A typical example is access provided at a terminal in a public library.

Lynx

is a text-only *browser*, see page 37. It is particularly useful for users whose computer does not have facilities to display pictures.

Mosaic

is a UNIX-supported graphics *browser*, see page 37, which can be used to find many types of information on the Internet's *WWW*, see page 37.

A9   Communications

Other related terms may be found in sections A8 Internet,
B6 Networks, B7 Communications Devices and Control Devices and
C17 Communications Technology.

The internal architecture of a computer involves electronic signals being passed from component to component. It is a natural extension of this idea to send signals *out* of the computer, to another computer, perhaps thousands of kilometres away. The technology to achieve this is discussed in section C17.

The extension of these concepts and practices has produced the range of opportunities provided by the Internet. It has such a wide range of terms which are specific to it that section A8 is devoted exclusively to the Internet.

On an electronic scale, the distance of a few metres to your printer is so large that it raises a new set of problems (is the printer actually switched on? – what does the computer do if it isn't?): these problems are surprisingly not made *much* more severe if the printer is across the other side of the Atlantic. So it seems quite natural for a number of computer applications to have been developed that involve communication and information-provision over large distances.

Many of the applications have become so much a part of modern industrialised societies that it takes us aback to realise that they involve computing technology – taking cash from a cash dispenser in the middle of the night in a strange town, sending a fax, reading the sports results on Teletext, and so on.

Facsimile transmission (Fax)
including: fax groups
is the use of regular voice-quality telephone lines to send copies of documents, which may include drawings as well as text. The sender inserts the document into their own fax machine, and dials the receiving machine, which must be available at that time, and not busy sending or receiving another fax. The two fax machines need to be compatible. In order to simplify the process of identifying compatibility, fax machines are classified into *groups* with different technical specifications. The two machines need to belong to compatible groups.

The sending machine scans the paper on a line-by-line basis, and transmits the information to the receiving machine, which recreates the document using photocopier technology (for this reason, many fax machines can also operate as photocopiers). Many computers that can be connected to the telephone lines can send faxes directly, without the need to generate a paper copy first: this simplifies the problem of finding the receiving machine busy, as the computer can simply try again later, without human intervention.

Bulletin board

including: system operator (sysop), Campus
also known as: Bulletin Board System (BBS)

is the electronic equivalent of a notice-board, carrying short items that may be of interest to a wide number of people. Bulletin boards are sited on a computer, and the users access the computer by a *network* (see page 151), *electronic mail* (see page 38) or the *Internet* (see page 36). They can leave messages for anyone to read, review messages left by other users and sometimes take copies of software that has been placed on the board. The organiser of such a board is traditionally known as the **system operator** or more familiarly as the *sysop*. Larger bulletin boards are run by organisations such as newspapers, computer manufacturers or universities, and offer comprehensive information services as well as an opportunity to read or post messages. A popular large board accessed by many schools because of its educational focus is *Campus*.

Figure A9.1: *A typical bulletin board screen*

Computer conferencing

makes use of *electronic mail* (see page 38) to allow a group of people with a common interest, but geographically separated, to share advice, opinions, information and so on. The users are organised in a 'conference' and are able to examine messages left by other users, add their own comments, and generally participate in the work of the group. This is very similar to the idea of a *bulletin board* (see above), but there is a suggestion in a computer conference that users are all on an equal footing, and are all expected to contribute equally.

Computer-Supported Co-operative Work (CSCW)

including: work group

It is too early to tell whether this unwieldy description will find a permanent place in computer terminology: it describes the use of networked computer systems to enable **work groups** of employees to share documents, diaries and other computer files.

Closed User Group (CUG)

Not all information services on a *Viewdata* system (see page 52) are available to all subscribers. Commercial businesses, for example, may choose to provide information only to registered dealers or sales representatives: such a group is known as a 'closed' user group.

Electronic Funds Transfer (EFT)

including: debit card, EFTPOS, cash dispenser, automatic teller machine (ATM)
is the use of computer networks to transfer money. This may be done between banks, as an alternative to sending a cheque or a bankers' draft, especially where international transfers are involved. Most large companies now pay their employees by electronic transfer of funds into their personal bank accounts. Increasingly, it is being used in retail stores as an alternative to payment by credit card or cheque: the purchaser offers a *debit card* which is processed in the same way as a credit card, but which initiates the transfer of money from the purchaser's account directly to the shop's account. In this use, it is normally known by the cumbersome title of *Electronic Funds Transfer at Point-of-Sale* (*EFTPOS*). The same principles are involved in a cash withdrawal from a *cash dispenser* or *automatic teller machine (ATM)*.

Minitel

The French telecommunications agency has replaced printed telephone books by an on-line computerised directory enquiries service, called 'Minitel'. Simple terminals with screens are widely available in public places, and personal equipment may be bought or rented. As well as telephone information, a wide variety of commercial and public information is available and theatre and travel tickets can be purchased, as well as more conventional ordering of goods. This is essentially a public *bulletin board* (see page 50).

Telecommunications

a general term describing the communication of information over a distance. The method of communication is normally via a cable, *wire* or *fibre optic* (see page 162) or electro-magnetic radiation. See also *wireless communication*, page 161.

Tele-commuting

is the use of information technology to allow people to work in their own homes, while still being in easy contact with the office. Typically, this involves use of *electronic mail* and *fax* (see pages 38 and 49), as well as allowing remote users access to a central computer or network.

Tele-conferencing

including: video-conferencing
is the use of communication links to conduct meetings between people who are geographically separated. The links might be voice-only, or might include pictures, when it is usually referred to as *video-conferencing*.

Videotex

is the overall name given to systems that supply information on television screens. See *Teletext* and *Viewdata*, below, for fuller descriptions.

Teletext

including: Ceefax, Oracle

is a system that uses part of the broadcast television picture unseen to the regular viewer, to supply a variety of information, such as news stories, weather forecasts, train cancellations and so on. With a specially equipped TV set, the viewer can press buttons on a remote control handset to replace the TV picture by simple text pages. Each page is numbered, and all the pages are transmitted in sequence. A particular choice of page is requested by entering the number, after which there is a slight delay until that page is next transmitted; this waiting time limits the number of pages that realistically can be provided. Some pages are linked, and allow the viewer to pass from one page to another more rapidly. All TV channels in the UK offer this service; the BBC version is known as *Ceefax*. The commercial channels were originally known as *Oracle* until the name 'Teletext' was adopted as a brand name. Because the viewer cannot talk back to the provider of the pages of information, this is only a one-way information service. See also *Prestel*, below.

Viewdata

including: Prestel

is the general name given to a *Teletext*-like system (see above) which displays 'pages' of textual information on a television screen, but uses regular phone lines, rather than a broadcast television signal, to transmit information. It is then possible for the user to interact with the system, supplying information, requesting searches of the data, or even ordering goods and services by supplying credit-card information. Because pages are only transmitted after a specific request, very large collections of data can be offered, without penalty to other users. The best-known such system is the UK *Prestel* viewdata system.

On-line service

is a service, such as a *bulletin board* (see page 50) or an *email* service (see page 38), which is normally available at all times. It may be provided as part of a network or it may be accessed via external communications systems.

Header

is data at the start of a set of data which is used to identify the data. In communications, a header will contain data about the destination and route for the subsequent data.

Trailer

is data at the end of a set of data which indicates the end of the data in a *frame*, see page 307. Another kind of trailer is an *end of file marker*, page 259, for a file.

A10 Control

Other terms related to the use of computers in controlling processes and devices will be found in B7 Communications Devices and Control Devices and C17 Communications Technology.

The use of computers to make machines do what we want them to - called **control** - grew out of the extensive use of mechanical devices and electro-magnetic switches (relays). In telephone exchanges, traffic lights and lifts, control used to be achieved by the use of mechanically operated switching systems. Other methods were designed to control the operation of machines, made up of devices which reacted to conditions in the environment such as temperature, pressure, speed, position. Large manufacturing plants were built controlled by these methods.

The development of microprocessors and microcomputers made it possible to improve the reliability of existing systems and to make them more flexible. In a modern airliner the computer system is capable of controlling take-off and landing as well as automatically maintaining course, speed and altitude. The computers used in cars take over part of the control of the car engine from the driver. The operation of washing machines and video equipment is frequently managed by microprocessors.

Control may be exercised remotely, in which case control signals are sent from the controller to the device. These signals may be transmitted in any of the ways which are used to pass data for example through wires, or as radio or infra-red signals.

Control systems may be either passive or re-active. In a **passive system** the controlled device, once it has been set going, will perform a predetermined set of activities regardless of the circumstances. A **re-active system** will vary its behaviour in response to different situations. By using programmable chips, connected to suitable sensors, it is now common for systems to respond to the information provided by these sensors. Combining control and observation, through the use of sensors, has made it possible to extend the scope of automatic **process control**, for example in the manufacture and packaging of chemical products.

Automation
is the use of machines or systems to perform tasks as an alternative to using people.

CAD/CAM
including: computer assisted manufacturing (CAM)
is the use of the output from a computer aided design (CAD) process as input to control a *computer assisted manufacturing (CAM)* process. This can be an integrated process in which the manufacturing happens automatically and is important in the development of new products. See *computer aided design,* page 26.

Data capture

including: sampling, data logging
is the *sampling* (collection at specified intervals) of output from external sensors (see also *polling*, page 293). This data may be used to control a process. *Data logging* is the capture and storage of data for later use; thus data captured in a control process may be logged for later analysis of the process.

Feedback

including: closed loop feedback, open loop feedback
is the use of data from sensors as input to the controlling program. In this way the result of previous actions becomes input which contributes to selecting the next action. If the response to the feedback is automatic (there is no human operator involvement), the process is called *closed loop*; if an operator is involved, it is called *open loop*. In most situations where feedback is used to control position, for example stacking boxes on shelves, the correct position is achieved by an iterative process, in which a move is followed by a position check, each move bringing it closer to the required position, until the correct position is reached.

Fly by wire

is a method of controlling an aeroplane in flight. The flaps, rudder and other control surfaces of the aeroplane are operated by motors. These motors are controlled by (electrical) signals which are created as a result of actions by the pilot. This kind of flight control system involves the use of computers to analyse the pilot's intentions and thus work out the right amount of movement of the control surfaces; the computers can over-ride the pilot in situations which would endanger the aeroplane.

G-code

is a form of *intermediate code* (see page 246) which can be used by the control systems of machine tools.

Numeric control

also called: computer numeric control (CNC)
generally refers to the automatic control of machines such as lathes and milling machines. Some numerically controlled machines simply obey a preset program of instructions, while more advanced machines can react to *feedback* (see above) from *sensors* (see page 165).

Telemetry

is the use of communications (usually radio) and measuring sensors to achieve control of machines and instruments at a distance. For example, the control of satellites and space probes, or the monitoring and control of the performance of Formula 1 racing cars, where the technicians can adjust the engine control system on the car from the pits while the race is in progress.

Paper tape

including: paper tape punch, paper tape reader
is sometimes still used as the means of program and data input to machine tools. A pattern of holes punched in the tape is used to represent the data. In order to prepare the tape a *paper tape punch* is attached to the computer on which the program and data are prepared while a *tape reader* is used as an input device to the machine tool.

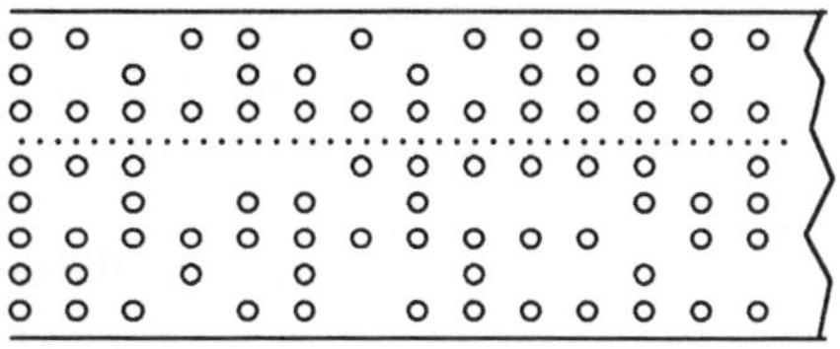

Figure A10.1: Punched paper tape

Process control

including: integrated manufacturing
is the automatic monitoring and control of an industrial activity by a computer that is programmed to respond to the *feedback* (see above) signals from *sensors* (see page 165). The operation controlled may be as small as a single machine packing boxes or as extensive as the control of an automated bakery, where the mixing, cooking and packaging are controlled within a single *integrated manufacturing* process.

Robot

including: robot arm
is a computer-controlled mechanical device which is sufficiently flexible to be able to do a variety of tasks. Robots are frequently used to do jobs where consistent performance is required (such as paint spraying motor cars) or where there is some danger to humans performing the task (such as the handling of toxic materials). A *robot arm* is a relatively simple fixed robot capable of picking things up, positioning them, etc.

A11 Numerical and Scientific Computing

The first computers were seen simply as calculating devices, able to carry out lengthy and tedious mathematical calculations without error and at high speed. They made existing trigonometric and logarithm tables unnecessary, as computers were able to calculate values when needed, as fast as they could look up stored values – although, at that stage, the individual scientist did not conceive of a personal computer, and continued to work with portable calculating devices such as slide rules and tables.

The focus of computing has now shifted away from the purely numerical, but nevertheless there are still major uses for mathematical programming. The statistical analysis of large amounts of data involves considerable amounts of computation, as well as the ordering and sorting of the data.

Another area involving numerical computing is the deciphering of codes – **cryptanalysis**. Strictly, a *code* is any scheme for substituting one representation of data for another, as in *character code*. The correct term for a coded message, where the intention is to conceal information, is **cipher**.

The process of enciphering messages – **cryptography** – also involves numeric computing because it is usual to turn textual messages into numbers (A=01, B=02, CAT=030120 etc.) and to perform mathematical operations on the resulting large numbers, in order to turn them into a cipher.

Some of the techniques encountered in numerical uses of computing belong to the mathematical branch known as **numerical analysis**. Some of these techniques are defined in this section. In calculating the values that appear in mathematical tables, the computer often uses power series; sometimes a calculation is done in an indirect way, using **iteration**, where a 'trial' answer is repeatedly refined, until it is approximately correct.

Algorithm

is a specific procedure for a computer that will either accomplish some task or solve a problem. An algorithm is roughly equivalent to a computer program. Algorithms may be described in any suitable form. These include instructions in words, such as Figure A11.1 on page 58, instructions in a computer language or diagrams. Algorithms, such as Figure A11.1, often involve the use of *loops*, see page 207.

Combinatorics

including: enumeration

is the branch of mathematics to do with counting or *enumerating*. In using computer systems to search for alternative routes through a road network, for example, it will be important to ensure that all possible combinations are considered, and that extra work is not done by considering routes that have already been looked at.

Combinatorial *algorithms* (see above) are designed to take care of details such as this.

Cryptanalysis

including: cipher breaking

is the '*breaking*' of *ciphers*. Nowadays, this is almost always done by computer. Captured cipher messages are analysed to see if patterns emerge that will indicate the method of coding, after which further analysis may indicate the precise *key* (see *cryptography*, below) used in the enciphering.

Cryptography

including: secret messages, cipher, key

is the science of sending *secret messages*, or *ciphers*. In communicating by code, it is usual for everyone to use the same method, but to have some personal (and secret) *key* that modifies the method in a way that makes the message remain secure, even if the method is known. Generally, textual messages are converted into numbers before being enciphered, resulting in a very large number of perhaps a hundred or so digits. The method is an *algorithm* (see page 56) that processes that number but uses the key number as a vital part of the calculation. See *public key cryptography*, page 58.

Data Encryption Standard (DES)

is a standard method of encrypting data, developed by the US Government. The method specifies how a *key* (see *cryptography*, above) is used to encode the message in a standard way. It is believed that the method alone is secure enough, without knowledge of the key, for it to be published. Making the method publicly available means that computer manufacturers can develop software and hardware for easy implementation of the method.

Monte Carlo method

A whimsical name which comes from the use of chance, usually random numbers rather than roulette wheels, in simulation. In exploring the behaviour of a complex system (which might be chemical, physical, biological, human, etc.), the overall behaviour of the system may be too complicated to specify confidently in mathematical terms. If the many small decisions in the system *can* be easily specified, then the behaviour of the system can be simulated, using random numbers to model a large number of small decisions. For example, migration of people between towns in the UK might be too complicated to specify mathematically, but information *is* available on how many people move from London to Edinburgh (say) each year. The overall behaviour of the population can be explored by selecting one resident of London, and generating a random number to see if that individual will stay or move, and if so, where to. By repeating this for the whole population of the UK, predictions about future population trends will be possible, even if the mathematics is not fully understood. See also *random number generation*, page 61.

Iteration (mathematical)

is a mathematical procedure for solving equations, where an initial estimate is made of the answer, and the result of using this (possibly quite poor) guess is used to improve the answer. If this process is repeated, or re-iterated, enough times, the desired answer can be found to any degree of accuracy. See Figure A11.1 for an example of iteration. See also *loop*, page 207.

CALCULATING A SQUARE ROOT

We know that the square root of 2 is 1.414214 to 6 decimal places. An iterative method of calculating this is to take a guess (even a very bad guess) such as 3. If this first guess is then used as x in the calculation:

$$y = \frac{1}{2}\left[x + \frac{2}{x}\right]$$

*you get an answer y=1.833, which is **closer** to the known answer than the original guess. The value of this method is that if you then repeat the calculation, using 1.833 as the guess, the next **iterate** is closer still, 1.46212. In fact, after only two further iterations, the method gives the known answer correct to six decimal places. Finding the formulas that 'work' in these situations is part of **numerical analysis**.*

Figure A11.1: An example of iteration

Public key cryptography

including: one-way functions, trapdoor functions, RSA algorithm

Some mathematical operations are easy to do, but in practice impossible to undo. As a simple example, it is easy to multiply together 11 and 13 to get 143, but it takes an amount of trial-and-error to work back from 143 to the (only) factors 11 and 13. If the numbers involved had hundreds or thousands of digits, rather than just two, the amount of trial and error involved would mean that even a fast computer might be unable to find the factors in an acceptably short time. Such operations – easy to do, and impossible to undo in a realistic time – are known as *one-way functions*. If the operation is one like the multiplication above, where some secret knowledge (like the numbers 11 and 13) provides a short-cut, they are known as *trapdoor functions*. These can be used as the basis for a simple but secure coding system, as shown in Figure A11.2, opposite. The best-known such function was developed by the mathematicians Rivest, Shamir and Adleman, and is, unsurprisingly, called the *RSA algorithm*.

	A public directory is published – for everyone in the code system, it tells the whole world what **key** is used to send messages to that person. This is a (big) number that can be used to encode messages. The *de*coding part is secret: only one person knows that!
	I want to send a message to you. I write my message out, substituting A=01, B=02 etc. and get a (long) number which represents my message.
	Now I look up your key in the public directory and use it to turn my message into another long number – this is done in a way that no-one except you can decode – even *I* can't, unless I look back at my original message.
	You receive my message, and using your very secret decoding method, turn it back into the original message.
	How do you know that the message was *really* from me? Anyone could look up your key in the public directory and send a misleading message that claimed to be from me! I can *prove* it was from me, like this:
	With my message, I include my name and address, but before I code this, I use my own secret decoding key to turn the name and address part into a scrambled version.
	Now I code the whole message – the message itself *and* the previously scrambled name and address.
	You receive this two-part message, and use *your* secret decoder to extract the plain message and the scrambled name and address. You read the message, and need to check that it is from me.
	You take the scrambled part, look me up in the directory and see what my public coding key is. Using this will unscramble the name and address, and you are confident that it *was* from me, because I am the only person in the world who knows what my *de*coding key is.

Figure A11.2: *How a public-key cryptosystem works*

Numerical analysis

is the branch of mathematics that studies the methods (such as *power series*, *iteration*, *recursion*) mentioned in this section. Numerical analysts are interested in methods of computing, but are not necessarily heavy users of computers in practice.

Power series

Some mathematical quantities (like π) can be computed using a series such as:

$$\pi = 4\left(\frac{1}{2} + \frac{1}{3} - \frac{1}{2^3.3} - \frac{1}{3^3.3} + \frac{1}{2^5.5} + \frac{1}{3^5.5} - \cdots\right)$$

Depending on how accurate an answer is needed, more or less of the terms being added together can be included. If you stop computing the series above after four terms, the answer 3.117284 is accurate to (only) 1 decimal place – if more are needed, adding in (say) four more terms increases the accuracy to 3 decimal places. *Numerical analysis* (see page 59) is the branch of mathematics that is used to design suitable power series.

Recursion

is a mathematical way of defining a computation in terms of a reduced version of itself. This may seem like a paradox, but because this method is close to the way some mathematical operations are programmed in a computer, it can be very efficient. See Figure A11.3 for two examples.

USING RECURSION

Factorials
The factorial of a number, written as 7!, 3! and so on, is defined as:
>   *7! = 7×6×5×4×3×2×1*
>   *3! = 3×2×1   and so on.*
*Factorials often turn up in **combinatorial algorithms**. Another way of defining a factorial is to say that:*
>   *7! = 7×6!*
>   *3! = 3×2!   or, in general, n! = n×(n-1)!*
*Thus, each factorial is defined in terms of a smaller factorial. This is a **recursive** definition. To make this work, it is necessary to give the smallest factorial 1! a specific value (in this case 1 itself).*

Sorting
A list (of numbers, or words — anything) often has to be sorted into order (numerical or alphabetic, say). One way of defining the process recursively, in a way that can be easy to program, is as follows:
>   *Find the earliest item in the list;*
>   *print that out, and remove it from the list;*
>   *now repeat the whole process, but using the new,*
>   *shorter, list.*
In a similar way to the factorial example above, it is necessary to program the computer to stop taking items off the list when you have shortened it so far that there is nothing left!

Figure A11.3: *Two examples of recursion*

Prime numbers

are numbers like 7, 19, 23 and so on, which have no factors other than themselves and one – that is, they cannot be made by multiplying other numbers together (as 24 can be made by multiplying 6×4, or 3×8, and so on). Prime numbers are important in computing because they form the basis of ciphers (see *cryptography*, page 57), and also because searching for new prime numbers is a good test of mathematical programming techniques. Other uses of prime numbers are in the design of algorithms for *hashing* (see page 192), and (*pseudo*) *random number generation*, (see below).

Random number generation

including: pseudo-random number generator

Many *simulations* (see page 30) on a computer need to make use of random numbers, in a similar way to 'tossing a coin' in order to make a decision. Most programming languages include a random number function that gives the user a suitable number, as if it had been chosen at random – numbers between 1 and 6, for example, to simulate the throw of dice in a game. Because computer programs cannot be truly random, a *pseudo-random number generator* is used, which gives numbers with the appearance of being random. See *Monte Carlo method*, page 57, for more information.

A12 Sound

Other related terms, especially those concerned with modulation, may be found in section C17 Communications Technology. Note that, throughout this Glossary, the spelling 'analog' has been preferred to the alternative 'analogue'.

This section is concerned with the use of computers to generate, store, communicate and manipulate sound.

Most of the terms used when working with computer-generated sound belong to the terminology of music or sound. There are however some terms whose use in a computing context need to be defined.

Electronic reproduction of natural sound has been available for many decades. The ability to generate natural sounds electronically – **sound synthesis** – was developed long before computers. Sound is produced by the continuous vibration of air. This means that it has analog properties. A microphone converts sound energy (air vibrations) into electrical energy (fluctuating voltage and current). In the opposite process a loudspeaker converts electrical energy into sound. These are both analog devices, since they create or use varying electrical energy. The earliest forms of sound synthesis worked by creating and manipulating varying electrical currents, they worked entirely on analog principles. With the use of digital computer techniques the more recent digital audio systems have been developed. These systems use digital methods to create, process and store sounds but receive analog input from microphones and produce analog output for loudspeakers.

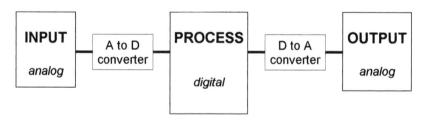

Figure A12.1: *A sound system*

The electrical output from microphones is analog (that is, it consists of a continuously fluctuating voltage). It has to be converted into a digital form if it is to be stored on a digital device (for example, a compact disc) or if it is to be transmitted or manipulated in a digital form. Loudspeakers or headphones require analog signals. The conversion of analog (sound) signals to digital is achieved by a sampling process while the conversion of digital to analog is achieved by adding the values of the bits in the digital representation.

Both analog and digital methods are used to transmit, record, manipulate and create sounds. Digital methods involve the use of computers (or microprocessors) to manipulate data. Thus many pieces of digital musical or sound equipment will contain microprocessors.

The use of computers to create sounds involve sound or speech synthesis. Many microcomputers have (or can be fitted with) appropriate chips so that they can output speech; for example the computer can 'speak' words as well as display them on the screen. The use of voice input is being developed, but there are difficulties yet to be overcome before it can be the normal method of communication between people and computers. As far as the computer is concerned sound is just another form of data which it can create, store, manipulate or output, provided the right input and output devices are available and connected. The manipulation of sound data may be done by software or by hardware within the computer or attached to the computer.

Sound synthesis

also known as: sound generation

including: analog and digital sound generation, subtractive synthesis, Frequency Modulation (FM), Phase Distortion (PD), Linear Arithmetic (LA), additive synthesis
is the use of electronic devices for creating sounds, sometimes called *sound generation*. The sounds may be generated using either analog or digital techniques. Electronically generated sound can create notes which are like those produced by a variety of musical instruments.

Analog sound generation has been used for a very long time (well over 50 years). Usually, the sound is produced by starting with a complex waveform, containing many harmonics, which is produced by an oscillator. Electronic filter circuits are then used to modify the sound by removing some of these harmonics. This process is called *subtractive synthesis*.

Digital sound generation is a recent development in which numbers representing sound waves are manipulated. A variety of methods are used to create the sounds, some of them unique to a particular manufacturer. The most commonly used synthesis methods are:

Frequency Modulation (FM) in which the digital representation of a number of pure waveforms are combined with each other to create a complex compound sound.

Phase Distortion (PD) in which the digital representation of a waveform is modified, by speeding up the rate at which the wave is generated, to produce a complex waveform. This complex waveform is then modified as in an analog synthesiser.

Linear Arithmetic (LA) in which sampled sounds are used as well as pure tones as the start of the process. Arithmetic operations are then carried out on the values of the bit patterns representing the sounds. (See *sound sampler*, page 66.)

Additive synthesis is a computer software method in which the user selects a mixture of harmonics and the computer calculates the values for the waveform at very small successive time intervals. In all cases the digital values for the sound are turned into sound signals by a digital-to-analog converter. Different methods of creating sounds produce different qualities of sound.

Music synthesiser

including: synthesiser, analog synthesiser, digital synthesiser, multi-timbral synthesiser, polyphony

is an electronic device for creating sounds. It is often called just a **synthesiser**. The sounds may be generated electronically using either analog or digital techniques (see *sound generator*, page 66). Most synthesisers have a piano-style keyboard and need to be connected to an amplifier with loudspeakers for the sounds they produce to be heard.

Analog synthesisers are usually intended to be used as musical instruments to be played, and most do not have the ability to store the sounds they create.

Digital synthesisers generally incorporate some form of digital storage and frequently have a built-in store of ready-made sounds. Digital synthesisers generally offer a much greater variety of sounds and a wider range of manipulation options than analog synthesisers. For example, a **multi-timbral synthesiser** can play two or more different sounds at the same time, or produce a number of different notes at the same time (**polyphony**), or a combination of both of these capabilities in the same synthesiser.

Envelope

including: ADSR (attack, decay, sustain, release)

is a shape which is used to describe the changes in volume (amplitude), pitch (frequency) and timbre (quality) of a note as it changes with time. The form of a sound envelope is normally used in *sound synthesis* (see page 63). One commonly used way of describing a volume envelope is known as **ADSR**, an acronym for Attack, Decay, Sustain and Release.

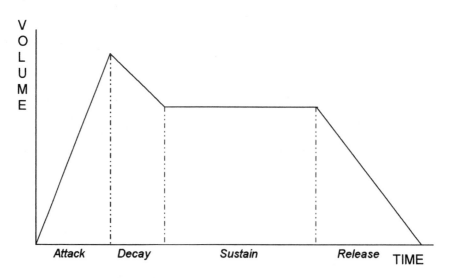

Figure A12.2: *Volume envelope*

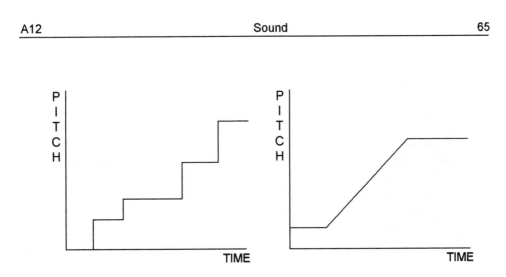

Figure A12.3: Two pitch envelopes

Attack is the rate at which an envelope rises to its initial peak before starting to decay. For example percussive sounds (piano or drums) have a high attack rate for their volume (amplitude). *Decay* is the rate at which an envelope falls from its initial peak to a steady (sustain) level. *Sustain* is the level at which an envelope remains whilst a key is still pressed after the initial attack and decay stages. *Release* is the rate at which an envelope fades away from its sustain level when the key is released.

MIDI (Musical Instrument Digital Interface)

including: MIDI channel, MIDI standard, MIDI code.

A musical instrument digital interface, MIDI (frequently, but incorrectly, referred to as a MIDI interface) is a particular form of serial *interface* (see *interface*, page 288 and *interface card*, page 297) built into or added to the parts of an electronic music system. The interface allows electronic music data to be passed in both directions between parts of the system. The links between parts of the system are called *MIDI channels*.

The form of the interface and the structure of the data are defined by the *MIDI standard*, which was agreed between the major manufacturers of electronic musical instruments in 1983. The standard defines the codes (*MIDI codes*) to be used for musical data, for example the pitch of a note and its volume. These codes allow music data to be passed between devices from different manufacturers in the same way that *ASCII codes* (see *character set*, page 252) allow alphanumeric data to be passed between different computers.

Music keyboard

including: keyboard

Any electronic music device which is controlled by a keyboard similar to a piano is called a music keyboard or a *keyboard*. The keys, which are arranged like the black and white keys on a piano, are frequently supplemented by switches, sliders or other ways of setting and changing the electronic signals produced by or used by the device.

Sound controller

including: musical instrument controller, audio controller

is a hardware device which controls sounds generated by a sound source. Controllers usually do not produce sounds themselves, though they may be made to look like (and be used like) a musical instrument, for example a piano keyboard or a guitar. These are called ***musical instrument controllers***. Some controllers use joysticks, sliders or wheels. These may be built into other controllers or attached to a musical instrument. Control of sounds is usually achieved by using *MIDI codes* (see *MIDI*, page 65). There are also ***audio controllers***, which can generate (MIDI) control signals from audio sounds. With an audio controller looking like a microphone, a user can sing into it while 'playing' a synthesised sound from a connected sound generator, and thus control the sound produced.

Digitiser (sound)

takes an analog sound signal and converts it to a digital signal. See also *signal converter*, page 163.

Sound generator

also known as: sound source

is a digital device capable of producing sounds as part of an electronic music system; it is sometimes called a ***sound source***. A range of such devices exist, which create sounds similar to those produced by particular musical instruments, such as drum machines, electric guitars or electronic organs. A *music synthesiser* (see page 64) is an example of a sound generator; it has a piano-type keyboard which is used to play it, but most sound generators have no direct means of being played as if they were musical instruments. Some have a collection of pre-defined sounds and some have synthesising capability. If the sounds can be altered then there will be controls to do so. The sounds may be accessed via *MIDI* (see page 65), to be used as input to a sequencer or a music controller, or the device may be attached to a computer as a dedicated peripheral.

Sound sampler

including: sampling rate, sampling resolution

is an example of a *digital sampler* (see page 164), in which the device receives sound signals from a microphone (or other sound source) and analyses them. It makes and stores the digital measurements from this analysis. By performing this process of analysis, measurement and storage very quickly and very frequently, the sampler converts the signal into a digital representation of the sound.

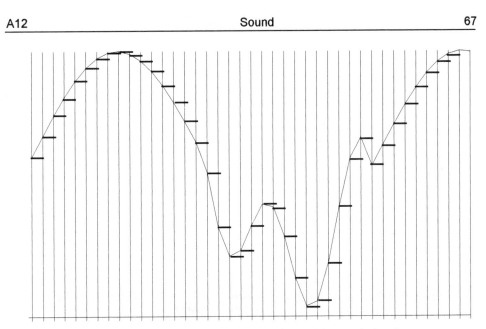

Figure A12.4: *A continuous waveform with sample levels*

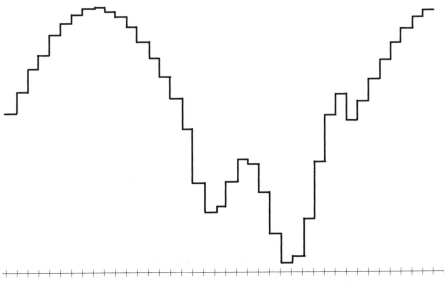

Figure A12.5: *The sampled waveform from Figure A12.4*

The succession of values from this sampling can be processed, stored or fed through a digital-to-analog converter to reproduce the sound. Sound sampling is the standard method of capturing sound for storage or manipulation in digital form.

The quality of sound produced using a sound sampler depends upon the sampling rate and the sampling resolution.

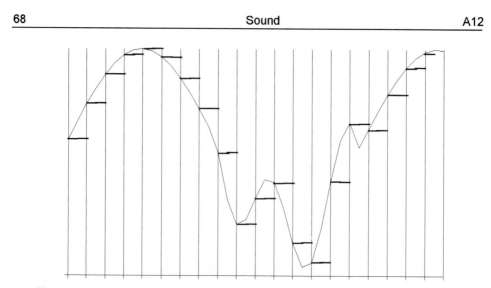

Figure A12.6: *The same waveform, sampling frequency halved - resulting in much cruder sound quality*

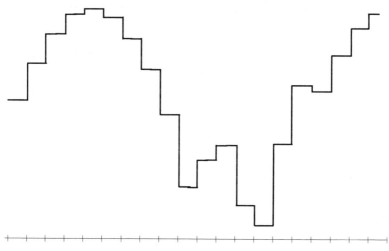

Figure A12.7: *The sampled waveform from Figure A12.6*

Sampling rate is the frequency at which samples are taken and is usually twice the maximum frequency of the sound being sampled.

Sampling resolution is the number of bits used for data storage, which is 16 bits for CD players but may be only 8 bits in some personal computers.

Sound mixer

including: channel, music channel

is an operator-controlled electronic device for combining sound signals. The operator selects how input signals are to be combined to form one or more output signals. The paths or connections for input and output signals are known as *channels* or *music channels*.

Sound processor

is the general term for electronic sound equipment which can take a sound signal as input, modify the signal and output the new signal. The processing may use either analog or digital techniques, but the use of digital methods is now more common. Most sound processors have a particular function, for example echo units, reverberation units, graphic equalisers, noise reduction units. All of these work in *real-time* (see *sequencer*, below).

Sound processing software on a suitable computer can do the same things that individual sound processing items achieve. Thus a computer may be used as a general-purpose sound processor.

Sequencer

including: real-time entry, step-time entry

is a digital device which can store a set of representations of notes, rhythms and other musical data for replaying at a later time. It may also include facilities for editing or for producing repeated patterns. Sequencers may range from the very simple, capable of storing only a small number of notes or a single chord, to the complex, capable of simultaneously handling many independent musical parts. Sequencers are often built into *synthesisers* (see *music synthesiser* page 64) and drum machines or other electronic music devices. One example of the use of a sequencer is to play a piece of stored music at different speeds without the distortion of pitch, which happens if the speed of a tape recorder is varied. Another is to change the sound of a series of notes previously entered, rather like changing the colours of parts of a computer-generated picture with an art program.

Music parts can be entered into a sequencer in one of two ways, *real-time* or *step-time*.

Real-time entry has the musical information provided by playing the notes with the correct relative time intervals. They need not be the actual intervals since the sequencer can modify the speed (tempo).

Step-time entry has the time interval between each note defined by the person entering the musical information.

Computer-based music system

including: digital sound system

is an arrangement of electronic music devices and a computer linked together so that music and other sounds, such as speech and singing, can be captured, stored, manipulated, generated or reproduced. These systems will probably contain both digital and analog components. Where only digital processing components are used it is referred to as a ***digital sound system***.

Music workstation

is a collection of connected music-generating and sound-manipulating equipment. A typical arrangement will include a keyboard, a synthesiser and a sequencer. They are increasingly likely to include a computer with appropriate software. See *computer-based music system*, page 69.

SMPTE codes

SMPTE is an acronym for the Society of Motion Picture and TV Engineers (USA). The codes are an agreed set of standards which make it possible to synchronise sound and video signals.

Speech recognition

also known as: voice recognition

is the process of analysing a spoken word and comparing it with those known to the computer system. Speech recognition software enables data to be input as words to the computer, for use by software such as a word processing package. The cheapest speech recognition software available for personal computers cannot distinguish between words in continuous speech and, to be effective, words have to be spoken consistently and separately. Specialist vocabularies for particular types of user, such as accountants or pathologists, are available. However, the differences between the same words spoken by different people still make this an unreliable process and the software has to be 'trained' to work with each user. Software which will recognise continuous speech requires substantial memory and processing power.

Speech synthesis

including: speech synthesiser, voice synthesiser, phoneme

is the production of sounds resembling human speech by electronic methods. A *speech synthesiser* (or *voice synthesiser*) achieves this either by the use of software or by using standard sound-generating hardware. An example of a speech synthesiser is a talking word processor. The sound is produced either by selecting an appropriate sound from a collection of stored sounds or by breaking down the input data into its individual speech components which are output in sequence. These speech components are called *phonemes*. For example the vowel sound in 'meet' and in 'meat' are the same phoneme.

A13 Hypermedia Systems

Hypermedia systems are interactive computer systems which are concerned principally with the storage of data (and its associated information retrieval) for reference purposes. They are usually organised so that the user can obtain information in a number of ways. Often called **hypertext** systems, they store text in such a way that users are able to construct their own links between different parts of the text. The multi-level approach to text acquisition, storage, analysis, comparison, retrieval and editing includes a comprehensive command structure which allows users to move through a document. This may be achieved by the use of pre-programmed links, through techniques such as *browsing*, or by searching for specific words. The system will remember the path taken.

Hypermedia is an extension of hypertext and also includes related graphics (still, animated and moving video) and sound.

The data is held in a non-linear structure using nodes and, for each node, a small number of links (typically 2, 3 or 4) are available to related nodes. Using on-screen menus, often presented on a menu-bar, it is possible to move through the system in a variety of search patterns. Starting with a main index, the user can choose a path which introduces the context of a particular subject and then, having noticed some point of special interest, can change the search pattern to follow the context of that new subject. The system might also allow the user to search for associated themes by using key words in the particular screen being displayed at that time.

The change in the type of information generated by calls into such a system can be dramatic. For example, in a system which was apparently associated with an art gallery, the user might choose to look at information about one particular artist which could include a screen display of that artist's pictures. Then, seeing a subject of interest depicted in one of the paintings, choose to look at paintings by other artists on the same subject. If the subject happened to be people playing musical instruments, the next step might be to choose to hear some music associated with those instruments. This might then lead to a topic dealing with the production of sound, and then to information about the physics of wave motion.

The usefulness of such a system is dependent on the type of data structure which it employs, the size of the database and the access time. The ease of use might be related to the physical process of using the menus, where a touchscreen might have considerable advantages over a mouse or the arrow keys.

Multimedia

is the presentation of information by a computer system using graphics, animation, sound and text. The data may be stored in a variety of ways using conventional computer storage devices, together with a picture database on CD-ROM. Output might be through VDUs, sound-generators and laser projectors.

Integrating a tutor program could allow the system to be used as a training resource. The performance of the user could then be monitored by recording the choices made in response to questions and evaluating this response using an expert system. This performance output might then be sent to a remote trainer who would assess the trainee's progress.

Interactive video

involves the use of a computer linked to a large capacity data store such as a Compact Disc (CD) to provide random access retrieval of images (including stills and continuous video) and sound. Data, once recorded, is not easily changed or added to and access times can sometimes appear long. However, any disadvantage arising is generally outweighed by the amount, variety and quality of data which can be retrieved from one active device.

HyperCard
including: card, stack
is an application-building tool provided with Apple Macintosh computers which allows for interactive storing and retrieving on-screen *'cards'*. These can contain text, graphics, sound and video clips, and are grouped together in one or more related *stacks*.

Browse

is a feature of hypertext systems which allows users to build their own route through an application rather than following a pre-determined one. The route so chosen may be remembered by the system so that it can be re-traced back to the starting point of that route. This kind of browsing is particularly useful in such applications as computerised manuals, computer aided learning packages and large databases.

Video clip

is a short section of film or video stored in digital form (both sound and pictures). It is easily incorporated in computer displays and hypermedia systems. The video clip would normally be stored in compressed form, otherwise the storage cost would be prohibitive. See also *video data compression*, page 311.

A14 Computer Assisted Learning and Training

The foundations of computer assisted learning were laid during the early 1960s with the development of **programmed learning systems**. These early systems did not use any form of computer technology (the microcomputer was not to appear for many years) but were either paper-based or used electro-mechanical devices known as **teaching machines**.

A basic principle of programmed learning was one of 'value added'. Before any teaching programme was constructed, a pre-test and a post-test for the unit to be taught were written. A learner would sit the pre-test, undergo the programmed instruction and then sit the post-test. The value added to the learner could then be deduced by comparing the two scores. It was assumed that the learner could never be at fault. If the improvement in score was only small, then it was assumed that there was a problem with the programmed instruction.

The programmes could be either linear or branching. A **linear programme** would be a sequence of very small learning steps punctuated by a test question. The learner would know at once if they had answered correctly or not, but there would be no remedial instruction. A **branching programme** would not let the learner continue to the next step if a test answer was wrong. In this case one of several remedial instruction paths were followed depending on the nature of the error.

Some of the teaching machines were multimedia, controlling slide projectors and tape recorders. They were all expensive and unreliable. The paper form of the techniques were more successful. Books were written as branching programmes.

This approach to learning had some success with well defined skills or confined areas of training. The armed services based many of their instructional manuals on programmed learning principles and for a time it seemed that the Royal Air Force could have a significant influence on the educational system. Attempts to write programmes to deal with areas that required a creative and critical approach were poor and by the end of the 1960s interest in the approach had diminished.

Once the microcomputer arrived, the same principles were revived under the title of **Computer Aided Learning (CAL)**. Although now the technology was no longer a problem the learning programmes were just as difficult to write. The early CAL systems did little better than the programmed learning systems. One major useful contribution to learning was the development of *adventure* games. Another was the use of controllable computer simulations of situations which were too costly or too dangerous to create in real life. The general approach started to become effective when video and CD-ROM images could form part of the instructional material. It is now understood that an effective learning system must have the ability to adapt in a major way to the response of the learner. This can happen if the system is able to learn about the learner. **Expert systems** can do just this but, as with all effective software, they are expensive and difficult to write.

The processing speeds and data capacity of computers are ever increasing. Coupled with the development of even more adaptive software, it is to be expected that CAL will move onto the more creative areas of learning.

If the computer has so far proved to be limited in its role as a teacher it is much more effective as a manager of the learning process. **Computer Managed Learning (CML)** is very much concerned with the recording of what a learner has achieved and directing the learner to the next unit of study. Computers are good at recording well-structured data and making decisions based on well-defined rules; CML is essentially recording and branching. The growth of a modular approach to learning courses has been made practical by the use of CML systems.

CAL authoring system

is a computer system that is set up to execute an authoring language for the creation of instructional material using a *Computer Aided Learning* approach (see the introduction to this section on page 73).

Adventure game

is a computer game in which the player explores a computer-generated environment, usually having to solve puzzles in order to make progress. Early adventure games (named after the first one, which was called simply 'Adventure') used only text; the player typed instructions such as 'GO SOUTH', 'OPEN DOOR', 'PICK UP GOLD', and the computer responded with a description of the new scene. Later games make substantial use of graphics, and may be playable over a network with several players taking part. See also *multi-user game*, page 43.

Because of their problem-solving nature and the way in which they stimulate the imagination, adventure games have been widely and successfully used in education.

Computer Aided Learning (CAL)

including: Computer Based Training (CBT), Computer Managed Instruction (CMI), Computer Managed Learning (CML)
is the use of a computer to provide instructional information to a student, pose questions and react to the student's response.

Computer Based Training (CBT) is the use of a computer as an instructional system in a training environment. The approach is the same as computer assisted learning but the learning area is confined to a well defined training objective.

Computer Managed Instruction (CMI) is the use of a computer to manage a student's progress through a course of instruction. The student's performance is recorded by the computer and new modules of instruction are defined or delivered as determined by the curriculum. A computer managed instruction system may or may not contain computer assisted learning material.

Computer Managed Learning (CML) is the use of a computer in a similar fashion to computer managed instruction, but with additional emphasis on providing help which depends upon the responses given by the student. Some computer managed learning systems can build up a detailed learning profile for each student. This profile can be used for both reporting and directing the studies of an individual student.

Buggy

is a simple robotic device exclusively used in a computer education context. The device can move in two dimensions and supports light and touch *sensors* (see page 165). The student can program the device to exhibit certain behaviour or the device could form part of a multimedia *computer managed learning* system (see page 74).

Many buggies are controlled by an external general-purpose computer. This allows the use of a variety of programming languages to construct the controlling programs.

Turtle

is a simple robotic device initially designed to exploit the graphical aspects of the programming language *LOGO* (see page 250). It is designed to have a pen attached to it so that a hard copy of its walk can be recorded. Students can program the device with any suitable language but it could form part of a *computer managed learning* system (see page 74) associated with certain aspects of learning mathematics.

Roamer

including: Bigtrack

is a simple robotic device exclusively used in the computer education context. Unlike many *buggies* (see above) Roamer has a computer built into it. This computer controls the movement of Roamer by responding to a sequence of instructions. These instructions form a program which the student has stored in the device by the use of a set of keys which are part of Roamer. **Bigtrack** is a device that has a similar educational purpose to Roamer but it moves by laying tracks (like a tank) rather than wheels.

A15 Artificial Intelligence and Expert Systems

Artificial intelligence (AI) is a recognised discipline within computer science. It attempts to design software (sometimes with associated hardware) that behaves in a way which, if it were human behaviour, would be described as intelligent.

The earliest artificial intelligence systems, in the 1960s, concentrated on such activities as playing chess and proving (mathematical) theorems. However the techniques built up are now being applied to aspects of behaviour not normally thought of as requiring great intelligence, such as recognising objects, understanding simple text, speech recognition and general visual interpretation.

These activities although often relatively straightforward for people are, in fact, not so straightforward for computers. It is a challenging problem to write programs for a computer to perform these activities - so much so that we are still far from successfully writing the programs, except in the most simple cases.

One recent development in artificial intelligence is neural networks. These draw from and emulate the structure of the brain in terms of neurons. The networks are made to 'learn' from training sessions and then repeat what has been learnt when given new data.

An **expert system**, sometimes known as an **Intelligent Knowledge Based System (IKBS)**, is an example of an 'intelligent' system applied to a real life application. The computer performs at or near the level of human experts.

Examples of expert systems include PROSPECTOR, which advises geologists when they are out in the field. The system asks for certain data about the environment where the geologist is considering drilling bore-holes and provides advice based on this data and on 'knowledge' already stored in its knowledge base.

Other well known expert systems include XCON, which gives advice on how to configure a VAX computer system – that is, how to make sure the correct units are specified and how they should be connected together for a certain application. There are a number of systems in the medical area; one of the better known is MYCIN, which gives advice on which drugs to use for certain types of bacterial infection.

Artificial intelligence (AI)

is the study and development of computing applications for tasks which would be described as requiring intelligence if they were done by people. Many of these applications involve systems capable of learning, adaptation or self-correction.

Cognitive science

covers a wide range of subjects which are concerned with the thinking processes (cognition) and are, to a great extent, people-oriented. Some, such as *artificial intelligence* (see above), computer vision and *human-computer interaction* (see page 80), are concerned with computers. Others are concerned with how people function: for example, cognitive psychology which includes the study of the mental processes of memory, language processing and vision. Some cognitive scientists find it helpful to describe how humans function in terms of a computer model of information processing.

Neural net

is artificial intelligence software which allows a system to learn to recognise features or characteristics of situations which are input to it. The technique is based on a model of the logical properties of interconnected sets of nerve cells.

A neural net is made up of a network of very many junctions, or nodes. Each of these nodes will 'learn' features according to its input. Once the learning phase is completed, the neural net can be used to recognise features of the same type that were originally presented to it.

Neural nets have been used for visual recognition and also for financial prediction.

Pattern recognition

is the process of identifying objects in a digitised picture, or in some cases digitised sounds, through analysis of the digital representation of the objects and comparison with stored knowledge about similar objects.

Cybernetics

including: robotics

is the study of the control of processes by a computer, for example an industrial process or a robot. *Robotics* is the study and design of robots. See also *control,* page 53, and *robot,* page 55.

Expert system

also known as: (Intelligent) Knowledge Based System (IKBS), (KBS)
including: knowledge base, heuristics, rulebase, knowledge engineer, knowledge acquisition, knowledge elicitation, explanation, inference engine, shell
is an application of artificial intelligence to a particular area of activity where traditional human expert knowledge and experience are made available through a computer package.

Knowledge base is that part of an expert system which holds knowledge about the application area (or domain), such as drug side effects. Much of the knowledge is held as **IF ... THEN ...** type rules. For example:

```
IF a patient has high blood pressure
              AND is anaemic
THEN avoid the use of a certain kind of drug.
```

From time to time the knowledge base is updated.

Heuristics are rules which are not derived purely from logic but are derived from the experience of a person. These are known as 'rules of thumb'. Many of the rules in an expert system are of this type.

Rulebase is the part of the knowledge base which is made up of all the rules known to the expert system.

Knowledge engineers are the people who collect the information in the knowledge base. This information is collected from a variety of sources in a variety of ways; one of the most important is collecting information through talking to experts. The collected knowledge is then formulated as a set of rules and facts.

Knowledge acquisition or *knowledge elicitation* is the process of gathering information for inclusion in a knowledge base.

Once the knowledge base has been constructed, the expert system is ready to be interrogated or consulted. The system requests the user to provide information and then searches the knowledge base to find appropriate advice for the user.

Explanations can be requested by the user. The system will provide the user with the reasoning behind the advice given. This is often in the form of a list of the rules tested by the system.

Inference engine (or *inference processor*) is a piece of software in an expert system which does the searching of the knowledge base. Searching the knowledge base uses standard searching methods which are independent of the application, for example a top-down or a bottom-up search.

Shell is a piece of software, which is an 'empty' expert system without the knowledge base for any particular application. The user enters the appropriate rules and facts.

Expert systems have a clearly identifiable internal structure, which is illustrated in Figure A15.1.

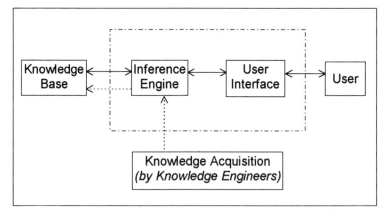

Figure A15.1: *An expert system structure*

The User communicates with the system through the User Interface, which passes requests for advice to the Inference Engine. The Inference Engine processes the request, obtaining information – rules and facts – from the Knowledge Base as required and finally returns the answer to the User Interface, and hence to the User. In the Knowledge Acquisition phase, the Inference Engine stores the information from the Knowledge Engineers in the Knowledge Base.

A16 User Interface

Cooks usually try to make their meals tasty and attractive as well as nutritious. In the same way, software writers try to make their products attractive to the user as well as being effective and easy to use. Much time and effort is spent on designing ways in which the user interacts with the computer and the software. Most software users are more concerned with what a package can do than with how it works. They expect to be able to see and understand what the software can do, they want to be able to communicate their instructions easily and have quick and understandable responses from the computer.

As the scope of computer applications has increased and the number of computer users has also increased, a variety of ways have been evolved for communication between the user and the computer; this is called the **user interface** or **user environment**. There are fashions in user interface design, just as there are in car or clothes design, but what is important is that the interface should achieve its objectives as efficiently as possible.

All user interface designs are limited by the capabilities of machines and people. Each design seeks to make the most of the strengths and avoid the weaknesses of computer equipment and its users. Aspects of computer hardware, for example processing speed, memory capacity, input and output devices, restrict what software can achieve. Speech is the most common form of communication between people but is not yet in everyday use for communication between people and computers, although systems are now available for personal computers. Communication through text is limited by the speed at which people can read text presented on a screen and the time taken to type responses accurately on a keyboard. Recent improvements in hardware have greatly enhanced the graphics capability of small computers. Many software designers have chosen graphical ways of presenting the activities or concepts available for selection at any time: icons (small pictures with an easily understood meaning) are widely used, since graphical information is independent of the user's language and can be used wherever the meaning of the icon is understood. All user interface designs are compromises between what it is desirable to provide and what it is possible to achieve.

It is the combination of those parts of the hardware and software of a system with which the user interacts which make up the user interface. User interfaces are described in a variety of ways, whose names highlight their main features; for example, **graphical user interface (GUI), menu selection interface, windows environment, forms dialogue**. There is no single kind of user environment which suits all applications or all users; the choice of an appropriate user interface depends on the amount of information to be presented or elicited, the experience of the users and their familiarity with the particular software.

Since taste and personal preference largely determine people's reactions to different user environments, there will always be scope for variety in their design. For those people who spend a long time working at a computer it is very important that the user interface they experience makes a positive contribution to their efficiency. It is increasingly common for the user to be able to adapt (**customise**) the facilities provided by the system to fit the situation in which the system is used.

Where there is an unusual user environment, such as where provision has to be made for disabled people, special arrangements are often made. These may include the provision of customised input and/or output devices, such as touch-sensitive keyboards, and the appropriate additional software.

Human-Computer Interaction (HCI)

sometimes: interface rather than interaction
including: Graphical User Interface (GUI), Man-Machine Interface (MMI), user environment
is one of a number of terms used to describe the communication between people and computer systems. Other terms for this are: *Man-Machine Interface (MMI)*, *user interface* and *user environment*. Any of these terms is likely to be used in discussions of how people and computer systems interact and the ease of use of a system.

One way of classifying interfaces is by the style of communication they provide. Some are purely textual whilst others, known as *Graphical User Interfaces (GUI)*, replace some or all of the words by icons. See also the introduction to this section.

Keyboard

including: qwerty keyboard, numeric keypad, function key, embedded keyboard
is the typical input device used with all general-purpose computers. A keyboard will have a number of keys, which is not the same for all computers nor is the arrangement the same.

Part of the keyboard is likely to be arranged in the same way as a traditional typewriter; this is called a *qwerty keyboard*.

Part of the keyboard may be a block of keys for the digits 0-9, possibly including the arithmetic symbols for add, subtract, multiply and divide, and an enter key; this is called a *numeric keypad*.

In addition to the keys for letters, numbers and punctuation marks, a typical keyboard will have special keys including, at least, enter (or return), escape (esc), control (ctrl) and some *function keys*. What these keys do will depend on the software being used rather than the hardware.

It is sometimes possible for the user to assign part of the keyboard for special purposes. This part of the keyboard is called an *embedded keyboard*. For example, keyboards with a restricted number of keys, such as laptop computers, allow a group of the keys to be assigned the role of a numeric keypad if the user wishes.

WIMP environment (Windows Icons Menus Pointer)

from: Windows Icons Menus Pointers
including: desk top
is a method of accessing the computer making minimum use of the keyboard by using a mouse (or similar device) to move a pointer over icons or text menus displayed on

the screen. For example, selecting an icon may open a window and start a task. For definitions of these individual terms, *window* and *icon*, see below, *pointer* and *menu*, see page 82, and *mouse*, see page 83. A combination of windows and icons is sometimes referred to as the *desk top*.

Window

including: active window, pane

is a temporary area opened on the screen displaying the activity of a program. There can be several windows on the screen at any one time which can be moved if required or removed completely (restoring the original information on the screen). At any one time only one window will be *active*, that is accessible for input by the user. Things may be happening in other windows, for example a clock may be showing the time, but this does not mean that the window is active. If several activities are being run at the same time, each will be in a separate window but only one can be worked on at a time. It is possible to have more than one window visible and shift from one task to another by moving the cursor from one window to another. A window may be divided into parts, called *panes*, which can be used separately; for example headers and footers in a document.

Icons

also spelt: ikons

are small pictures or symbols, with an easily understood meaning, displayed on the screen as a method of offering a choice of activity. A pointer is moved to a selected icon using, for example, a mouse, cursor control keys or a trackerball, and the activity is started by clicking a mouse button or pressing an appropriate key. This method has advantages over text-based input for inexperienced users. Icons can be independent of the user's language, provided the symbols are generally recognised.

Menu selection interface

is a form of user interface in which the computer displays a list of options from which the user must make a choice, either by typing the code displayed against the option, or by moving a highlight to the option (using cursor keys, a mouse or a trackerball) and then pressing a particular key or clicking the mouse button. The response may be to carry out the choice, to request further information (using any of the communication styles) or to report an error. See also *WIMP environment*, page 80.

Highlighting

including: inverse video

is changing the appearance of a part of a screen display by altering it in some way so that it stands out; for example by changing colour arrangements or by putting shading around an area of the screen. One commonly used method involves the use of inverse video, in which black becomes white and colours change to the colour represented by the inverse bit pattern, for example the inverse of 00011011 is 11100100.
Highlighting changes:

HIGHLIGHT into HIGHLIGHT

Pointer

also known as: mouse pointer

including: cursor, cursor movement key, arrow key, caret

is an icon (sometimes in the form of an arrow) on the screen. It moves around the screen in response to the movements of a mouse (or other similar device), or the use of keys. The pointer often changes its shape depending on its position on the screen, or the situation in an application. When the pointer indicates a position in text it is usually called the *cursor*.

Cursor is the screen symbol which indicates where on the screen the next action will begin. To make it easier to find and follow in text handling situations, the cursor may be made to flash on and off or the present position might be emphasised by using *highlighting* (see page 81). When entering text, the cursor automatically advances to the next typing position after a key is pressed. Actions other than entering text require the movement of the cursor about the screen. These movements are controlled by a mouse (or other similar device), or by the *cursor movement keys*.

Cursor movement keys (up, down, left or right), which are sometimes referred to as the *arrow keys* (↑, ↓, ←, →), are one way of directing the movement of the cursor about the screen.

Caret is the name for a symbol used by printers to show that text needs inserting; for this reason the name is used for the screen cursor for inserting text which is often in the form of a 'I'. Unfortunately, *caret* is also the correct name for the character ∧ which is one of the symbols available on many keyboards.

Menu

including: submenu, action bar, menu bar, pull-down menu, pop-up menu, status bar

is a range of options offered to a computer user so that a choice can be made. A menu may simply be a screen display which lists a number of choices. The user is expected to press an appropriate key to select one of them; one of the choices offered is likely to be another menu, known as a *submenu*. Sometimes a special panel appears when a choice has to be made. This hides part of the screen, but the screen is restored to its original state after the choice has been made.

Menu bar or **action bar** is a line of titles for menus across the screen (usually at the top, but sometimes at the bottom). These are the menus which the user can choose at that point. Clicking when the *mouse pointer* (see above) is on the appropriate word, or else pressing an appropriate key, selects a menu. The choice is usually displayed as a *pull-down menu*.

Pull-down menu is a menu that appears on request after its title has been selected from the menu bar. It gets its name because it usually appears immediately below the menu title.

Pop-up menu is a menu that appears on the screen wherever the user happens to have positioned the cursor. It may be called up as the result of pressing a *hot key* (see page 86), or because the program needs to offer the user a choice as a result of what is being done at that instant.

Status bar is a line of information displayed on the screen, usually either at the top or at the bottom, which shows some of the conditions in the task at the moment, such as the page and line number in a word processing application.

Mouse

including: mouse button, mouse event

is a computer input device, usually connected to the computer by a thin cable. Using a hand to move the mouse in contact with a flat surface causes a cursor, or pointer, on the display screen to move. A mouse has one, or more, finger-operated press switches, called *(mouse) buttons*. When a mouse button is pressed it causes a 'click' sound and passes a signal to the computer; the same thing happens when the switch is released. What effect these have will depend upon where the pointer is on the screen and what software is being used. Mouse operations, such as *clicking* (see below), dragging (see *drag*, page 86) or combining these with the use of keys on the keyboard, provide a wide range of possible options at any moment. Actions, such as pressing or releasing the mouse buttons, are sometimes called *mouse events*. See also, *event*, page 199. Alternatives to a mouse are a *trackerball* or a *trackpad* (see below).

Trackerball

sometimes called: trackball

including: trackpad

is an input device which is used to do the same things as a *mouse* (see above). It is a ball, set into a cup, which can be made to roll in any direction by using a finger or the palm of a hand, depending on the size of the ball. The movements of the ball are mirrored on the screen by a pointer, and finger-operated switches work in the same way as *mouse buttons* (see above). Trackerballs are frequently used on *laptop computers* (see page 110/1), being easier to use in this position than a mouse. An alternative to a trackerball is a *trackpad*, where movements of a finger over a sensitive plate are used to control the movements of the screen pointer.

Clicking

including: double clicking

Pressing a mouse button is called clicking, because this usually produces a 'click' sound. If the user clicks when the pointer controlled by the mouse is on an *icon* (see page 81), or a *screen button* (see page 85), then the operation represented by that icon (or button) is selected. For example, clicking on the picture of the flag of a country may cause its national anthem to be played.

Some software expects the mouse button to be pressed twice in quick succession which is called *double clicking*; a single click may have one effect while double clicking may have another.

Dialogue box

including: text box, list box, check box

is a window which appears when information about a choice is needed, or when options have to be selected. For example, choosing PRINT from a FILE menu may cause a dialogue box to appear, requiring answers to such questions as the name of the file, how many copies, etc. Normally, a dialogue box will offer the chance to cancel the request as well as the option to proceed. Dialogue boxes are intended to make it easy to obtain the necessary information quickly.

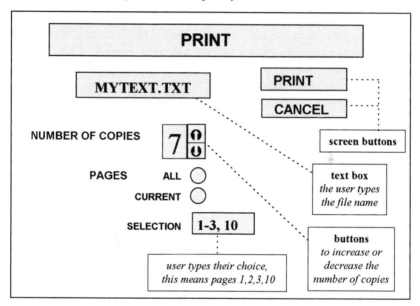

Figure A16.1: Dialogue box

In the dialogue box, shown in Figure A16.1, the *text box* for typing the file name, **MYTEXT.TXT**, could be replaced by a *list box*, in which the application shows a list of file names from which the user selects with the pointer.

Some list boxes stay the same size, others drop down to show several items.

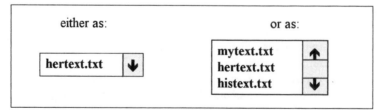

Figure A16.2: List box

In a *check box*, the feature is either activated if the box is marked or is not activated if the box is left blank. Clicking on the box will toggle its state. See *toggle*, page 85. See also the diagram, Figure A16.6, in *conversational interface*, page 88.

Screen button

is the name given to an area of the screen which is used to select an action. Selection is usually achieved by moving the pointer to the button and then pressing (and releasing) a *mouse button* (see page 83). A screen button may be an icon or the picture of a button switch with an icon or a word on it. See also *toolbar*, below, and *dialogue box*, page 84.

Scrolling

including: scroll bar

is the action of 'rolling-up' a screen. As each new line appears at the bottom, the existing top line disappears off the top. Where an application occupies more than a single screen, it is usual to provide a ***scroll bar*** to move the displayed portion of the application up or down the screen (vertical scrolling) and sometimes left and right across the screen (horizontal scrolling), see Figure A16.3).

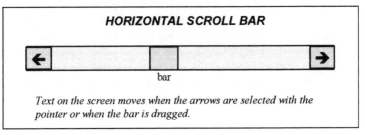

Figure A16.3: Scroll bar

Toolbar

including: tool, toolbox, toggle

is a line of *screen buttons* (see above) which represent the actions, ***tools***, that are currently available to be carried out within an applications package or a system. This line of buttons is called a ***toolbox***. For example, clicking on an icon for a brush in a drawing program will select a paintbrush tool. It is normal to make the icons behave like press switches (buttons), so that it is possible to see which tool has been selected or if the tool is still selected. Clicking on a selected tool again will cancel the selection; this means that the switches are ***toggles***, changing each time they are 'clicked'.

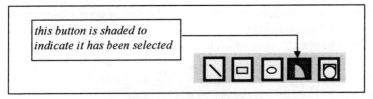

Figure A16.4: Toolbar

Toolbox is sometimes used to describe a collection of *utility programs* (see page 274).

Macro recording
including: script
is the action of recording a sequence of keystrokes, which achieve a particular purpose, and saving the recording, known as the *script*, for future use. By assigning a *hot key* (see below) to stand for this recorded sequence (see *macro*, page 218), it is possible to make frequently required actions easier to perform. For example, a single key combination could be used to type the whole of a frequently used phrase.

Drag
including: drag-and-drop editing
is the use of a mouse (or other similar device) to move an area of a screen display, which may be text or some part of a graphic display, bodily from one location to another. Before such movement can take place, the area concerned has to be defined in some way such as *highlighting* text (see page 81), or marking the boundaries of a graphics item. Moving things around in this way is sometimes referred to as *drag-and-drop editing*, which may also be used to copy, as well as move, part of a screen display. One example of dragging is moving the icon for a file from one sub-directory to another as a way of repositioning the file within the directory; another would be moving a graphic item from an application running in one window on the screen to a different application running in another window. Drag is sometimes used to mean moving the mouse while holding down a button.

Hot key
also known as: quick key, short cut key, keyboard short cut
is a function key or a key combination (frequently combining *control* or *alt* with other keys), which causes an action (such as calling up a menu, or running another program) whatever the user is doing. The name suggests the urgency of beginning a new action without fully breaking off from the existing task, or without the need to progress through a sequence of menus. The uses of *function keys* (see page 80) are sometimes defined as a menu on the screen or may be defined on a *keystrip* (see page 93) for the application.

Directory
also known as: folder
including: sub-directory, directory file, root directory
is a group of files or a group of files and *sub-directories*. A sub-directory is a directory within a directory, its contents may be files or other sub-directories or both. A directory is held, in the form of a list of file and sub-directory names (the *directory file*), on the backing store to which it refers; stored with it will be information needed for files to be retrieved from the backing store. Directories are usually represented in a tree structure, where the *root directory* is the entry point to the tree, as shown in Figure A16.5. See also *tree*, page 254 and *file*, page 187.

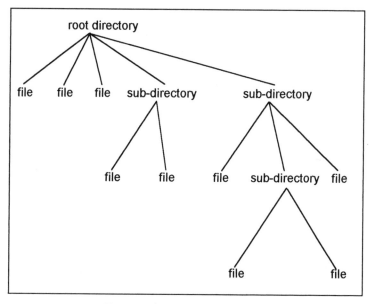

Figure A16.5: Directory tree

Screen saver

is software that removes the image from the display, either as a security measure or to reduce the risk of damage to the interior surface of the display screen. If the screen display is not changed for long period of time, the coating of the screen can become damaged.

Wildcard

is a symbol used in some commands or search instructions to stand for a range of characters. For example, **?** is often used to stand for any single character, hence the command **type d????.doc** would cause all files of type **.doc** whose names have five characters beginning with a **d** to be typed. The character ***** is usually used to stand for any group of characters (or perhaps none), hence **delete *.*** may be an unwise command, since it could cause all files to be deleted.

Command line interface

including: command sequence

is a form of user interface in which the user types commands for the computer to carry out. As the term suggests, the command is usually restricted to a single line of text, which may consist of any sequence of acceptable commands. The user has to know the conventions of the *command line interpreter* (see page 276). The commands may be combined to make up a *command sequence*, which can make this a convenient way of getting the computer to perform a sequence of actions (see *macro*, page 218). This form of interface can be efficient in the hands of experienced users, but can be very frustrating for those who do not know the right commands to use.

Conversational interface

is a form of user interface in which the computer and the user appear to be holding a conversation or dialogue, using the screen for output and the keyboard for input. The user may be seeking information from the computer, but the computer may need to ask its own questions before it is able to provide the answer to the question originally asked. The example below, which could be a dialogue about a request to print a file, gives an indication of the kind of communication that might be experienced:

```
        PROMPT (computer)                RESPONSE (user)
           ~~~                              ~~~
           ~~~                              ~~~
        name of file to print ?          MYTEXT.TXT
        print all 10 pages ?             no
        which pages ?                    1 to 3 and 10
        print pages 1-3,10: correct ?    yes
        how many copies ?                3
           ~~~                              ~~~
           ~~~                              ~~~


        each line will appear one after another
```

Figure A16.6: *Conversational dialogue screen*

Interactive computing

including: conversational mode

is a mode of operation in which the user and a computer system are in two-way communication throughout the period of use. In practice, most personal computer applications are interactive, whereas some applications on terminals attached to large central computer systems, for example in supermarket branches, are still run in batch mode with data and command instructions supplied through the terminal. See also *batch processing,* page 172.

When a terminal user on a network appears to be in continuous communication with the central computer, getting replies almost immediately, it is described as *conversational mode.*

Forms dialogue interface

including: response field

is a user interface in which the computer outputs separate *prompt* (see page 89) and response fields for a number of inputs.

Response field is the place in a dialogue screen (Figure A16.7) where users may type their responses, in any order. There may be automatic movement of the cursor, depicting the entry point, from response field to response field. The process is similar to filling in a form on paper and allows the entries to be changed at any stage until the 'execution' key or button is pressed.

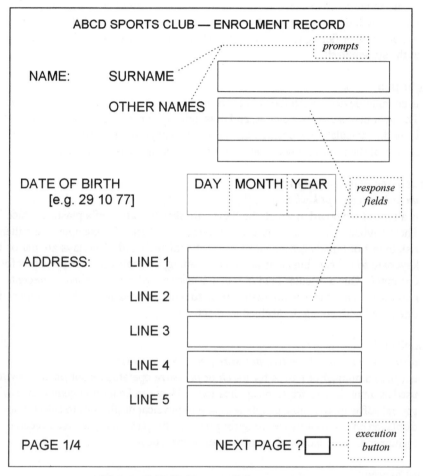

Figure A16.7: Forms dialogue screen

Prompt

is a character or message displayed on a screen to indicate that the user is expected to do something, usually to input data into the system. Sometimes a visual prompt is emphasised by a sound.

Screen editing

is the process of changing (editing) stored data or programs using a computer screen. The characters which are the data or programs are altered on the screen by adding, removing or changing individual characters or groups of characters.

Error message

is a message to the user indicating that something has gone wrong; it may include instructions on what action is needed. Well designed applications packages will include comprehensive error-detection routines and helpful error messages. These routines will detect errors resulting from user mistakes, such as letting the printer run out of paper or failing to put the right disk into a disk drive, as well as errors occurring in the system itself.

Light pen

is an input device, which looks like a pen with a wire connecting it to the computer. The light pen is used to point at, and thus indicate, a position on the screen. Software is used to calculate this position and perform an appropriate action. One application is the use of the pen to draw on the screen rather like an artist drawing on paper.

Touch-sensitive keyboard

including: concept keyboard

is a type of keyboard in which the 'keys' are sensitive areas of a plastic surface. These keyboards are generally used in special situations, for example where there is a risk of dirt or liquids getting into a conventional keyboard. Overlays are put on the keyboard to indicate the areas and their meaning, and software interprets this for the computer. One particular kind of touch-sensitive keyboard is called a *concept keyboard*. This has programmable areas to input information to the computer. It is often used with young or disabled learners.

Touchpad

also known as: touch switch, pressure pad, pressure switch

is one of a number of names for *touch* or *pressure* operated sensor *pads* or *switches*, used as input devices for some applications. They can be used in conjunction with special software to enable people with severe physical disabilities to select items displayed on a screen by touching (or pressing) the pad when the item needed is highlighted. See also *touch-sensitive keyboard,* above.

Touchscreen

is a special screen that is able to detect the position on the screen which a user's finger is touching or pointing at. One way of doing this is by having two sets of fine wires on the screen (one set across and the other down) which sense the finger position. Another way is to have vertical and horizontal patterns of infra-red light beams which are interrupted when a finger (or pointer) is close to the screen. With both these methods, the software can calculate what position has been touched.

Profile

is a file which holds data on how the system is to be presented for an individual user each time they log on. These customised interfaces are often available on network operating systems and on-line services.

User friendly

describes a system, either hardware or software, which is kind to its users. Since the user interface largely determines what a user experiences, it is the software system which is generally being described. However, some aspects of hardware, such as the feel of a keyboard, can improve or spoil user friendliness.

User transparent

sometimes: transparency

describes actions by a computer system, hardware or software, which are not apparent to the user. Nearly all hardware actions, other than those affecting the screen, are transparent, and most operating system actions take place without the user being aware of them. Well designed user interfaces achieve high levels of *transparency*.

Wizard

also known as: assistant

is a feature of some applications packages, which helps users to perform a task. By asking the user some questions, a wizard provides help in making best use of the available facilities. For example, a table wizard might help to create tables by offering a number of possible types, or a letter wizard might show how you could set out a letter for a particular situation.

A17 User Documentation

Other terms related to documentation will be found in C2 Systems Documentation, and C8 Program Documentation. As User Documentation is concerned with making the computer easy to use, terms in section A16 User Interface may also be of interest.

Software Documentation. When a computer software package is bought, whether it is a computer game, a spreadsheet or a programming language, user documentation will also be received. This may be anything from an instruction leaflet to a series of manuals. This 'user documentation' is designed to introduce the package and to tell the user how to use the software to its best advantage. This documentation may be totally in printed form or it may be seen on the screen when running the package. There may also be files on the accompanying disks called "Readme" or "Help".

There must be an overview of the package describing what it is capable of doing in fairly broad terms but also include some specific uses and features that are important with the package. This may include some sample screen displays and printouts to show the users what to expect.

An early section should be on how to install the software (to make the software available on the user's system). These instructions might well include

- how to make extra copies of disks (in case the working disk is damaged)
- how to copy on to a hard disk and configure the software (where the user has a choice of options as to how the software is to work and what hardware will be used, such as the type of printer)
- how to make hardware adjustments that may be needed. These may be described for the user to do or may require the help of a dealer.

Some of these operations may refer to hardware documentation. For example reference may be needed to printer documentation.

It may be that the software has already been installed, so installation and configuration may not seem to be of interest. However, if the printer is changed, the configuration process will probably need repeating, either by the user or the supplier.

It is important that the novice user has access to tutorial material consisting of written instructions or similar sequences given as an on-screen tutorial. This is designed to speed the user through the simple aspects onto the more advanced usage that may have been in mind when the purchase was made. Equally for the more experienced user there should be some summary sheet or quick reference guide. It is useful to have a reference to the use of specific keys (such as the function keys), perhaps in the form of a **keystrip** (a piece of card or plastic that is fitted onto the keyboard).

One of the first actions of the user should be to register the purchase with the publishing software company so that any upgrade or fault information can be passed on. With more sophisticated packages there might be a telephone help line.

An index to the documentation should help the user to find how to do specific tasks and to find more detailed explanations of error messages.

Hardware Documentation. Any piece of hardware will need some instructions on how to use it. Usually a physical connection will need to be made between items of equipment, for example between a monitor and computer. This will specify details of the connecting leads and where they are to be connected.

Most computers can have 'add on' peripherals, such as scanners or hard drives, to attach to existing systems. Some hardware needs minor physical adjustment before connecting it to a computing system. Some hardware devices are attached via a SCSI (Small Computer Systems Interface) and these devices need a unique device number. These could be set by the use of plug-in wire connectors (jumpers). Printers commonly have switches which are controlled *either* by software *or* by hardware. **DIP switches** (see Figure A17.2 for an example) are commonly used to specify the details of paper to be used, the characters to be printed and the type and speed of communication between computer and printer. These details may alternatively be specified by a special sequence of key presses on the device. Printers also may need to have paper feed mechanisms fitted.

With a new computer system the user documentation will also give the options that are controlled by software. These might include the type of monitor to be used, the type of printer and the speed of response of the mouse. Instructions on using the mouse, general care of the computer and use of disk drives are usually included. These will include how to format and copy disks and precautions that should be taken to prevent accidental damage and loss of data. Documentation may contain details on how your hardware may be customised for improving performance in a variety of circumstances. There is often a section on troubleshooting faults should your system not respond as it should, for example what to do if the printer produces gibberish or the screen remains blank.

More technical detail is usually available (at extra cost) from the manufacturer or a third party. The quality of such literature varies in its accuracy and clarity.

Keystrip

is a piece of card or plastic used with a keyboard. It labels the operations performed by function keys within specific programs. For example, in a word processor the function key F4 might have Search/Replace above it (see Figure A17.1).

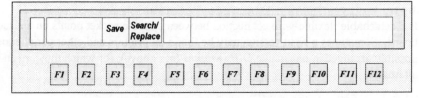

Figure A17.1: A keystrip

User documentation

gives the user any information necessary for the successful running of a piece of software or hardware. This does not generally include many technical details which will usually be found in *maintenance documentation* (see page 177).

Tutorial

provides the user with a guided tour through the software. It is a sequence of tasks to be carried out. This will help the user to find out how to use the software by experimenting with it and seeing the results.

README file

is a file which is provided on the medium with the software. It contains the latest details of using or loading the software.

HELP system

including: context sensitive help

is a means of providing helpful messages to guide a user when using a software package. It will give indications of how to answer prompts from the software and how to perform relevant operations. If the message responds to what the user appears to be doing currently, then it is called *context sensitive help*.

DIP switch

is one of a set of small slide-operated switches mounted together in a bank (Figure A17.2). These are used to set options on hardware, such as printers. For example, they may control what language alphabet to use or the size of font. (DIP stands for Dual In-line Package.)

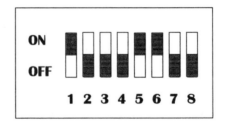

Figure A17.2: Bank of eight DIP switches

Jumper

is a detachable flexible-wire connection between suitable socket points on a circuit board. Sometimes a rigid version may be found on printers and other peripherals, possibly arranged in banks like *DIP switches* (see above), for which they are an alternative.

Install

is to transfer software onto the medium from which it is to be run. Installation is normally onto a hard drive but could be onto a floppy disk or a network.

Deinstall

is to remove software from a medium – the process is the reverse of *install*, see above. This should remove all traces of the software and release the space from the storage medium. If the license is to install a limited number of copies, then deinstallation re-credits the disk (normally called the *key disk*, see page 107).

Control panel

is a small display/keyboard on a device that enables the user to set options. On a printer this may be used to set the print style or change the paper source.

Dongle

is a piece of hardware used to reduce the possibility of software piracy. It usually plugs into a standard interface on a computer. Without the correct dongle the protected software will not run.

A18 Computer Personnel

*Further definitions related to the area of human-computer
interaction are found in section A16 User Interface.*

Computer systems are the concern of people and human-computer interaction is
extensive.

It is people who ask for systems, specify systems, design and build systems. They
develop and enhance existing systems, implement systems, manage and use systems.
People – as described through their personal information – are often both the direct
source and the subject of the computer's database. The demand, by people, for
information is the main reason why computers are needed.

In many organisations, the 1990s have seen an increase in both the number and the
types of task which computers have been required to perform. To enable this
expansion of use to be managed in a controlled and professional manner, not only have
computer-related job descriptions and responsibilities changed but many jobs on the
user side of the interface have similarly been affected.

This section gives an indication of the types of job related to computer use and
offers a brief description of some of those jobs. A more detailed description of the
wide range of IT (information technology) jobs, and the skill levels involved, can be
obtained by examining the British Computer Society's **Industry Structure Model**.

Recently, some large organisations have changed their operational methods and,
instead of employing teams of IT specialists themselves, have signed contracts with
outside firms who agree to supply these specialist staff as and when required. This is
known as **outsourcing**.

Computer support personnel
also known as: support personnel
are those involved in the day-to-day running of an organisation's computing
installation.

Computer operator
is the person who operates the computer and, where appropriate, responds to requests
from the operating system and from remote users in a time-sharing system.

Data processing manager
is the person responsible for the overall running of a data processing department.

Database administrator
is the person in an organisation responsible for the structure and control of the data in
the organisation's database. See also *database management system*, page 20.

Decision support specialist

is responsible for organising database interrogation procedures to allow business managers to access management information in appropriate formats.

Network controller

also known as: network manager

is the person responsible for the smooth running of a network. This will generally include communications (software and hardware), access (user identifications and passwords) and shared resources such as common data storage. (Compare with *network controller - types of computer*, page 114.)

Data preparation staff

are those responsible for organising and entering data into the computer system.

Hybrid manager

combines business understanding, IT technical competence and organisational knowledge and skills. Typically, the IT skills component will be gained after the acquisition of the business and organisational components.

Programmer

including: systems programmer, applications programmer, information systems engineer, coder

is the person responsible for writing and testing computer programs. Those involved in the writing of operating systems, general utilities (such as sort routines) and specialist tools (such as a graphical user interface) are usually called *systems programmers*, whilst those writing programs for specific user applications are known as *applications programmers*.

Those programmers working on the design and testing of programs are often called *information systems engineers*, whilst those who are mostly involved in translating statements into machine-readable form are called *coders*.

Systems analyst/systems designer

is the person responsible for the analysis of a system to assess its suitability for computerisation. Where computerisation is decided upon, the systems designer will be responsible for building on the analyst's results to create the new computer-based system and will normally work up to the point where programmers can sensibly take over.

Persons who have been responsible for the analysis and who then work on the new system design, are referred to as *analyst/designers*.

Technical support staff

are computer specialists who are concerned with the integrity and functionality of the computer system. They may be hardware rather than software oriented.

Computer service engineer

known as: computer engineer, maintenance engineer, service engineer
is the person responsible for the maintenance of the hardware, and is often employed by a specialist contract servicing company.

Software support staff

including: help desk, hot line
are usually employed by software houses or specialist vendors in order to respond to questions relating to the use of particular pieces of software. They are often referred to as a '*help desk*' and may be contacted quickly using the telephone '*hot line*' to give advice on problem solving.

Information systems manager

is the current term for the person who manages the interface between the computer system and the organisation's user community.

Data Protection Officer

is the named person in an organisation who is responsible for seeing that the organisation's registration (under the *UK Data Protection Act 1984*, see page 101) is adhered to.

Industry Structure Model (ISM)

Designed by the British Computer Society, this sets out, as a series of competences, what is expected of a person performing computer-related task at each stage in a variety of career paths.

A19 *Computer Abuse, Security and Related Law*

*This section includes terms from legal aspects of computing and
terms relating to the security and control of data in computer
systems.*

Modern society is very dependent on computer systems and the data they contain.
This dependence provides opportunities for anti-social behaviour ranging from the
annoying to the criminal. This section considers security measures and legislation
which attempt to deal with computer abuse.

Computer abuse describes a wide range of anti-social behaviour, such as:
* unreasonable use of personal data, for example to use cross-referencing
  to reveal new, unrelated and perhaps embarrassing information;
* electronic vandalism where software or data is deliberately damaged;
* creating viruses which cause random damage to software or data;
* theft of valuable information.

These problems are dealt with through the deterrent effect of legal punishment
under the Data Protection and Computer Misuse Acts and through using a variety of
security measures to make abuse difficult.

The **Data Protection Act** protects individuals from unreasonable use of stored
personal data. This data may be very embarrassing or could be used for blackmail –
even if the individual has done nothing wrong. Computer data is potentially more
dangerous than paper documents because:
* data can be retrieved electronically from a computer anywhere in the
  world;
* it can be searched very quickly to find patterns that are not obvious but
  which could be personally damaging or embarrassing;
* data from a range of computers can be combined and so apparently
  unrelated data can produce damaging information.

The **Computer Misuse Act** defines electronic vandalism and theft of information.
It makes these activities criminal. There are penalties for individuals who attempt to
interfere with another person's use of computers, such as:
* hackers who try to beat security measures as a 'game';
* vandals who damage the software or data of a computer;
* virus writers whose viruses can cause random damage;
* thieves who break into computer systems to gain access to valuable
  information.

Security measures that can be taken may use either physical or software methods.
Physical methods include:
* providing workstations with locks or keycards to prevent unauthorised
  use;

- locking offices containing workstations;
- positioning screens so that visitors are not able to see the contents of the screen;

Software methods include:

- using screen savers to hide the contents of the screen if the user leaves the workstation.
- passwords to ensure users are authorised;
- changing passwords frequently;
- limiting the range of tasks that can be carried out at a workstation;
- setting access rights so that only some users can carry out some operations;
- having special barriers to restrict access to a computer system by external users.

In addition to data protection and computer misuse legislation there are also copyright laws which enable software producers to protect their investment in software development. These laws provide the means to penalise people who copy unprotected software without permission.

Computer systems in manufacturing, real-time processes and safety critical applications need to meet particular design standards and their implementation may have to conform to quality assurance standards. Product Liability and Consumer Protection legislation, particularly in the USA, imposes severe penalties on the producers of poor quality computer products.

Data protection

including: data consistency, inconsistent data, data integrity, data privacy, data security

is ensuring that data is correct and is kept confidential and safe. These concepts apply to all data, not just data which is confidential or about individual people.

Data can be corrupted, stolen or lost in many different ways which are unexpected. It is essential that these are prevented (as far as possible) and that the data can be recovered if required. Failing to protect data can be disruptive and often very expensive.

Data protection involves the issues of :

Data Consistency is the relationship between the input data, the processed data and the output data, as well as other related data items. If the system is working properly the data will be correct at each stage (allowing for the processing done) and is said to be consistent.

Inconsistent data happens either when the result of a process is wrong (for the data input) or if two pieces of related data have the wrong relationship. For example if a person's age is not the same as their age when calculated using their date of birth, this would be inconsistent. This inconsistency could be caused by the age or the date of birth being input wrongly, an error in the calculation program or a variety of technical faults.

Data Integrity describes the correctness of data both during and after processing. Data may be changed by the processing but will still have integrity. Safeguards are needed to make sure that the data has integrity by detecting any accidental or malicious change to the data (see also *corruption*, page 192).

Data Privacy describes the need of some data only to be accessed by, or disclosed to, authorised persons. The Data Protection Act (see below) provides legal protection for individuals' data. Data privacy requires systems managers to build safeguards into their systems (both physical arrangements and software checks) to reduce the risk of unauthorised access.

Data Security involves the use of various methods to make sure that data is correct, is kept confidential and safely (providing data protection). Data security includes ensuring the integrity and the privacy of data, as well as preventing the loss or destruction of the data.

Data Protection Act 1984

including: data user, Data Protection Registrar, data protection principles
is the United Kingdom Act of Parliament which sets out requirements for the control of data stored about individuals on computer systems. The Act covers many aspects of data privacy (see *data protection*, page 100). The Act also defines *data users* who are responsible for the uses made of the computerised data.

Data users are required to register with the *Data Protection Registrar* and provide details about the data they hold for the data protection register. This register enables any individual to find out if personal data relating to them is likely to be held and they have the right to ask for a copy of the data from the data user. If the data is incorrect, the data user must correct it. The few exemptions to the Act mainly relate to data held by government agencies, the police, the courts and the security services.

The Act defines eight *data protection principles* which are given here in a simplified form:
1. Data should be collected and processed, fairly and lawfully (for example there should be no deception in the collection);
2. Data should be used for specified registered purposes;
3. Data should not be used or disclosed for any purpose other than those registered in the data register;
4. Data should be relevant and not excessive;
5. Data should be accurate and kept up to date;
6. Data should not be kept any longer than necessary;
7. Access must be provided for individuals to check and correct their data;
8. Security measures should prevent unauthorised access or alteration of the data.

The Act only applies to data about individuals – 'personal data'. The 1984 Act is due to be replaced with new legislation which complies with European Union requirements.

Computer abuse

has no legal definition but it is generally taken to be the wrongful use of computer systems and software for improper, anti-social or illegal purposes. Examples of computer abuse are the spreading of *viruses* (see page 105), data terrorism (actions against computer systems and data), computer-based fraud and computer pornography. Almost all examples of computer abuse involve breaches of laws such as the *Data Protection Act* (see page 101) and the *Computer Misuse Act* (see below).

Computer Misuse Act 1990

including: computer misuse

is the United Kingdom Act of Parliament aimed specifically at *hackers* (see *hacking*, below). It defines *computer misuse* as the unauthorised use of computer systems and relates both to hardware (for example using a computer without permission) and software (for example accessing parts of a computer system without authorisation). The act also defines offences relating to unauthorised computer access and the unauthorised access to, the modification of, or the deletion of data.

Hacking

is attempting (with or without success) to gain unauthorised access to a computer system. This may be the unauthorised use of a computer or simply unauthorised access to particular programs or data stored on a computer (see *access rights*, page 104).

The term hacking is also used to describe an unplanned approach to the design and use of a computer system. A hacker uses unusual and complicated techniques to solve problems as they arise. The resulting software is prone to errors and difficult to fix and maintain. This approach is often successful in gaining unauthorised access to computer systems, hence the new meaning of the term.

Electronic signature

is the special encryption of the data, used to indicate that the data is genuine. If the recipient of the data can correctly decipher the electronic signature then the data should be correct (and forged data is unlikely to have been substituted).

Logging in

also known as: log in, logging on, log on

is the procedure needed for a user to gain access to a computer network, a multi-access computer system or a specially set-up standalone workstation. Logging in is a part of the security procedures to prevent unauthorised access.

Logging out

also known as: log out, logging off, log off

is the correct procedure followed when ending a session on a computer network, multi-access computer system or a specially set-up standalone workstation. Logging out is a part of the security of the system preventing the workstation being used until an authorised user logs on again.

Firewall

including: proxy server

is a computer program used in a large computer system to prevent external users (even if authorised) getting access to the rest of the system. Network users' access is restricted to a small part of the system and the firewall software prevents a user (including unauthorised users) accessing data or executing any programs in the rest of the system.

If a user needs data from the main system it can be provided by a *proxy server*. This program receives requests from users, verifies them, accesses the required data and communicates with the users. The users cannot run programs but rely on the proxy server to access data for them. Instructions to the host computer itself are limited to specific types of requests, the effects of which can be controlled.

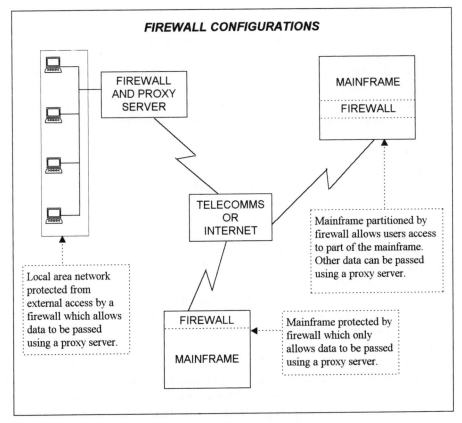

Figure A18.1: Firewalls

AUP (Acceptable Use Policy)

is the basis on which an *Internet service provider* (see page 42) makes its service available to its customers.

User ID (User Identification)
also known as: user name
including: password, personal identification device (PID), keycard, swipecard,
personal identification number (PIN)
is a unique name or code used to identify a user to a computer system when gaining access (known as *logging on*, see page 102). The *systems manager* (see page 98) or systems management software allocates user IDs to new users.

　　Checks must be made to verify that the person logging on is the correct 'owner' of the user ID. Methods of checking include passwords, personal identification devices, personal identification numbers.

Passwords are words or codes known only to the user. A password is linked to a
　　specific user ID. Although a user ID may be generally known to others, access
　　can only be gained with the correct combination of user ID and password.
Personal Identification Device (PID) is usually a plastic card which identifies the
　　user and acts as an electronic key. Most cards have a magnetic stripe which
　　stores information. This information can be read by a computer and used as a
　　user ID. Unauthorised access is made difficult because an unauthorised user
　　must have the personal identification device. Additional protection can be
　　provided by the use of a *personal identification number* (see below). *Keycard*,
　　or *swipecard*, are other names for a personal identification device in the form of a
　　plastic card.
Personal Identification Number (PIN) is a number used as a password, particularly
　　with bank cards and credit cards. For example a bank card is the personal
　　identification device, which provides the user ID, and is used with a personal
　　identification number to obtain cash from an *automatic teller machine*, page 51.

Access rights
including: password protection
control whether a particular user can use or edit a program or data file. Each user is assigned rights which determine the files that can be accessed. A user may be allowed complete access to a file (including altering the data), or may be restricted only to reading the data (or part of the data). Technical personnel will have more substantial rights. Access rights can also restrict the use of a file to a particular workstation or user.

　　Some files have additional access restrictions provided by *password protection*. When a user attempts to gain access to one of these files a *password* (see above) will be requested before access is allowed. This provides extra security since knowing a user's password is not enough to gain access to the data. The password is often used as the *encryption key* (see below) to encrypt the data, making the data meaningless even if unauthorised access to the system is achieved.

Encryption
including: scrambled data, decryption, encryption key, decryption key
makes data in a computer system unintelligible. The encrypted data appears to be meaningless and is sometimes described as *scrambled data*. Encryption provides

security for the data (by preventing it being understood), both when stored electronically and when transmitted between computer systems. *Decryption* is converting the unreadable data back into an understandable form.

An *encryption key* is a word or code selected by the user to govern the encryption process. A *decryption key* is needed before the data can be understood.

In conventional systems both encryption and decryption keys are the same and therefore all users must have a copy of the key. If the number of users is small and the concern is for the security of stored data, a single encryption key is usually sufficient. If transmission, rather than storage, requires extra protection then different encryption and decryption keys may be used. See *public key cryptography*, page 58, and *data encryption standard*, page 57.

The terms encryption, enciphering, coding and encoding are often used loosely with the same meaning, as are decryption, deciphering and decoding.

Virus
including: parasitic virus, worm
is a program designed to make a computer system unreliable and to copy itself between and within computers. The virus includes instructions to do the copying automatically, via a disk or network. The virus may also include instructions to damage data (in the memory or on a disk) or affect the computer's operation, such as displaying silly messages. These effects are activated when some pre-determined conditions occur (such as on a particular date). Most viruses are specific to a particular operating system.

A *parasitic virus* hides itself by attachment to a file which already exists until a specific event causes the virus to take action, perhaps destroying data or illegally copying data. A *worm* is a virus which, once activated, can copy itself automatically and very quickly particularly between computers on a network.

Anti-virus program
also known as: vaccine utility
including: infection, anti-virus monitor, virus checking, disinfection, computer hygiene
is used to detect and remove viruses.

Infection occurs when a virus has copied itself onto a computer system, usually to its hard disk. Because of the potential damage a *virus* (see above) can cause it has to be removed. Detection and removal of viruses is often difficult and has several aspects:

Anti-virus monitors are programs loaded permanently in memory and continually monitor programs for changes. If any change is detected, the file is prevented from being run and a warning message is given. New data read into the computer is also screened for viruses and appropriate action taken.

Virus checking scans the files on a computer system to detect viruses.

Disinfection is the removal of viruses that have been detected.

Computer hygiene is the term used to describe the prevention and cure of problems caused by viruses.

Trojan horse
also known as: Trojan

is a program which performs a normal process in the computer but will also perform another, possibly harmful, process at the same time. Trojans have been used by hackers (see *hacking*, page 102) to copy data from secure files or record information about security measures.

Software copyright
including: software licence, single-user licence, multi-user licence, site licence, public domain software, freeware, shareware

is the legal protection that authors and publishers have regarding the use of their software. It is not always realised that computer software is covered by similar copyright laws to those which apply to books and other publications. The Copyright, Designs and Patents Act 1988 protects 'intellectual property' and establishes the rights of the author.

When software is purchased there will be a *software licence* which sets conditions for the use of the software. These conditions vary considerably between products. Any use of the software not allowed by its licence is illegal. In practice, this means that copying software bought by someone else is likely to be an offence. Special licences are needed for some cases, for example multiple use on a network.

Various types of licence are used and the specific terms of each licence must be adhered to. Examples of the types of licence include:

Single-user licence where the software can be used on only one computer. This is the usual type of licence.

Multi-user licence where an organisation may install the software on an agreed number of computers. A reduced fee is paid for each computer.

Site licence where any number of computers may use the software at a single location. One payment is made to allow the multiple installation. These are not common outside the UK educational sector.

Public domain software has a licence waiving all rights and allowing free use of the software. This is a US legal concept which rarely applies in the UK. See *freeware*, below.

Freeware has a licence allowing free use (and usually distribution) of the software. The licence usually does not allow alteration or sale. The author usually provides little, if any, help and support. In the UK freeware is often called *public domain software*, see above.

Shareware has a licence allowing free use (and usually distribution) of the software for a trial period. If the user wishes to continue using the software a fee must be paid, usually in return for improved versions, manuals and support.

Commercial Internet Exchange (CIX)

is an accepted set of accounting agreements on charging for the use of the Internet by commercial organisations

Piracy

also known as: software piracy

including: protected software, unprotected software, copy protection, installation disk, key disk, FAST (Federation Against Software Theft)

is the illegal copying of software whether for personal use or re-sale. Software publishers lose considerable potential income due to illegal copying of their products and take a variety of measures to prevent it.

Protected software is supplied in a form designed to be difficult to copy. It may have copy protection or use a *key disk* (see below). *Unprotected software* has no special precautions against copying and relies on the legal authority of the *software licence* (see page 106).

Copy protection uses some physical changes to the data on the disk to prevent copies of the disk being made.

Installation disks contain the software in encrypted form. The software is copied onto the computer's hard disk before it can be used. The installation program may only allow the software to be installed a limited number of times. It may also make further copying difficult by embedding the owners name or computer serial number within the installation disks.

Key disk is a floppy disk or CD-ROM disk used to install software which contains credits that are reduced by one on each installation. It may also be a disk that is required every time a program is run to ensure it can only be used by one computer at a time. See also *software copyright*, page 106.

FAST (Federation Against Software Theft) is an organisation which operates on behalf of software publishers. It actively pursues breaches of software copyright.

Part B
What Computer Systems Are
Made Of

Computer systems can be assembled out of a variety of different pieces of equipment in a whole variety of different arrangements. This part of the Glossary defines terms which will be encountered when considering how computer systems are arranged, organised and connected to other computer systems. Terms related to the uses of computers are in Part A and terms concerned with the internal workings of computers are in Part C.

B1 Types of Computer

This section includes those terms that are descriptive of computers in general.

A computer is an automatic, programmable, digital data processor. Every part of this definition is crucial to our understanding of what the modern computer is, and how it works. **Automatic** means simply that it operates without human intervention, except where this is expressly pre-planned and provided for. This feature alone distinguishes the computer from the simple pocket calculator, where each computation results from a manual key-press. **Programmable** means that the instructions to be followed automatically are held (as a 'program') within the store of the computer. If a repetitive calculation (a 'loop') is necessary, the same instructions can be used and re-used. The instructions are usually held in the same storage area as that used for data – computer programs and the data they operate on can comfortably co-exist in the same sort of storage. Often (usually), the instructions can be replaced with other instructions: either as a part of developing a program to completion, or as a wholesale replacement of one program with another. **Digital** means that the computer operates with quantities that take only distinct values from a known range: often, but not always, these are binary quantities that take only two values, 'on' and 'off'. The power of digital data is that the computer (and the programmer) knows in advance what the data will look like: this is very similar to the human knowledge that all numbers, no matter how large, can be expressed as a combination of the ten digits 0, 1, 2, 3, ... 9. In principle, humans can add together (or multiply, divide – whatever) *any* two numbers. The 'hundreds, tens and units' method can easily be extended to numbers as large as we please. Notice that, because programs and data can occupy the same storage in the computer, programs are also expressed digitally. Although digital processing is now universal, computers did not always work this way – see *analog computer*, page 112.

Finally, **data processor** simply expresses what a computer *does* – it operates on digital data, and produces some actions as a result.

Types of computer

including: mini-computer, mainframe, computing power, Lisa, Macintosh, personal computer, PC, microcomputer, micro, compatible, clone, home computer, portable computer, laptop computer, notebook computer, palmtop computer, personal digital assistant (PDA), desktop computer, tower, mini-tower, multimedia computer, super-computer

Newer computers tend to be smaller than those they replace. Names are needed to distinguish each new type of computer. Originally 'computer' meant something that filled a room, needed air-conditioning and several operators to run it. When computers with the same power became available in a much smaller package, the rather ill-defined term *mini-computer* was introduced to describe the newcomer, while *mainframe* was reserved for the original monster. *Computing power* is a measure of the speed at which the computer works and the complexity of the operations performed.

The most significant development of the late 1970s was the introduction of a type of computer small enough and cheap enough to be bought by individuals. Apple Computers led the way commercially with their range of computers which evolved through the *Lisa*, offering the first convenient *graphical user interface* (see page 80), to the *Macintosh*. Later still, when IBM introduced the *Personal Computer* (or *PC*), a general name was needed for these types of small computer.

Microcomputer (or simply *micro*) became the general name, with 'PC' the name for computers based on the original IBM design. These have become known as IBM *compatibles*, or *clones*, and can run the same software without needing any changes to the software.

Home computer is generally a PC with some sound and video capabilities.

Portable computers were the next development.

Laptop computers run off battery power and are suited for use while travelling, or at business meetings.

Notebook computer (sometimes called a *palmtop computer*) is very compact and designed to be carried in a pocket. Because they are useful in situations where mains-powered computers are not appropriate, most laptop and notebook computers include software to transfer data to a PC or a larger machine. See also *docking station*, page 297.

The current trend is for smaller and even more portable computers.

Personal Digital Assistant (*PDA*) is a pocket-sized device without a keyboard (it is accessed through a pen-like stylus moving over the display, and the software recognises handwriting) but has failed to take the market by storm. The future in this area remains extremely unpredictable.

Desktop computer is used to describe the conventional personal computer needing a power supply and used at a desk. See also *desk-top publishing*, page 10

The box containing the central processor, disk drives and other storage may be in the shape of a *tower* designed to stand on the floor by a desk or be small enough to stand on the desk beside the monitor, when it is called a *mini-tower*.

Multimedia computer has facilities for processing data as text, graphics, video moving images and sound, and can interface with a range of input and output devices for these different forms of data.

These names are all relative to one another, and are often ill-defined. Most personal computers now are more powerful than the earlier mainframes.

Super-computer is a very large machine which processes hundreds of millions of instructions per second. It is likely to have many parallel processors to achieve this. Data is processed simultaneously (in the parallel processors) as well as sequentially to complete tasks very quickly.

Analog computer

including: hybrid computer

is a different design of computer from the digital computers we normally use. Instead of operating on digital data, these use continuously varying quantities, such as voltages, or positions, to represent numbers, and combine these electrically or mechanically as a way of processing. This term is now mainly of historic interest. Inevitably, some computers, known as *hybrid computers*, used both analog and digital technology in combination.

Computer

is an automatic, programmable, digital data processor. This definition is expanded and explained in the introduction to this section; the definition also excludes the *analog computer* (above).

Computer generations

including: first-generation computers, EDSAC, EDVAC, ENIAC, DEUCE, Pegasus, LEO (Lyons Electronic Office), Univac I, second-generation computers, Atlas, third-generation computers, ICL 1900, IBM 360, fourth-generation computers, fifth-generation computers

are a convenient way of distinguishing major advances in computer technology. The first three generations have well-accepted meanings, but the later generations tend to be used by manufacturers to stress the more modern features of a particular machine.

First-generation computers were the earliest designs. They used valves, mercury delay lines, electrostatic memories and had very limited storage. Important first-generation computers include the experimental *EDSAC*, *EDVAC* and *ENIAC* (which lacked stored-program facilities, and would now fail our definition of computer) and the production scientific computers *DEUCE* and *Pegasus*. Commercial machines were *LEO* (*Lyons Electronic Office*) and *Univac I*. These machines were all large, typically filling one or more rooms, and consumed large amounts of power.

Second-generation computers arrived when the transistor replaced the valve as the basic component. They were consequently much more reliable, and consumed less power. They were cheaper, but still out of reach for most businesses and certainly for individuals. One of the most significant machines was *Atlas*.

Third-generation computers saw the transistor replaced by the integrated circuit (the 'silicon chip'). They were again cheaper, and consumed less power and became even more reliable. One consequence of new design methods was the ability to produce whole families of similar, but differently-powered, computers – the *ICL 1900* series, or the *IBM 360* family, for example.

Fourth-generation computers are those commonly encountered today. There is no single technological advance that distinguishes fourth-generation computers from the third-generation, except possibly the much greater use of *large-scale integration* (see page 298/9) of components on silicon chips, which resulted in increasing similarity of machine design. A dramatic fall in the cost of internal memory, and increases in the speed and capacity of external storage, led to new applications and new methods of programming. In addition there was a growing realisation that standardisation of software, particularly operating systems, is necessary.

Fifth-generation computers are (still) something between an experimental prototype and an advertising agency's slogan. Many new computing concepts, that seemed to be significant advances on the previous generation, attracted this label: the use of formal mathematical logic in programming, for example, or the move away from a 'traditional' *Von Neumann* architecture (see page 293); increased use of *distributed processing* (see page 156), *parallel processing* (see page 286) and so on. New methods of interacting with a computer – speech, touch – also came to be known as 'fifth-generation'. The term should be used with caution, until the sixth-generation arrives, and we fully understand what was in the fifth.

Computer system
including: configuration
is the complete collection of components (hardware, software, peripherals, power supplies, communications links) making up a single computer installation. The particular choice of components is known as the *configuration* – different systems may have the same configuration or not.

Front-end processor
is a computer dedicated to managing communications devices or other computers linked to a more powerful computer system, generally a *mainframe* (see page 110/1). The front-end processor receives messages and commands from the communications devices, and organises these before passing them on to the larger computer for processing.

Hardware
is the physical part of a computer system – the processor(s), storage, input and output peripherals, etc. This is in contrast to the *software* (see page 6) which includes application packages, and the data in the storage.

Multiprocessor system
is a computer system with several *processors* (see page 281). These will work co-operatively, handling specific tasks (managing the screen display, doing arithmetic computation, handling peripherals) or simply sharing out the processing to enable parts of a task to proceed simultaneously (in parallel). See also *parallel processing*, page 286.

Word processor
is a computer dedicated to, or primarily for, word processing. Some have displays which are the proportions of conventional paper sizes; some offer black text on a white, or coloured, background; most provide an extended keyboard with function keys for the software provided with the computer. Nearly all these facilities are now available as standard on general-purpose computers.

Network controller

including: controller

is a computer dedicated to organising a computer network. It handles the communications between users and the shared resources, such as disks and printers. Some network topologies, such as the *star network* (see page 153), where the central computer is the network controller, can only operate with a controller; other arrangements may not use one. See also *server*, page 157.

   Controller is sometimes used to mean a network controller, but normally means a computer used in control applications to monitor *sensors* and control *actuators*, see page 165.

B2   Peripherals

Peripherals are devices that can be attached to a computer system to do specialised jobs and which are frequently necessary for the effective use of a computer system. They are not necessarily provided as part of the computer. The range of devices is varied and many peripherals have been covered in other sections:

> *Additional memory*, *and terms relating to it, will be found in B3;*

> *Display devices and related terms will be found in B4;*

> *Printers and related terms will be found in B5;*

> *User interfaces often rely upon extra equipment being attached and details of such equipment will be found in A16;*

> *Sound, communications and control each have their own peripherals and details will be found in A12 (for sound), A9, B7 and C17 (for communications) and A10 and B7 (for control).*

This section is concerned with those peripherals which do not find a place in the sections listed above.

There is a vast range of peripherals available but each performs one or both of the functions of **input** or **output**. At one time all memory, apart from immediate access memory, and all input and output devices were seen as 'peripheral'. This has changed, especially in personal computer systems, and equipment that used to be seen as special input devices, such as a mouse, are now a fundamental part of the system.

Peripheral device
is the term used to describe an input, output, or backing storage device which can be connected to the central processing unit.

Input/Output device (I/O device)
is a peripheral unit which can be used both as an input device and as an output device. In some instances, 'input/output device' may be two separate devices housed in the same cabinet.

Input device
is a peripheral unit that can accept data, presented in the appropriate machine-readable form, decode it and transmit it as electrical pulses to the central processing unit.

Document reader
is an input device that reads marks or characters made in predetermined positions on special forms.

Scanner

including: flat-bed scanner, hand-held scanner, optical character recognition software, colour scanner

is an input device which scans a drawing or text on paper and sends to the computer an image of the drawing or text as a *bit map* (see page 286). It works by shining light on the drawing or text and measuring the reflected light. In a *flat-bed scanner*, the object to be scanned is placed on a flat surface (usually glass) and a light source and sensors move backwards and forwards over it. A user moves a *hand-held scanner* over the object to be scanned. See also *bar code reader*, 117.

   Optical character recognition software, which may be part of the systems software, can convert text in the scanned image into a text datafile, which can then be edited. The software is not foolproof but it does include error messages to highlight characters which were not recognised. For most people scanning a piece of text and editing it is much quicker than typing the text. See also *optical character recognition*, below.

   A *colour scanner* directs a beam of strong laser or high-intensity light at the image, and uses filters to separate out the colours and intensities in terms of the *CMYK model* (see page 144), then stores them in a computer.

Machine readable

including: magnetic stripe, (magnetic) card encoder, (magnetic) card reader, mark sense reader, optical mark reader (OMR), optical character recognition (OCR), magnetic ink character recognition (MICR), bar code reader/scanner, wand

describes data that can be input to a computer without the need for any preparation. This data may be stored magnetically on a credit card or travel ticket, or printed on paper which is also readable by humans.

   There is a variety of ways of reading printing into a computer, but in most cases there has to be software to analyse what has been read, in order to recognise it. For example, after a page of typed text has been entered as an image using a *scanner* (see above), it requires complex processing by software to turn the image into the codes for the individual characters.

Magnetic stripe is the strip of magnetic material on cards such as credit cards and
   travel tickets used to hold machine-readable data. The data is written on the
   stripe by a *(magnetic) card encoder* and read by a *(magnetic) card reader* or by
   a *scanner* (see above).

Mark sense reader is an input device that reads special forms (or cards), by detecting
   the marks made in predetermined positions. The marks may be put on the form
   by hand or may be printed in some way.

Optical Mark Reader (OMR) is an input device that reads marks made in
   predetermined positions on special forms (or cards) by a light-sensing method; for
   example, the numbers recorded on a National Lottery entry form.

Optical Character Recognition (OCR) is machine recognition of printed characters
   by light-sensing methods. For example, the reading of typed post codes when
   mail is automatically sorted or the machine-readable section of a European
   Community passport.

Magnetic Ink Character Recognition (*MICR*) is machine recognition of stylised characters printed in magnetic ink. The commonest application is the data printed on a bank (or building society) cheque: the cheque number, the branch number and the account number. These characters are both machine and human readable.

Bar code reader or *bar code scanner* is an input device used to read information in *bar code* form (see page 3). Sometimes the reader is built into equipment such as a supermarket checkout terminal, where it is usually referred to as a scanner. This form of reader shines laser light beams onto the object being scanned and interprets the patterns reflected by the bar code. An alternative form is a hand-held device, which is usually called a *wand*; this also works by sensing light reflected by the bar code.

Key-to-disk system
including: key-to-tape system
is an input device for accepting data from a keyboard and writing it straight onto magnetic disk. This method of data input for large computer systems has mostly been replaced by entry into microcomputers acting as terminals to the system or by automatic data capture systems, for example hand-held key-pads for meter readers. Where the data is written to tape it is called a *key-to-tape system*.

Output device
is a peripheral unit that translates signals from the computer into a human-readable form or into a form suitable for re-processing by the computer at a later stage.

Computer Output on Microfilm (COM)
is a technique for producing computer output directly on microfilm, for example the creation of computer-generated microfiches. This provides a very economical method of storing archive copies of documents and diagrams as well as making them generally available in microfiche form.

Operator's console
is the *terminal* (see page 156) used by the computer operator to control the operation of a mainframe or mini-computer.

Original Equipment Manufacturer (OEM)
including: badging
is a firm which makes basic computer hardware for other manufacturers to build into their products. For example, a manufacturer using a microprocessor as a control device in a washing machine, or a computer manufacturer fitting another manufacturer's disk drive mechanisms into their computer. Many components of computer systems are made by only a small number of manufacturers, and are then built into systems which are sold by other manufacturers under their own brand name: this practice is known as *badging*.

Plug compatible

including: plug and go

is used to describe any peripheral equipment, made by a manufacturer other than the computer maker, which is intended to be connected to the computer and will work successfully without any adaptation being needed. This has happened successfully only rarely in the past, and a group of hardware and software companies have co-operated to define a set of standards (known as *plug and go*) to make this more effective.

Timing information

including: index mark, clock mark, clock track

is required because mechanical devices cannot operate with the precision needed by computers. So, for example, an *index mark* in the form of an *index hole* (see page 122) is found on some floppy disks to provide a fixed reference point for reading and writing data. Another example is the *clock marks* making up the *clock track* which synchronise the reading of the items on a mark-sense document.

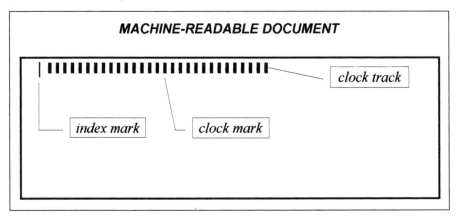

Figure B2.1: Clock track on a machine-readable document

Footprint

is the amount of space (area) taken up by a peripheral or a computer on a desk.

B3 Memory

Memory is the name given to that part of a computer system in which data is held. This data is made up of files, either program files or data files. Computer memory serves two purposes. The first is to hold programs or data that the processor needs immediately; for this reason it is sometimes called **immediate access memory**. The second is to hold data that may be needed at some time; it is often called **backing store**. Immediate access memory must be able to be read (and be written to) very quickly, since most computer instructions require that data is moved around in the immediate access memory. Backup memory can have distinctly slower reading and writing times. Immediate access memory is usually about 1000 times as fast as backing store. The immediate access memory is located very close to the processor, so that signals take the shortest possible time in coming from and going to the processor; but backing store can be in separate units connected to the processor by cables.

Memory and storage have meanings that overlap and are often used as interchangeable words; but memory suggests data is immediately available whereas storage suggests that data has to be retrieved. Sometimes memory is described as **primary**, for the immediate access memory; **secondary**, for the principal backing store; and **auxiliary,** for other forms of backing store. A variety of other names are used for immediate access memory, such as IAS, main memory, the memory, the store and for backing store, such as backup memory, peripheral memory, off-line storage.

Throughout the development of computers there has been a continual search for ways of improving memory technology. The search has been for reliable, compact storage devices with low energy consumption. Whenever a suitable new device has been developed, ways of cheap mass-production have been found.

Because of the different requirements for the two functions of memory, it is usual for completely different kinds of technology to be used in a particular computer system. For immediate access memory, most present-day computers use some form of random access memory integrated circuits, in which very large amounts of data can be stored in a single plastic encapsulated chip. For backing store most use some form of magnetic storage, such as disks or tapes, and may also have read-only storage, such as CD-ROM.

Immediate access memory is sometimes in two parts. One part, called **cache** memory, is made up of a small capacity but exceedingly fast memory and is located next to the processor. The other part is much larger, and a copy of some of its contents is put into the cache memory in readiness for instant use. The choice of size for the main memory of a computer is partly determined by the addressing methods used and the cost of memory components. It is usual for computers to be sold with the potential for later memory expansion.

Backing store consists of the medium (the material on which the data is stored) and any associated mechanisms. Most computers use magnetic backing store (tapes or disks), while some use integrated circuit semiconductor memory, and optical systems are increasingly being used. As far as the user is concerned, the medium may be removable, for example tapes, floppy disks and optical disks; or fixed, for example hard disks. The advantage of using removable media is that an expensive mechanism can be used for a variety of purposes with cheap media. Fixed disks provide faster access and greater capacity than removable disks and are used to store programs and data that are frequently needed. Most computer systems now have both fixed and removable disks. A large computer system will have fixed disks, removable disks, tape storage and, possibly, optical storage. A personal computer will have at least a hard fixed disk and a floppy disk unit and, possibly, an optical disk unit.

Memory may be **volatile** or **permanent**. Volatile memory loses its data when there is no power supply to it, whereas permanent memory does not require power. All magnetic and optical media provide permanent memory as do some forms of integrated circuit memory. However the most widely used form of integrated circuit memory for immediate access store is volatile; this means that, when the computer is switched on, programs and data have to be loaded from backing store. If power is cut off, for some reason, then all data in memory will be lost.

Memory is often described by the type of *access* that is possible. For example, all the storage locations in immediate access memory can be directly accessed and the access time for all locations is the same; this is described as **random access memory**. In contrast, the data stored on a tape can only be reached by going through the tape, in sequence, until the right place is found; this is described as **serial access memory**. Storage on a disk is in concentric rings and is a collection of small sequential lengths of storage. Since disk storage can be so quickly accessed, it is generally thought of as direct (random) access storage.

Some forms of memory can only be read (**read-only**) and normally cannot be written to except during manufacture. Some semiconductor memory chips are manufactured as a blank memory array that can have data 'programmed' into it at a later time. One advantage is that some of these programmable memory chips can have the data erased and rewritten if necessary. Uses for programmable chips include storing programs for controlling traffic lights or lifts, and computer games programs. Most current optical disk technology is read-only, of which compact disc read-only memory (CD-ROM) is one example. Experience of technical advances suggests that it is only a matter of time before read-write optical devices become generally available at low cost. Some storage devices use a laser system to etch data onto a blank disk; the recorded data can then be read as often as needed but cannot be rewritten. They are called write-once read-many (**WORM**) devices.

Storage

also known as: memory
is a general term covering all units of computer equipment used to store data (and programs).

Store

also known as: memory
including: store location, address (store), main store, immediate access store (IAS),
primary store, (memory) cell

The store, or memory, is the part of a computer system where data and instructions are held for use by the central processor and where the central processor puts results it generates. The computer store is made up of a large number of identifiable units, called *(store) locations*. Each store location has a unique label, called a *(store) address*, which is recognisable and used by the central processor. Those store locations that can be addressed directly by the central processor are called the *main store, immediate access store (IAS)* or *primary store*. A store location, sometimes called a *(memory) cell*, is capable of holding a single item of data, a *byte* (see page 254).

Backing store

also known as: secondary store, mass storage
including: magnetic disk storage, magnetic tape storage, optical disk storage,
magneto-optical storage

is a means of storing large amounts of data outside the *immediate access store* (see above). A computer system will have at least one form of backing store. Most backing store uses magnetic storage, but increasing use is being made of optical storage systems. Backing store is sometimes referred to as *secondary store* or *mass storage.*

Magnetic disk storage is backing store in which flat rotatable circular plates, coated with a magnetic material, are used for storing digital data. The data is written to and read from a set of concentric circular *tracks* (see *magnetic disk*, page 122).

Magnetic tape storage is backing store which uses plastic tape coated on one side with magnetic material. Digital information is stored on the tape as a set of parallel *tracks* (see *magnetic tape*, page 125), which are written or read simultaneously.

Optical disk storage is backing store which uses plastic disks on which the data is stored as patterns on the surface. One method uses hollows etched into the surface of the disk for pre-recorded data in the form of *CD-ROMs* (see page 130). Other methods, such as *phase change optical disks* (see page 130) provide read/write optical storage.

Magneto-optical storage is backing store which uses plastic disks on which data is stored by a combination of optical and magnetic methods.

Magnetic disk

also known as: computer disk, disk
including: hard disk, floppy disk, disk pack, exchangeable disk pack, diskette, index
hole, track (disk), cylinder

is a circular disk, usually made of plastic, coated with a layer of magnetic material on which data can be stored by magnetically setting the arrangement of the magnetic material. This is done by electro-magnetic *read/write heads* (see page 129). Disks may have data stored on one side only (single sided) or on both sides (double sided). The disk may be rigid (a *hard disk*), or flexible (a *floppy disk*). Where a disk drive has multiple disks (a *disk pack*) these are generally rigid, hard disks, on a common spindle with read/write heads for each disk. If the disk pack is removable so that it can be exchanged for another complete pack, it is called an *exchangeable disk pack*.

A floppy disk (sometimes called a *diskette*) has to be protected by an outer covering which prevents the magnetic coating from being damaged and keeps out dirt. Floppy disks are made to agreed standard designs, which can be used on any drive for the same size of disk. The commonest size is 3½ inch, but the earlier 5¼ inch standard is still significantly used.

Floppy disks need to have some way of showing where the tracks start. In 5¼ inch disks this is done by an *index hole*. This is a small hole near the central hole, which lines up with a gap in the casing once every revolution. In 3½ inch disks, it is only possible to fit the disk onto the drive in one position. Floppy disks provide one of the most common ways of passing data and programs from one computer user to another.

The general layout of recording surfaces on a disk and on a multi-surface disk pack is shown in Figure B3.1.

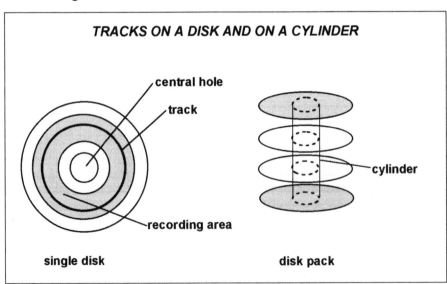

Figure B3.1: Track and cylinder

Data is stored on disks in concentric rings, called **tracks**. In a disk pack, a set of tracks one above the other, for example the tenth track on each disk, is called a **cylinder**. It is normal to store data which needs to be kept together, on a cylinder rather than on one disk, because the read/write heads will not need to move to access the data.

Disk drive

also known as: magnetic disk drive
including: fixed head disk unit, hard disk drive, Winchester drive, floppy disk drive, CD-ROM drive, CD-ROM jukebox
is the unit made up of the mechanism that rotates the disks between the *read/write heads* (see page 129), and the mechanism that controls the heads. Most disk drives have one set of read/write heads for each surface and have to be moved to the required track. A disk unit with one set of heads for each disk track is called a *fixed head disk unit*. This arrangement gives much faster access to data on the disk(s) but at increased cost.

Hard disk drives use rigid magnetic disk(s) enclosed in a sealed container. This has the advantage of allowing high recording density because the recording heads can be very close to the magnetic material on the disk. A small hard disk drive, sometimes known as a *Winchester disk (drive)*, is widely used in microcomputer systems as the principal back-up store in addition to one or more floppy disk drives.

Floppy disk drives use flexible disks which can be removed from their drives by the user, unlike hard disks which are permanently mounted. See *magnetic disk*, below.

CD-ROM drives (sometimes called CD-ROM players) are very similar to audio compact disc players and read CD-ROM disks. A *CD-ROM jukebox* is a CD-ROM drive with a mechanism for automatically changing the current disk for another selected disk; it is similar to the old-fashioned jukebox for playing gramophone records.

Disk array

including: RAID (Redundant Array of Inexpensive Disks)
is set of hard disk units used as if they are a single mass storage device. By using two disks to hold the same data, a disk drive fault will be unlikely to have any effect on the operation of the whole system. By writing some of the data to each of a number of disks, storage and retrieval of data can be speeded up. This method of organising backing store for large computer systems is known as *RAID*, which stands for *Redundant Array of Inexpensive* (or *Independent*) *Disks*. RAID systems provide a low-cost method of ensuring that losses of data are nearly impossible.

Disk format

including: (disk) formatting, sector, hard-sectored disk, soft-sectored disk, disk verification

is the arrangement and organisation of the *tracks* (see page 122/3) on a disk. Each track is divided into a number of equal-length portions, called *sectors* (see Figure B3.2). A sector is the smallest addressable portion of a track and is the smallest unit of data that is written to or read from a disk. Normally each sector on each track holds the same amount of data, even though outer tracks are longer than inner tracks, so the *packing density* (see page 128) depends upon the distance of the track from the centre of the disk. Some disk systems use variable speed disks which have different amounts of data on each track.

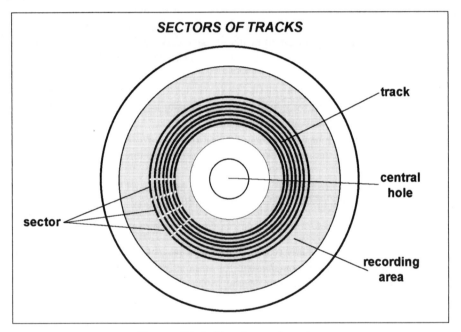

Figure B3.2: Tracks and sectors

If the sectors are partially or wholly created when the disk is made, the disk is called a *hard-sectored disk*. If the sectors are created by software on an unformatted disk, the disk is called a *soft-sectored disk*. Floppy disks may be either hard- or soft-sectored.

The initial preparation of a blank disk for subsequent writing and reading by adding control information such as track and sector number is called *(disk) formatting*. When a disk is formatted, it is also *verified*; it is checked to ensure that all the tracks and sectors are fit for recording data. Formatting a disk that contains data will erase all the data on it. Floppy disks for personal computers need to be appropriately formatted for the machine on which they are to be used, although some machines may be able to read disks in a variety of formats. It is possible to buy floppy disks which are already formatted.

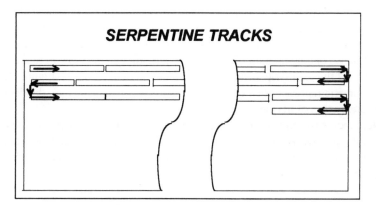

Figure B3.6: Blocks in serpentine tracks

Large amounts of data can be stored on a single tape. Tapes are used as backup or archive storage and are very useful for storing data which is required only on planned occasions, or when the majority of records will be accessed in any processing, for example data which is updated monthly or quarterly. Applications which have very large storage requirements are increasingly using high packing density tapes for on-line purposes.

Cache memory

also known as: the cache

including: disk cache

is a part of the main store, between the central processor and the rest of the main store. It has extremely fast access, so sections of a program and its associated data are copied there to take advantage of its short fetch cycle (see *fetch-execute cycle*, page 283). The use of cache memory can greatly reduce processing time. It is sometimes called the *cache.*

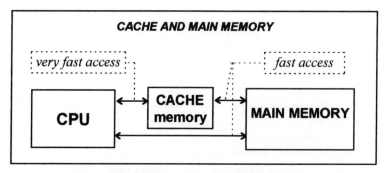

Figure B3.7: Cache memory

A way of speeding up the transfer of large amounts of data from disks is to use a *disk cache*, which is a section of memory for holding data that has been read from disk storage. See also *buffering*, page 287.

Data is written to the tape in blocks, with a gap between each block, called an ***inter-block gap.*** The gap is needed for the tape to accelerate to the correct speed for reading or writing or to stop after reading or writing. Since the data is stored sequentially, finding an item of data will require that all the tape up to the data item is wound past the read/write heads until the required item is found. Figure B3.3 shows a diagrammatic representation of data on this form of magnetic tape; the data is stored as discrete areas of magnetism along each track.

More recent systems use the same technology as video recorders, where the data blocks are written on diagonal tracks (Figure B3.4) across the tape by a rotating head. This gives very high density and greater read/write speeds than the earlier tape systems.

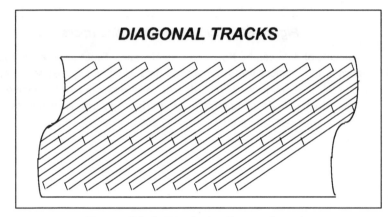

Figure B3.4: Blocks in diagonal tracks

Other tape formats include blocks arranged side by side on multiple tracks (Figure B3.5) and blocks one after another in a 'serpentine' arrangement with alternate tracks written in opposite directions (Figure B3.6).

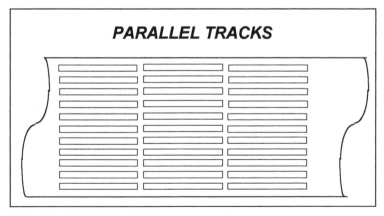

Figure B3.5: Blocks in parallel tracks

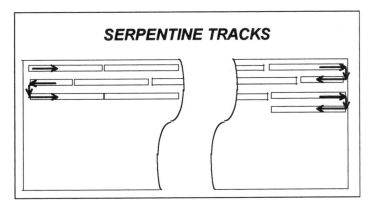

Figure B3.6: Blocks in serpentine tracks

Large amounts of data can be stored on a single tape. Tapes are used as backup or archive storage and are very useful for storing data which is required only on planned occasions, or when the majority of records will be accessed in any processing, for example data which is updated monthly or quarterly. Applications which have very large storage requirements are increasingly using high packing density tapes for on-line purposes.

Cache memory
also known as: the cache
including: disk cache
is a part of the main store, between the central processor and the rest of the main store. It has extremely fast access, so sections of a program and its associated data are copied there to take advantage of its short fetch cycle (see *fetch-ecute cycle*, page 283). The use of cache memory can greatly reduce processing time. It is sometimes called the *cache.*

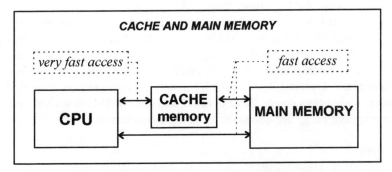

Figure B3.7: Cache memory

A way of speeding up the transfer of large amounts of data from disks is to use a *disk cache*, which is a section of memory for holding data that has been read from disk storage. See also *buffering*, page 287.

Tape streamer

is a small tape drive unit, usually using tape cassettes, with very large storage capacity. They are frequently used to make backup copies of data for security purposes.

Packing density

including: bits per inch (bpi), disk density

is a measure of the quantity of data that can be held per unit length of track on a storage medium. It is usually measured in ***bits per inch*** (***bpi***) and is the number of binary digits (or bits) stored in one inch (2.54cm) along each track.

Terms such as single density and double density (**DD**), quad density (**QD**) and high density (**HD**) are used to describe the packing density of magnetic disks (***disk density***). The interpretation of these terms is not uniform, since the size of the disk, the age of the drive and the sophistication of the operating system cause differences in meaning.

Semiconductor memory

also known as: integrated circuit memory
including: MOS, CMOS

is a form of memory which uses integrated circuit semiconductor chips. The storage capacity of this form of memory is very high, the time taken to read a data item is very short and the access is direct. There are a number of different forms of semiconductor storage; the more common ones use ***MOS*** (***metal-oxide-semiconductor***) or ***CMOS*** (***complementary MOS***) technology. The advantage of CMOS types is that they require little power to retain their contents; powered by small batteries they can be used as *non-volatile memory* while the computer is switched off. See *volatile memory*, page 132. Most current computer designs use semiconductor memory for immediate access storage.

RAM (Random Access Memory)

including: static RAM, dynamic RAM (DRAM), memory refresh

is memory that has the same access time for all locations. Each location holds one *byte* (see page 254) and is directly addressable. RAM may be either ***static***, which holds its memory so long as there is a power supply, or ***dynamic***, which has to be ***refreshed*** by reading and rewriting the contents very frequently (about every 2 milliseconds). Dynamic RAM (***DRAM***) is more widely used than static RAM because it needs less power. Both dynamic and static RAM are *volatile* (see *volatile memory*, page 132). See also *semiconductor memory*, above.

RAM disk

also known as: silicon disk

is memory which is addressed as if it were a very fast random access disk. It behaves as an extremely fast backing store for the user but is usually volatile and has to be loaded from backing store. It is normally an area of main memory reserved for this use.

ROM (Read-Only Memory)

including: PROM (Programmable Read-Only Memory), EPROM (Erasable PROM), EAROM (Electrically Alterable Read-Only Memory), EEPROM (Electrically Erasable PROgrammable Memory), flash PROM, cartridge

is memory for which the contents may be read but cannot be written to by the computer system. Read-only memory is used for both data and programs. There are optical ROM systems (see *CD-ROM*, page 130), and semiconductor (integrated circuit) ROM systems (see *semiconductor memory*, page 128).

The term **ROM** is frequently used to mean the (integrated circuit) read-only memory used to hold programs and associated data for building into computers. Software in ROM is fixed during manufacture, but there are other ways of putting programs and data into ROM.

PROM (Programmable Read-Only Memory) is a type of ROM which is manufactured as an empty storage array and is later permanently programmed by the user.

EPROM (Erasable PROM) is a type of PROM whose data can be erased by a special process (e.g. by exposure to ultraviolet radiation) so new data can be written as if it were a new PROM.

EAROM (Electrically Alterable Read-Only Memory) and *EEPROM (Electrically Erasable Programmable Read-Only Memory)*, sometimes called *flash PROM*, are other similar types of read-only memory.

Some small computers and games computers use software on (integrated circuit) ROM which is packaged in plug-in modules called *cartridges*. This is a convenient way of preventing the software from being copied.

Read/write head

including: disk access time, seek time, latency, head crash, park

is the set of electro-magnets and necessary circuitry used to magnetise the magnetic material used for storage. Tape units have fixed heads and the tape moves past them. Most disk units have the set of heads on an arm which moves them from track to track, but fixed head disk units have a set of heads for each track, which greatly reduces the time taken to access data on the disk. Double-sided disks require a set of heads for each side. The time taken to get data from a disk, the *disk access time*, includes the time taken to move the heads to the correct track, called the *seek time*, and the time taken for the disk to rotate to the correct part of the track, sometimes called *latency*. However, some people use latency to mean the total waiting time.

Head crash is when the read/write heads hit the surface of a disk. This can cause serious damage to the mechanisms and loss of data. To avoid this happening with personal computers, for example when a machine is moved, the read/write heads are often automatically put in a safe position, *parked*, whenever they are not being used to access the disk. Following the proper procedures of closing all files before ending a session of work will ensure that the disk is properly parked. Some early personal computers required the user to give the command for parking the disk.

Optical storage

including: CD-ROM (Compact Disc Read-Only Memory), videodisk, laser disk, EB disk (Electronic Book disk), WORM (Write-Once, Read-Many), multisession-CD, photo-CD, magneto-optical disk, phase change optical disk

uses laser technology to etch the surface of a storage medium to form minute patterns which represent the data. The scattering effect on a narrow laser beam is used to read the data which may be digital or analog. At present, the process of making optical disks requires costly equipment, but this may change. The digital technology is the same as that used in audio compact discs (CDs).

CD-ROM (*Compact Disc Read-Only Memory*), which uses the same size of disk as audio CDs, is a read-only form of backing store used to hold large amounts of data. CD-ROM disks are pressed from a master disk in the same way that audio CDs are made. A *videodisk*, sometimes called a *laser disk*, is an equivalent analog form, which uses large disks like long playing gramophone records, for which the domestic equipment is quite rare. A recent development is the *EB disk* (*Electronic Book disk*), which uses a 3 inch disk. The data on CD-ROM may include programs as well as sound, graphics or text data. CD-ROM with a computer capable of manipulating, storing and outputting high quality sound and graphics is a multimedia system. See *multimedia computer*, page 110/1.

WORM (*Write-Once, Read-Many*) is an optical (compact) disc system, which allows the user to write data on the next available portion of the disk. A portion of the disk can only have data written on it once, but this data can be read as often as required. Some worms allow the overwriting of data so as to spoil or erase it. *Multisession-CD*, which is designed to capture and store materials created during separate work sessions, is one example of a worm; another form is *Photo-CD*, which stores conventional camera images on optical disk.

Magneto-Optical Disk is a re-writable optical disk which uses magnetic and optical techniques. Writing uses a laser beam to heat a small part of the surface of the disk and, at the same time, a magnetic field arranges the magnetic material in this heated area in one of two ways. Reading uses the effect that the magnetic field on the surface of the disk has on a weak laser beam.

Phase Change Optical Disk is a re-writable optical disk which uses a laser to read and write data. It uses three strengths of laser signal. The weakest signal is used to read data; the other two signals are used to write data, by making parts of the material of the disk surface reflective or non-reflective to the weakest signal.

Content-addressable storage

also known as: associative storage

is a physically separate module of storage, designed to allow access to a location by its contents rather than by an address label. The normal address *decoder* logic (see page 326) is replaced by logic which compares the contents of part of each store with the address item. The remainder of each store contains indications of where the required data is stored.

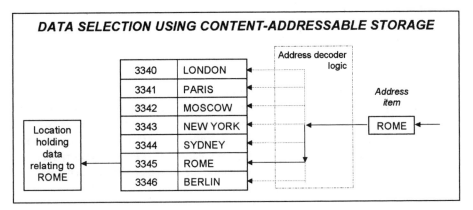

Figure B3.8: Content-addressable storage

Block

including: bucket

is the name for the smallest unit of data which is transferred between backing store and main store in one operation. In large computer systems, a *bucket* defines a unit of storage in random access memory. A bucket will contain a (variable) number of blocks. Access to the data is by reference to the bucket it is in.

Memory map

including: disk map, file allocation table (FAT)

describes the way storage is organised in a computer. For example, sections of memory may be allocated to the screen display, program code, or variables. The memory map for disk storage is called a *disk map.* It describes how the information held on the disk is organised, and is kept on the disk. It may be held as a *bit map* (see page 286). Details of where files are stored in backing store is kept in a *file allocation table (FAT)*, which is a file also kept on the backing store. See also *directory*, page 86.

Scratch pad

also called: work(ing) store

including: scratch file, scrap file, work(ing) file, scratch tape

is a section of immediate access store reserved as a temporary working area for use by an application. It is also called a *work store* or *working store*. An area of file space on backing store assigned for this purpose is called a *scratch file, scrap file, work file* or *working file*. If tape is used, it is called a *scratch tape*. See also *clipboard*, page 9.

Virtual storage

is a means of apparently extending main storage by using backing storage if it were main memory. See also, *virtual memory*, page 284/5.

Volatile memory

including: permanent memory, non-volatile memory

is a form of storage which holds data only while power is supplied. This is in contrast to **non-volatile memory**, which keeps its contents even when the system is switched off. All currently used forms of magnetic storage and optical disk storage are non-volatile, but most other forms of storage are volatile. **Permanent memory** retains its contents regardless of power supply and cannot be erased or altered; many forms of read-only memory (ROM) are permanent.

Write protection

including: blocking ring, write-inhibit ring, write-permit ring, request verification

is the prevention of unintentionally overwriting data on backing store. This can be achieved *either* by hardware features *or* by provisions in software.

Hardware write protection is built into floppy disk drives and floppy disk cases; for the older, 5¼ inch disks a cut-away portion of the case has to be covered over with an adhesive patch, while for 3½ inch disks there is a sliding cover for a hole in the case. There are no similar standards for large disk units; each manufacturer provides their own system. There is no hardware write protection for small hard disks in personal computers. Tape units have removable **blocking rings** behind the tape spools which act either as **write-inhibit** or as **write-permit rings** depending on the system used; cassettes or cartridges have sliding tabs.

Software methods include double checking a request (**request verification**) if it will over-write or delete a file, checking the characteristics of file names to see if they are protected and asking for passwords before overwriting or deleting any data.

B4   Display Devices

Human beings possess a very high resolution, multicolour and fast-moving vision system. Thus it is understandable why so much technical effort has gone into producing displays from computer systems that can exploit the facilities of the human eye.

Much of the current display technology uses the cathode ray (television) tube. The tube looks like a large electric light bulb with a flat end. The user sees only the flat end. The electronics of the system makes the end glow with patterns of dots. It is the number and nature of these dots that determines the quality of the picture that the user sees.

For such applications as word processing then perhaps a monochrome (one colour) display is all that is needed but at the present state of development the software that would be used to produce the word processed document would no doubt require a colour display. We are now at the stage where colour display is considered to be the norm.

All the colours of the rainbow can be made by mixing various amounts of red, green and blue light. A colour display screen is coated with substances that glow when they are hit by electric particles (electrons).

The coating is arranged in horizontal lines of **triads**. A triad is a cluster of three dots that will glow; one will glow red, one green and one blue. The electronics of the whole system will excite different members of the triad to a greater or lesser amount, so as to produce a glowing dot (**a pixel**) of the required colour and brightness. It is an arrangement of a large number of these pixels that produces the final picture. The screen picture needs to be able to change quickly, anything from just simple text editing to a fast-moving graphics image. This ability to change is achieved because the picture is redrawn many times a second (in the range of 25 to 72 times) even if it is not actually changing. This screen **refresh** process is done by the electron beam making a horizontal sweep over each line of triads. It is technically easier, and thus cheaper, for the screen refresh to be done in two passes; every other line of triads is refreshed on a first pass, then the other lines are refreshed at the second pass; this is called **interlace** scanning. Interlace scanning is the method normally used in domestic television but a system that refreshes all the lines of triads in sequence, called **non-interlaced** scanning, is used in a number of designs for computer display screens.

The electronics that pass the information from the computer to the screen device are generally specific to the type of screen device. These electronics have to be installed by fitting a specific electronics board, called a **display adapter**, into the computer. For example, when a system has a VGA display this means a VGA screen device and a matching VGA display adapter in the computer.

The development of laptop computers has required high-performance flat-screen display systems. This has been achieved by major enhancements to liquid crystal technology, which was originally developed for pocket calculators. In its basic form, liquid crystal display consists of a thin layer, a film, of fluid sandwiched between two sheets of glass or plastic. Complex wiring is used to apply voltages to different small areas of the film of liquid. The applied voltage alters the ability of the liquid to reflect or transmit light. Thus a pixel display is built up of light and dark dots of varying intensity. One way of producing colour is to have three layers of different types of liquid, with different colour characteristics, where each layer has its own associated wiring. Some systems rely on reflected light and cannot be used in poor lighting conditions. Back lighting systems, where the liquid films transmit light from a light source behind the screen, give a more easily viewed display than reflective systems.

Monitor

including: monochrome monitor, colour monitor, scan rate, multiscan monitor
is the term generally used for any device that displays information using a cathode ray tube. Although this definition could include a standard television set, a monitor normally does not have the receiving part of a television set. All monitor displays are made up of illuminated dots on the screen. Monitors may be monochrome or colour.
Monochrome monitors give a display of varying intensity of a single colour, for
　　example white, green or orange on a dark (black) background.
Colour monitors give a display with a range of colours determined by the colour
　　circuitry in the monitor and the computer.
　　Monitors may have a fixed or variable *scan rate*, that is how often the image is redrawn or refreshed (see *screen refresh*, page 137). Monitors that can operate at different scan rates are called *multiscan monitors* or *multisync monitors*; they can adjust to different scan rates set by a *video adapter* (see page 137). Multiscan monitors first appeared in 1985 and are essential for modern high definition display systems, such as *SVGA* and *EGA* (see page 136).

Frame

including: interlace
is used to describe a screenful of information treated as a single unit. An example is a response frame for the input of data in a screen input data capture system.
　　In electronics, a frame is one complete screen picture. In a standard television set, this consists of 625 separate lines; a new frame is transmitted every 1/25 of a second, as two *interlaced* fields: the first field is the odd-numbered lines and the second is the even-numbered lines.

Raster graphics

including: raster, scan, interlaced scan, non-interlaced scan, scan frequency, screen resolution, dot pitch, low-resolution graphics, High-Resolution Graphics (HRG)
is a method of producing an image on a display screen. The image is drawn on a cathode ray tube (a CRT) by illuminating *pixels* (see page 135) as horizontal lines of dots covering the whole screen; this is called the *raster*. An electron beam sweeps over these lines of pixels, drawing the display many times a second, in the same way that a picture is drawn on a television set (see *frame*, above).

Sweeping over the lines of the raster display is called *scanning*. The scan may be done by drawing alternate lines (line 1 followed by line 3, and so on) on a first pass and then the rest of the lines on a second pass. This is called an *interlaced scan*, and is the method used in television sets. Alternatively the scan may draw each line successively (line 1 followed by line 2, and so on), called a *non-interlaced scan*. How often the screen is scanned is called the *scan frequency*.

The quality of a raster display depends upon the *screen resolution*, which is usually quoted as the number of pixels in a row × the number of rows (horizontal × vertical), and the *dot pitch*, which is the size of a dot (pixel) on the screen. Values of between 0.28mm and 0.38mm for the dot pitch are considered acceptable; this is between 100 and 70 dots per inch.

To provide an acceptable image on a large screen, the pixel resolution has to be increased to give the same dot pitch as on a smaller screen. On a 14-inch screen with 1024 × 768 pixels the dot pitch is 0.28mm (approx. 90 dots/inch); to achieve similar quality of image on a 17-inch screen requires a resolution of 1280 × 1024 pixels (dot pitch 0.26mm, approx. 98 dots/inch).

In general, raster graphics will produce untidy display of any line which is neither vertical nor horizontal. If high quality screen display of line drawings is required, then *vector graphics* (see page 138) is the appropriate system.

A number of general descriptions of display resolution are used:

Low-resolution graphics is generally applied to graphical display units where simple pictures can be built up by plotting large blocks of colour or by using special graphics characters. It is used for *teletext* images (see page 52).

High-Resolution Graphics (HRG) is generally applied to graphical display units capable of plotting around 300 or more pixels in the width of a *monitor* screen (see page 134).

Pixel
is a contraction of 'picture-element'. As used in graphics, it is the smallest element of a display. A pixel will have one or more attributes of colour, intensity (or brightness) and flashing.

Pixel graphics
is where a picture is constructed of a rectangular array of dots. Each dot may be any of the colours available to the computer but it is not possible for a dot to be split into smaller pieces. This means that it is impossible to have detail smaller than the size of the *pixels* (see above).

Palette
is the range of display colours available in the computer system. Any particular display system may not be able to support the total number of colours, hence a selection is made from the possible palette. The user may be allowed to change this selection.

VIDEO GRAPHICS ADAPTERS

NAME	DESCRIPTION	RESOLUTION and CHARACTER SIZE (rows × characters) (pixels: width × height) (pixels: width × height)		COLOUR PROVISION
Monochrome Display Adapter (MDA) Released 1981	text but no graphics: (for monochrome monitors)	text: graphics:	25 rows of 80 characters not available	monochrome only
Hercules Graphics Adapter Released 1982	text and graphics (for monochrome monitors)	text: character size: graphics:	32 rows of 80 characters 10 × 9 720 × 320 pixels	monochrome only
Colour Graphics Adapter (CGA) Released 1981	colour text **two** colour graphics modes: (MDA compatible)	text: character size: graphics: graphics:	25 rows of 80 characters 8 × 8 640 × 200 pixels 320 × 200 pixels	16 foreground + 8 background two colours four colours
Enhanced Graphics Adapter (EGA) Released 1984	improved version of CGA text and graphics bit mapped	graphics:	640 × 350 pixels	16 colours
Video Graphics Array (VGA) Released 1987	improved version of EGA text and graphics bit mapped	graphics:	640 × 480 pixels	256 colours
Super Video Graphics Array (SVGA) Released 1988	analog display system: needs multiscan monitor	graphics:	800 × 600 pixels	16 colours infinite range of shades of grey
Extended Graphics Array (XGA) Released 1991	analog display system: needs multiscan monitor	graphics:	1024 × 768 pixels	256 colour text theoretically infinite range of colours; in practice usually limited to $262,144 \ (= 2^{18})$

***Table B4.1:** Graphics adapters*

See also *pixel* (page 135) **and** *monitor* (page 134) **and** *bit map* (page 286).

Video adapter

also known as: display adapter, graphics adapter
is the circuitry which generates the signals needed for a video output device to display computer data. The data may be text only or text and graphics. The circuits are contained on a circuit board which is installed in the computer with output via a cable to the display unit (the monitor). A variety of adapters have been devised and sold. Most are associated with one computer manufacturer and require the use of a particular design of *monitor* (see page 134). There is a range of adapters for IBM PCs (and IBM compatibles), some of which are described in Table B4.1 (opposite). These specifications were all promoted by IBM.

A number of other manufacturers have developed adapters with different screen proportions and higher resolutions such as 1280 × 1024 pixels. There are video adapters from other manufacturers which can be installed in PCs. Computers which are not IBM compatible frequently use their own video adapters with different standards.

Screen refresh

including: refresh rate, Vertical Refresh Rate (VRR)
is the process of continuously energising the glowing substances on a cathode ray tube device to keep the display visible. The screen is refreshed between 25 to 72 times per second (known as the *refresh rate*) depending on the display system used. The technique allows the easy display of changing images.

Vertical Refresh Rate (*VRR*) is related to the horizontal sweeps that the electron beam makes in a cathode ray tube (CRT) display. Once an image has been entirely repainted by horizontal sweeps then it has been vertically refreshed. A low vertical refresh rate tends to produce flicker. A VGA monitor has a vertical refresh rate of 60 - 70 scans per second and the standard for SVGA monitors is 72 scans per second. See also the table of *video graphics adapters* for IBM PCs, Table B4.1, opposite.

Video RAM (VRAM)

is a separate high-speed memory into which the processor writes the screen data, which is then read to the screen for display. This avoids the use of any main memory to hold screen data.

Graphical Display Unit (GDU)

is an output device, incorporating a cathode ray tube (CRT), on which both line drawings and text can be displayed. The term has become used for display systems specifically for high quality graphics work. A graphical display unit is often used in conjunction with a light-pen to input or re-position data. High quality graphical display units normally use *vector graphics* (see page 138).

Vector graphics

is a screen display method using a cathode ray tube (CRT) in which each line of a drawing is drawn on the screen individually. A line can be drawn in any direction (although there is a minimum width of a line) and so the display is a more accurate presentation of the picture with no jagged edges. The resolution of vector graphics screens is usually very high so that the size of pixels is small, which gives the high quality display. Vector graphics is an expensive technique to implement with the result that most displays use *raster graphics* (see page 134).

Liquid Crystal Display (LCD)

is a display technique that uses the phenomenon that certain liquids alter their ability to reflect or transmit light if a voltage is applied to them. Originally used for pocket calculators it is now common for laptop computers.

Light Emitting Diode (LED)

is a display that uses the property of some semiconductor diodes to emit light when a voltage is applied to them. Their power consumption is negligible and they give off no heat. They are commonly used as indicator lights on devices such as disk drives. They are also useful for monitoring the logic state of lines in control applications.

Colour display

including:RGB (Red Green Blue)

is the form of display from a colour monitor. This display is usually produced by a colour cathode ray tube, as in a television set. In a cathode ray tube, coloured dots on the backing of the screen are made to give off light. The coloured dots are red or green or blue. Different levels of brightness of the three colours combine to produce the range of colours on the screen.

RGB (Red Green Blue) describes a method of connecting a computer to a (colour) display monitor in which the colour information is transmitted as three separate signals. RGB signals do not need to be decoded, as does a *PAL* signal (see below). Thus, definition is generally better using an RGB connection.

PAL (Phase Alternating Line)

is the UK standard method of encoding colour information in a television signal. If a domestic television set is used as a display device via the ordinary aerial socket, the computer must contain a PAL encoder for colour.

B5 Printers

A printer is connected to a computer for the sole purpose of transferring the information from the computer to paper or other media. The version printed out on paper is often referred to as **hard copy**. There are many types of printer that can be connected to a computer system varying in quality, cost and purpose. Their output may be in black on white, known as **monochrome**, or in colour. Modern printers contain embedded microprocessors to control their operations.

Colour printers are becoming more common for a number of reasons; their cost is reducing whilst their quality is improving, colour monitor screens are in general use, and multimedia material usually requires colour. This can be advantageous, since information and graphics in colour are more interesting, remembered longer and can contain more detail than the same material printed in monochrome.

Colours from a printed page are produced by reflected light, whereas colour from a computer screen is emitted. Colour printers create the different colours by combining different proportions of the three secondary colours, cyan (C), magenta (M) and yellow (Y). It is no simple matter to ensure that the colours displayed on your monitor will be matched by the output of your printer. Human sensitivity to colour varies so that no two people are likely to see a given colour or combination of colours exactly the same.

Printers in common use are **character printers**, **ink jet** and other **matrix printers**, and **laser printers**. There are also specialist printers, such as **thermal wax** and **dye sublimation printers,** and **plotters.**

Character printers print complete single characters one at a time. **Ink jet, dot matrix** and **laser** printers all deliver an image which is made up of patterns of dots, either black or coloured. It is possible to produce any character or shape simply by arranging for ink dots to go in the right places. This method can be used for printing out a copy of a piece of computer graphics (for example a picture or a design) as well as for printing text.

Ink jet and dot matrix printers produce the dots using a mechanism (a print head) which travels in steps across the paper. If the dots are very small and the steps are small enough the quality of printing can be very fine. Because the dots are positioned at points on a grid (a **matrix**), these printers are called matrix printers. For example, the letter h can be crudely formed by a simple pattern of dots, shown in Figure B5.1 (overleaf). But by using a matrix with many more squares, it is possible to produce a perfectly shaped letter h.

Historically, **character printers** were really a development from typewriters, often with all the characters on a single element (a ball or a daisy wheel). These printers were mechanical in action and they are seldom used today as other printers can work faster, produce quality printing, do it quietly and are more versatile.

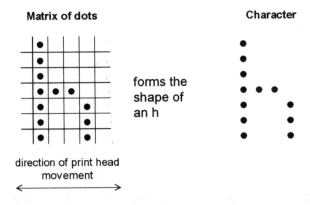

Figure B5.1: *A character formed by a pattern of dots*

Dot matrix printers, which use pins striking an ink ribbon to make marks on the paper, are relatively cheap. They will work with almost any quality of paper, are generally able to print on either continuous paper or single sheets, and can print multiple (carbon) copies at the same time. They are frequently used in supermarket checkouts and in industry. The quality of printing may be poor.

Ink jet printers (also known as **bubble jet printers**) produce print quality rivalling that produced by a laser printer (but not as quickly). They may be small enough to be easily portable and models exist which can print very large sizes of paper.

Laser printers essentially use the Xerographic technology of the modern photocopier. Their advantages are their speed and high quality of printing. They are used in offices as they are robust and the printed image is waterproof. Colour laser printers are available, but they are still rather expensive.

The quality of monochrome printing will depend mainly on the **resolution**, that is the size of the dots and the number of possible positions for them. In colour printing, there are several factors which affect quality; these include the resolution, the range of colours the printer can produce **(colour palette)** and the software which controls the printing process **(colour management)**.

In summary, deciding upon a printer is not easy as all printers today can print anything that your computer can produce. Probably cost, quality of print, and colour or monochrome are the three main areas to focus upon – and noise, if you are likely to be printing a lot or late at night.

Printer

including: monochrome printer, colour printer, print head

is an output device producing characters or graphics on paper. *Monochrome printers* use a single ink colour, normally black on white paper. *Colour printers* use coloured inks, to produce the coloured image, as well as black ink. There are many methods of printing and of organising the operation of a printer, for example some smaller printers use a moving *print head* which travels backwards and forwards across the paper and carries the printing mechanism. For a summary of information about printers see Table B5.1 pages 146/7.

Character printer

including: daisy wheel printer, golf ball printer
is one which prints characters one at a time. A moving print head holds the mechanical part, a wheel (daisy wheel) or ball (golf ball), on which the set of characters are arranged, and can travel from side to side across the paper. The character is lined up with the striking position and then struck against a ribbon onto the paper. A change of font is achieved by replacing the mechanical part.

Bi-directional printer

is a printer where the return movement of the *print head* (see above) is also used to print, speeding up the printing often at the expense of quality.

Impact printer

is a term applied to any printer which creates marks on the page by striking an inked ribbon (or carbon paper) against the page. The object that strikes the ribbon may be the shape of a complete character or may form a pattern of dots, which combine to reproduce a character or to produce a graphic image.

Matrix printer

is a printer which forms characters or graphics images out of ink dots in a rectangular matrix of printing positions. The image is made up of dots in the same way that a screen image is generated using *pixel graphics* (see page 135).

Dot matrix printer

also known as: pin printer
including: thermal printer
is a *matrix printer* (see above) which uses pins to print the dots. A print head moves in straight lines across the paper. Inside the print head is a vertical line of pins each of which can print a dot on the paper. The dots are printed by pins striking a ribbon against the paper. By making the pins hit the paper at the right moment it is possible to print a pattern of dots that looks like any character that is wanted. Some dot matrix printers can print in colour by using a special ribbon containing the four *CMYK* colours (see page 144). They are reliable, cheap and can make multiple (carbon) copies. The quality of print is not as good as from other printers.

A **thermal printer** uses wires arranged like the pins of a dot matrix printer which are heated to form dots on heat-sensitive paper. Thermal printers are very quiet, light and portable but do not produce good quality printing. They are used in older facsimile machines.

Ink jet printer

also known as: bubble jet printer
including: ink cartridge, print cartridge
is one which uses small bubbles of quick-drying ink to produce the printing. The ink is held in small containers, called *ink cartridges* or *print cartridges*. The printed image is created by forcing droplets of ink from the cartridge through fine holes onto the paper, forming the characters by patterns of dots. It can print text or graphics. A monochrome ink jet printer will print characters in black and diagrams using shades of grey. Colour ink jet printers have four separate cartridges for cyan, magenta, yellow and black (see *CMYK model*, page 144).

The print quality of most ink jet printers is much better than *dot matrix printers* (see page 141), however they tend to saturate the paper with ink, which can spread giving a fuzzy outline and causing the paper to crinkle – special paper for ink jet printers removes this problem, but at a cost.

Laser printer

is a page printer which uses a laser to 'write' the image to be printed onto a light-sensitive drum. The drum then uses electrostatics (as in a photocopier) to attract toner, a fine plastic powder, to coat the image with powder. Paper is then pressed against the drum transferring the toner to the paper. The paper is then heated to melt the toner onto the paper. The computer software sends the image to the printer's memory, which requires that a laser printer has to have a fairly large amount of memory in order to print a page – at least 1 Mb, but preferably more.

A monochrome laser printer will use black powder, a colour version uses the equivalent of four monochrome lasers for each of the four secondary colours cyan, magenta, yellow, and one for black (see *CMYK model*, page 144).

Thermal wax printer

including: dye sublimation printer
is a printer which works by melting coloured wax dyes onto special paper from a wax-coated roll. *Dye sublimation printers* work in a similar way but with slight differences in the print head and formulation of the dye. They are used for high quality realistic colour reproduction. Both types are expensive, and until recently were normally used only with large systems or installed on networks so as to "share" the cost. They are now sometimes used with *digital cameras*, see page 28.

Line printer

including: barrel printer, print hammer, chain printer
is one that prints a complete line of characters at one time, and hence is generally faster than a character printer. The printers described below are large machines capable of printing at very high speeds and are generally only used with mainframe computers.

In a *barrel printer* the complete character set is provided at each printing position, embossed on the surface of a horizontal barrel or cylinder, and each printing position has a *print hammer*, which is used to press the paper against a ribbon to print a character. The barrel turns and as the correct character for a position occurs, its print hammer strikes the paper against a ribbon and onto the character, causing the character to be printed.

In a *chain printer* the characters are carried on a continuous chain between a set of print hammers and the paper. The chain moves along the print line and as the required character appears at a print position the print hammer strikes the paper against a ribbon and onto the character.

Unless these printers are well maintained the quality can be poor with the characters badly aligned. Although they have mostly been replaced by other types of printer, some are still in use.

Page printer

is one which forms and prints a whole page in one operation, for example a *laser printer* (see page 142).

Graph plotter

also known as: plotter

including: flat-bed plotter, digital plotter, X-Y plotter, incremental plotter

is an output device which draws lines on paper by moving a pen in a holder relative to the paper on which the drawing is being made. In some designs the paper is on a roller and both the pen and the roller move. In others, known as *flat-bed plotters*, the paper is fixed on a flat surface, and all the movements are made by the pen. Colour is achieved by changing the pens. The software to control plotters is different from the software for printers.

Digital plotters receive digital input specifying the co-ordinates of the points to be plotted, together with information about how the next point to be plotted is joined to the current point.

X-Y plotters create the drawing by plotting data at points defined by their x and y co-ordinates. They are used by architects and engineers for *computer aided design* (see page 26) because they are very accurate.

An *incremental plotter* receives input data specifying increments to its current position, rather than data specifying co-ordinates.

Font

including: printer font, printer driver, font cartridge

is the set of printing or display characters in a particular type, style and size. Printers may offer a choice of *printer fonts*, either by exchanging the printer head or by software control as with dot matrix, ink jet, or laser printers. The font options, which can be selected by the user, may be stored in the computer and accessed through *printer drivers*, which are part of the system software that formats data for printing. Alternatively fonts may be stored in read only memory (ROM) *font cartridges* installed in the printer. Printer fonts may be produced by the same software as screen fonts and appear identical on the screen and in printed output. See also *Postscript*, page 149.

Printer resolution

also known as: resolution

including: dots per inch, dpi, low resolution, high resolution, print quality, correspondence (or letter) quality, draft quality, condensed type

is the term for the clarity of text and graphics as they appear on paper. Resolution is measured in *dots per inch*, or *dpi*. The smaller the dots making up the printing and the closer they are together, the clearer the image will be. *Low resolution* images have coarse dots, a "grainy" appearance and diagonal lines are jagged. *High resolution* images have fine dots and produce clearer images with diagonal straight lines and curves appearing smoother and less jagged.

Laser and inkjet printers normally have a resolution of 300 dpi, while high resolution of 1200 dpi is used on typesetting machines.

Print quality is a description of how well formed the characters are when printed. The descriptions are in terms of the standards expected of printed output for different purposes. *Correspondence quality*, also known as *letter quality*, is similar to the quality of a traditional typewriter, or of an ink jet or laser printer. *Draft quality* is an option on some printers; the characters are not well shaped, but can be printed quickly. *Condensed type* is produced by some printers which can reduce the width of a character, so that more text can be fitted on a line.

CMYK model

also known as: CYMK model

including: subtractive model, spot colour

is a method for specifying the separate colours used in colour printers for use with computers. When white light illuminates the printed page, coloured pigments on the paper absorb some of the light (the primary colours) and reflect the rest (the secondary colours). Colour printers create colours by combining different proportions of the three secondary colours, cyan (**C**), magenta (**M**) and yellow (**Y**). For example, Cyan pigment absorbs (subtracts) red light and reflects green and blue light, which the eye sees as cyan. Black could in theory be produced by combining the three secondary colours, but this often appears as a muddy brown. Printers normally add black (known as K for key, derived from blac**K**) to produce a true black, giving the **CMYK** or *subtractive* model. See also *colour display*, page 138. Sometimes an additional colour, known as a *spot colour,* is needed to produce exact colour matching. For commercial printing, a film is produced for each of the four CMYK colours and any spot colours.

Colour palette

is the collection of distinct colours that a printer can produce. The palette may be extended by combining varying amounts of the colours in the palette. Colour mixing is software controlled. See also *colour management*, page 145.

Colour management

including: Colour Management System (CMS)

is the software process which controls the colours printed, by managing the transfer of colour data between devices. The flow of data is shown in Figure B5.2.

The management of the transfer of colour data associated with different devices such as screens, scanners, CD-ROM readers and printers is handled by software known as a ***Colour Management System***, or ***CMS***. The CMS may be included in the operating system or provided and installed separately. It works by comparing the colours for a device with independent colour standards, and translating the colours for different devices so that they appear similar. When they cannot be exactly matched, for example the differences between a screen using the RGB system and a printer using the CMYK system, the CMS will select the nearest match.

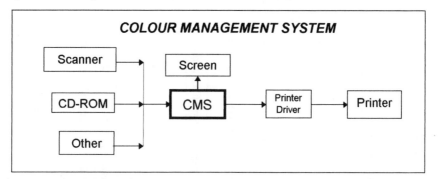

Figure B5.2: *Data flow in a colour management system*

Pantone is a system in which numbers are allocated to colours for exact colour matching. The Pantone numbers may be held in a *look-up table* (see page 200).

Colour separation

is the process needed for selecting colour data for printing. In order to print in colour, a coloured image has to be separated into its component colours. This is part of the process of preparing the data for a colour printer.

To prepare material for printing, for example from a photograph, the photograph will need to be scanned using a *colour scanner*, page 116.

Media

is the collective name for materials (tape, disk, paper, cards, etc.) used to hold data.

Hard copy

also known as: printout

is computer output printed on paper.

PRINTER TYPES AND CHARACTERISTICS

CHARACTER PRINTERS	MATRIX PRINTERS	PAGE PRINTERS
line printers (barrel, chain), golf ball, daisy wheel	*pin dot matrix printers, ink jet printers*	*laser printers*
impact on a ribbon or carbon paper is used to form the characters	uses *pins* (impact or thermal) or *ink jet* to print the image	uses *photocopier* principles
prints individual characters, text only	can print text and graphics	can print text and graphics
characters are printed as complete characters in a single action	text and images made up of dots in a matrix pattern (similar to a screen image)	prints a complete page at a time
line printers etc. – poor print quality; *daisy wheel* etc. – very good print quality	print quality depends on the resolution (dots per inch)	capable of very high resolution
usually only a single (limited) font available at a time	wide range of fonts available through software	wide range of fonts available through software
restricted line spacing (often only full lines)	flexible line spacing	can print anywhere on the page print area (possibly excluding margins)
unlimited page length, fixed maximum width	unlimited page length, fixed maximum width	fixed maximum page length and width
can print multipart stationery	*pin printers* – can print multi-part stationery; *ink jet printers* – cannot print multi-part stationery	cannot print conventional multi-part stationery
usually only single colour, fixed intensity	can print in colour, *ink jet* can print a range of shades	can print colour, can print a range of shades
line printers can print at high speeds	slow to medium speed printing	can print at high speeds
Obsolescent technology but some *line printers* are still in use in large scale data processing contexts.	Replacement for typewriter-style printers; generally compact machines; wide range of speeds and quality.	Have almost completely replaced the older line printers for large volume printing. Sizes range from desk-top to very large, floor standing machines.

CHARACTER PRINTERS	MATRIX PRINTERS	PAGE PRINTERS
Line printers use a print hammer for each print position to strike the paper and ribbon/carbon paper against embossed type on barrels or chain loops when the right character is in position: *daisy wheel* and *golf ball printers* print a character and then move to the next print position and have easily changeable fonts.	Print mechanisms move backwards and forwards over the paper, which advances after each pass by the print mechanism. Print quality is determined by the number of pins or ink bubble size and the minimum size of head and paper movements.	Image of the page is 'written' by lasers onto a special drum as an electrostatic charge: the drum attracts toner particles which are transferred to the page and heated to set the image.
Application range: small office machines to large scale data processing	Application range: personal printers to network printers on small networks	Application range: personal printers to large scale data processing
Current speed range (approx.): **daisy wheel /golf ball** 5 cps to 35 cps **line printers** 200 - 2000 lines per minute	Current speed range (approx.): **pin (*impact*)** 25 cps to 250 cps **ink jet or bubble jet** 4 mins per page to 8+ pages per min	Current speed range (approx.): **laser** 4 ppm to 40+ ppm (up to 2500+ lines per minute)
Resolution: **daisy wheel /golf ball** some proportional spacing	Resolution: **ink jet or bubble jet** 300 to 600 dots per inch	Resolution: **laser** 300 to 600 dots per inch

Table B5.1: Printers

Feed

is the process of making paper move through the printer. See *paper feed mechanism*, below.

Paper feed mechanism

including: line feed, page feed, friction feed, tractor feed, pin feed, (cut) sheet feeder
is the means of making the paper move through the printing process. Many printers require *line feed*, that is the paper is moved after a line (or sometimes half a line) has been printed. Laser printers eject one page at a time, *page feed*.
Friction feed is a mechanism for advancing paper by gripping it between rollers.
Tractor feed, also known as *pin feed*, is a mechanism for advancing paper by the use of perforations down the side of the paper and a toothed wheel (a sprocket).
Cut sheet feeder (also known as *sheet feeder*) allows ordinary separate sheets of paper to be automatically fed in for printing. Where a sheet feeder is not provided as part of the printer, it may be available as an accessory.

Continuous stationery

including: fan-fold paper, multipart stationery, bursting, decollate
is printer paper which is perforated to make pages and folded in alternate directions at each set of perforations to form a stack, *fan-fold paper*. *Bursting* is the separating of continuous stationery into individual sheets by tearing the paper along the perforations; it may be handled mechanically or by humans. Continuous stationery normally has a tear-off margin on both sides with holes for a tractor feed mechanism to use. It can be a series of pre-printed forms.

For some applications it may consist of several sheets together, either with carbon paper in between or made of pressure-sensitive paper (termed *multipart stationery*) so that several copies are printed at the same time using an impact printer. To *decollate* is to separate the sheets of multipart continuous stationery. See also *pre-printed stationery*, below.

Pre-printed stationery

has certain fixed information already printed on each sheet so that the computer can fill in the gaps. This increases the speed of printing and improves the presentation. The paper may be cut sheets or continuous stationery. Common examples are customer accounts for gas and electricity, and computer printed cheques.

Printer buffer

is a store, usually in the printer but can be in a separate box between the computer and printer, which receives the information for printing and stores it until it is printed. It is able to receive the information at a much higher speed than the printer can print, thereby freeing the computer from the printing task a little quicker.

Page description language

including: Postscript

is a *high-level computer language* (see page 246) used to pass instructions to printers for setting up the data to be printed.

Postscript is a page description language used by some laser printers for complex graphics and desk-top publishing. The computer will code its printout requirements, for example the size, direction and style of a piece of text or the format for a diagram. These will then be interpreted by the postscript translator, which is in a processor in the printer, into the corresponding image of dots ready for printing.

B6   Networks

*Other terms and concepts related to networks and communications
are to be found in A8 Internet, A9 Communications,
B7 Communications Devices and Control Devices and
C17 Communications Technology.*

Connecting pieces of communications and information equipment together in a
network is not a new concept. The early telegraph systems, especially in America
where the distances are so great, provided the stimulus for telegram services and the
later development of telex communications, in which text information could be sent
between any telex machines on the world-wide telex network using telephone lines.
Passing messages internationally has been possible ever since the development of
international cable links which began in the 19th century. For over 70 years the
world's newspapers depended upon organisations that gathered news around the world
and delivered it to their client newspapers through the telex network. These services
are still provided by some of the same organisations but in addition there is now e-mail
and other services linking computers around the world.

In a computer network a number of computers are connected together in order to
exchange information. For example, an organisation having offices spread over a
wide geographical area might install a network to enable employees to examine
information held on computers in other offices many miles away.

The connections between computers may be wires, fibre optic cables, microwave
links, communication via satellite or any combination of these. The interconnected
collection of computers form the network. The computers may be large powerful
machines, small personal computers or terminals. They will all be capable of running
on their own but with the added advantage of being able to communicate with each
other.

In a traditional network, users must explicitly log on (that is, identify themselves to
the network) and explicitly move information around on the network by issuing the
appropriate instructions. A **distributed system** is normally thought of as a network in
which the existence of the other machines is not obvious to the user. Programs and
data held on other machines can be used as though they were held locally on the user's
computer.

A distinction is usually made between networks of computers that are all situated
relatively close to each other - for example in the same building or cluster of buildings
- known as a **Local Area Network** (a LAN) and those in which the computers are
geographically remote, known as a **Wide Area Network** (a WAN).

A network offers the possibility of sharing work between the different resources
available. For example, if one computer has a heavy load of processing, some of the
work can be moved to another machine on the network. A network makes all the
resources of the network (programs, data and equipment, such as printers and disk

drives) available to the whole network without regard to the physical location of either the resource or the user.

Reliability is another advantage of networking. The effect of hardware failures can be reduced by switching work from a failed device to one that is still functioning. This can be particularly valuable in systems such as banking where it is important that the system can continue operating even if there are some hardware failures.

Networks of small computers can be a cheaper way of providing computer power than a single large machine. If a network of small machines has access to outside facilities, whose use may need to be purchased, such as a large specialist databases, the potential of the network is greatly enhanced. Linking a network to other networks, which are themselves linked to yet further networks, makes it theoretically possible to have the whole of world knowledge available to any computer on such a network.

The Internet now provides this kind of linking of networks. It works because there are thousands of networks each connected to other networks in such a way that it is possible for messages (data) to be sent from a computer on one of the networks to any computer on any other network, provided that both networks have access to the Internet. How such data travels through this 'network of networks' is illustrated in Figure A8.1, page 35.

Network

including: distributed network

is a linked set of computer systems capable of sharing computer power and resources such as printers, large disk drives, CD-ROM and other databases. Sometimes network is used to mean the arrangement of links between the equipment that form the network. See *network topology*, page 152.

In a *distributed network* the sharing of resources is arranged by the (network) operating system without any action being required by the user.

Local Area Network (LAN)

is a network in which the computer systems are all situated relatively close to each other, for example in the same building or cluster of buildings, such as a school. Since the distances involved are small, direct physical connection is possible. The network connections are normally wire cables, such as coaxial cable, but fibre optic cable is being increasingly used.

Wide Area Network (WAN)

is a network in which the computers are geographically remote. Wide area networks make use of a range of connection methods including communication satellites.

Network topology

including: bus network, ring (sometimes called loop) network, star network, central node, hub, nexus, FDDI (fibre distributed data interface) backbone

is the theoretical arrangement of components of a network. The actual arrangement will almost certainly be determined by the buildings or other locations for the parts of the network. The network descriptions indicate how the devices on the network, the computers, printers, servers, etc., are connected to each other. Since networks communicate serially, the actual connections will be capable of *serial data transmission* (see page 302).

A *bus network* has each of the devices connected directly to a main communications line, called a bus, along which signals are sent. The bus will frequently be a twin cable of some kind, for example coaxial cable.

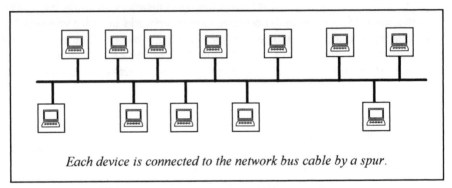

Each device is connected to the network bus cable by a spur.

Figure B6.1: A bus network with spurs

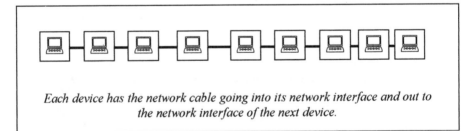

Each device has the network cable going into its network interface and out to the network interface of the next device.

Figure B6.2: A bus network

A *ring network* (sometimes called a *loop network*) has each of the devices on the network connected to a ring (or loop) communications line around which signals are sent. The devices may be connected to the ring by spurs, as in Figure B6.3 or the connections may pass through the *network interface* (see *interface*, page 288 and *interface card*, page 297) in each device, as in Figure B6.4; in this case, provision has to be made for the system to continue to work if one of the devices is switched off or fails to function properly.

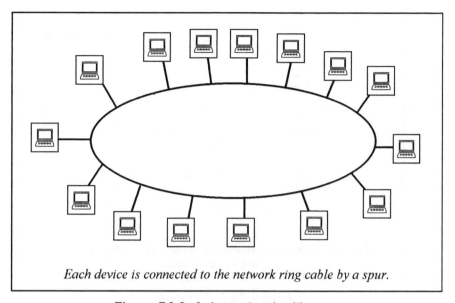

Each device is connected to the network ring cable by a spur.

Figure B6.3: *A ring network with spurs*

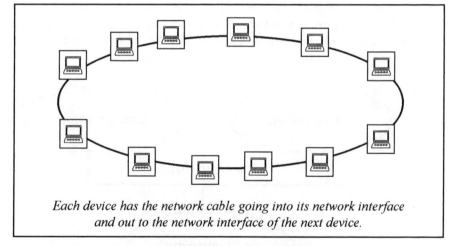

*Each device has the network cable going into its network interface
and out to the network interface of the next device.*

Figure B6.4: *A ring network*

A **star network** has all the network devices connected to one central computer which
is often used as the *file server* (see page 157). The **central node** of the network,
often called the **hub** or **nexus**, is a computer which has separate connections to
each computer or terminal.

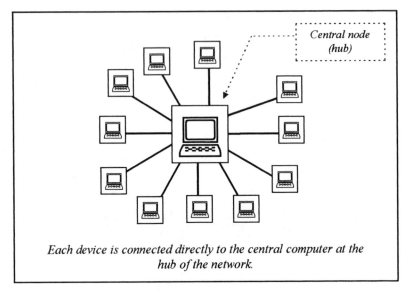

Each device is connected directly to the central computer at the hub of the network.

Figure B6.5: *A star network*

A *FDDI backbone* is a high-speed communication link used to provide the basis for a network consisting of small sub-networks. The connections are fibre optic cable. *FDDI (fibre distributed data interface)* is an ANSI defined standard for high speed fibre optic cable communications with transmission speeds of 100 Mbps

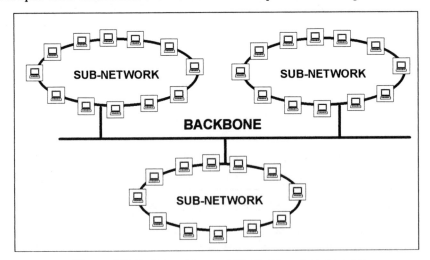

Figure B6.6: *A backbone with three sub-networks*

Backbone
is the top-level of a hierarchical network to which the main user networks are connected. See also *FDDI backbone,* above.

Cluster
including: cluster controller
is a group of computers in the same physical area, possibly on a network. A cluster sharing resources will usually be less formally organised than most networks. A *cluster controller* is the computer acting as controller for the cluster. See also *network controller*, page 114.

Token ring network
including: token, Cambridge ring
is a *ring network* (see pages 152/3) in which information is sent around the ring as variable-sized packets of data. In addition to the data, a packet will contain the address of the sender and the destination address. The *token*, which is a signal that passes round the network, can be thought of as a carrier for the packet. For a packet to travel round the ring it has to be attached to a token. This is a method of avoiding data packets colliding on the ring and creating unreadable signals. In principle, the packet travels round the ring attached to the token until it is taken off at the destination address or it returns unread to the sender, where it is taken off as unread. The token then becomes free and continues round the ring ready to have another package to be attached to it by one of the network devices. The token continually circulates around the ring picking up, carrying and dropping packets off at their destinations. Generally there is only one token.

A *Cambridge ring* is a token ring network which has a number of tokens travelling around the network passing each device at equal time intervals. A network device wishing to send a packet simply attaches it to the first available free token. The data transmission capacity of a Cambridge ring is much greater than a simple token ring network.

The network topology for token ring networks is shown in Figure B6.4, page 153.

Network number
including: station number
is the unique number assigned to a network when it is set up. All computers on the network have their own *station number* within the network, which is assigned through software. In addition, the *network interface* (see *interface*, page 288 and *interface card*, page 297) fitted in the computer has a unique number permanently stored in it. Communication between networks requires these unique numbers to ensure that messages get to the correct station in the correct network, since it is now possible for any network to communicate with any other network.

Econet
is an obsolete local area networking system designed to provide cheap computer networking for BBC and some Acorn microcomputers. Both the hardware (the cabling and computer interfaces) and the software (the *network operating system*, page 157) were non-standard and only worked with those computers. It has been used in a large number of British schools.

Ethernet

is a popular general-purpose *local area network* (see page 151). The network can be used by different types of computer system, even at the same time. Network interfaces are available from many manufacturers. It uses either wire connections (coaxial or twisted pair cable) or fibre optic cable. The software which makes up the *network operating system* (see page 157), has to be bought separately. Ethernet networks are frequently used in offices and schools. The transmission rate is 10 Mbits/sec and it uses the principles of *carrier sense multiple access/collision detection* (see page 310).

Peer-to-peer network

including: client station

is a description of a very simple network which provides shared resources, such as printers and storage, but may offer little in the way of additional facilities, such as file security. The name comes from the fact that all the computers on these networks have similar specifications and that all stations on the network have equal status. For example one station may act as a file server, another as the printer server, but both of them are also network stations capable of being used as client stations. A computer on the network, which is available for use by users of the network, is called a *client station*. See also *terminal*, below, and *server*, page 157.

Client-server relationship

is a method of network organisation in which stations make use of resources available at one or more *servers* (see page 157). This is the kind of organisation seen in a *star network* (see pages 152/3), in which one computer has the role of central resource manager for the network. But other forms of network can also operate with a client-server relationship.

Distributed processing

is the sharing of data processing tasks between physically separated processors on a network.

Terminal

also called: network terminal, network station, station
including: point-of-sale (POS) terminal

is a computer or computer-controlled device operating on a network. A stand-alone computer used to provide resources for the whole network is a form of terminal which is often called a *(network) station*. See also *server*, page 157.

A network may have a variety of different kinds of equipment connected to it. For example, a supermarket network will probably have standard computers for its offices as well as the *point-of-sale (POS) terminals* (the checkouts) all connected on the same network. This may be linked to a wider network for the whole supermarket chain. A point-of-sale terminal will have a variety of functions, which may include *electronic funds transfer* (see page 51), as well as *bar code scanning* (see page 116/7) combined with getting the costs from a database on the network to produce the customer's bill.

Server

including: file server, printer server, CD-ROM server, database server
is a station on a *peer-to-peer network* (see page 156) which provides a resource that can be used by any authorised *client station* (see 156). There are a number of types of server.

A *file server* provides central disk storage for any users of the network. The file server software identifies each user's files separately so that other users cannot use them. Users can access their own files from any client station on the network.

A *printer server* allows all the client stations to use a printer controlled by it and usually provides the facilities of a *print spooler* (see page 277).

A *CD-ROM server* allows all the client stations to obtain data from a CD-ROM disk currently being used by the CD-ROM server computer. Often a CD-ROM server will have access to many CD-ROM disks, either from a collection of several CD-ROM players, or from a *CD-ROM jukebox* (see page 123).

A *database server* manages a large database. Client stations can access data in the database and, if authorised, can maintain the database. The database processing is usually carried out by the server, with the query being sent by a client station to the server and the results assembled by the server and returned to the client station. This form of *client-server relationship* (see 156) can ensure the consistency of the database, even in the distributed environment of a *peer-to-peer network* (see 156).

Any expensive resource can be made available to a large number of users by a server computer. Other examples are a teletext server, which makes available the current data being broadcast by teletext services; a viewdata server, which provides and manages a local viewdata service for the network; a mail server to manage the electronic mail for the network; or even a weather station server obtaining and distributing current local instrument readings or satellite weather data.

Network operating system

including: Appletalk, NFS, Novell Netware, Windows for Workgroups, UNIX
is the software needed to enable a computer to communicate with other computers (stations) using a network. All computers on a network must have the same network operating system software to be able to communicate through the network. Additional software is required for any servers. In particular, a file server needs additional software to enable it to provide secure data storage for users. Widely used network operating systems include *Appletalk, NFS* (Acorn computers), *Novell Netware, Windows for Workgroups* and *UNIX*.

AFS

originally: the Andrews' File System, now known only as AFS
is a set of protocols which allows a user on a machine on one network to use files on a machine on another network as if they were on the user's own machine.

Host computer

is a computer used to control a multi-user, multi-access or distributed computer system. In particular the term is applied to computers which provide access to the Internet. A host computer manages the communications and storage needs of its users, who may be subscribers to an *Internet service provider* (see page 42).

Network accounting software

provides statistics about the use of a network by its users. This may be about the use made of terminals on a multi-user computer system or about the use of facilities on a *peer-to-peer network* (see page 156). The information can be used to charge users for their use of resources or to monitor improper use of the network.

The information recorded can include such things as the connection time and the processor time used, a list of times and dates when the computer has been used on a multi-user system, disk storage space used, printer use, and e-mail use on a peer-to-peer network.

The accounting software can present the overall activity on the network in a variety of ways (tables, graphs or a log) and thus assist the network manager to optimise the system and, possibly, devise charging structures.

Value Added Network Service (VANS)

is a wide area network with additional facilities such as a centrally provided database or information system for which users pay charges, which are usually based on their use of the facilities. An example is the charged pages of the *Prestel* service, see page 52.

Gateway

is a link between two dissimilar computer systems, which may be local area networks. The communications between the systems are usually sent via public telecommunications links. The gateway converts the data passing through it into the formats required for each system; in addition, it can monitor usage and limit access between the systems to authorised users. See also *bridge*, page 163.

Workstation

is **either** a *station* on a network (see *terminal*, page 156), **or** a location where a computer, with its associated equipment, is used, such as a designer's work area; this kind of workstation may be on a network or not.

B7   Communications Devices and Control Devices

This section is concerned with terms used in describing the transmission of data between computers within networks and terms found in the study of control systems. Other related terms may be found in A9 Communications, A10 Control, B2 Peripherals, B6 Networks or C17 Communications Technology.

Communications and control require that information is passed rapidly and accurately between parts of a system. The origins of present-day communication systems are the electric telegraph in which signals were sent as electric pulses, the telephone in which sound is passed as a varying electric current, and radio in which the signals are sent as electromagnetic radiation.

Modern communications systems are highly reliable, accurate and affordable. From the earliest days of computers until the late 1980s it was necessary to install special quality telephone lines between linked computers. Now it is possible to use standard voice quality lines for connecting computers and remote devices. This is partly due to the use of digital signal systems and partly due to the use of more reliable materials and devices for the transmission of signals in the public communications systems. The installation of digital telephone exchanges in many parts of the world, and the use of radio links where cables are not available, mean that it is impossible for a user to know whether a link between two telephones or two computers is by cables or via some terrestrial or satellite radio link. Where public communication links are not available, private links are installed.

The materials for connecting computers are wires of some form, fibre optic cables, radio links or infra-red radiation. Each has its advantages and its disadvantages. If wires or optic cables are used, then the individual locations of equipment may be restricted to sites served by the cables; if infra-red links are used then receivers and transmitters have to be in sight of each other; if radio is used then privacy may not be easily achieved. At present, nearly all local area networks are linked by some form of wire cable. Where these connect into the wider world, they require some device to make the connections to the outside world. These connecting devices arrange for the signals to be sent in an appropriate form, at the correct speed and with the necessary destination information attached. The computer user determines the content and destination of the messages but the linking devices determine the way in which the messages are sent and often the route.

Communications channel

also known as: data channel, data carrier, data link
including: data transmission
is a communication circuit along which data, in coded form, may be transmitted
between two points; it may consist of more than one line. **Data transmission** is the
process of using a data link. See also *facsimile transmission,* page 49 and *bus,* page
286.

Modem (MOdulator-DEModulator)

is a data communications device for sending and receiving data between computers
over telephone circuits. It converts the digital signals from the computer into audio
tones for transmission over ordinary voice quality telephone lines and converts
incoming audio signals into digital signals for the computer. It is normally plugged
directly into a standard telephone socket.

Fax modem

is a modem with the ability to send documents as if it were a fax machine.

Fax (facsimile) machine

is a machine for transmitting and receiving copies of paper document pages over
telephone circuits. The process involves scanning a document and transmitting the
resulting data to another fax machine which prints the copy.

Terminal adapter

sometimes called: adapter
is an interface which is plugged into a microcomputer serial port to link into an *ISDN*
(integrated services digital network) (see page 306).

Private Branch Exchange (PBX)

including: Private Automatic Branch Exchange (PABX)
is a private telephone exchange. It provides the interface between a group of telephone
extensions and the public network lines. There is usually a facility which allows any
extension to dial any other extension directly and to dial into the public network using
only a simple connect code and the outside number. Normally, external callers only
get the operator unless they know the direct dial number for an individual extension.

    Digital PABXs can control and interconnect a mix of telephones, fax machines,
teletext devices and computers all operating at different bit rates.

Multiplexor

sometimes spelt: multiplexer
including: time division multiplexor (TDM), time slice, statistical multiplexor,
intelligent time division multiplexor, frequency division multiplexor (FDM)
is a device that receives data from several independent sources for transmission along
a single route to a single destination. A two-way communication multiplexor must be

able to separate signals for each of the destinations. The de-multiplexor could be a *front-end processor* (see page 113).

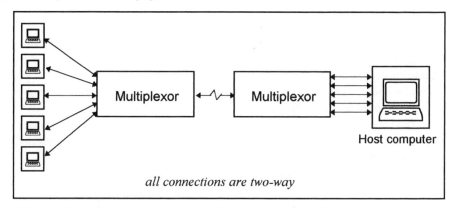

all connections are two-way

Figure B7.1: *Multiplexors connecting remote workstations to a computer*

A *Time Division Multiplexor (TDM)* transmits the signals from two or more sources in successive short time intervals, called *time slices*. Each source gets the same duration of time interval. Where the multiplexor time allocation is proportional to the activity of each source, it is called a *statistical multiplexor,* or an *intelligent time division multiplexor.*

A *Frequency Division Multiplexor (FDM)* uses the available route link to transmit the data from the different sources at the same time. This is achieved by dividing the available channel *bandwidth* (see page 305) into a number of narrow bands, each of which is used for a separate transmission but at a slower speed.

Wireless communication
including: infra-red, microwave transmission, satellite
covers a whole range of possible methods of data transmission, which can be used for linking computers within networks or for links within computer systems.

Infra-red communication uses the same systems as domestic remote control of televisions. Examples of its use include the control of robotic devices and remote keyboards. It is necessary for there to be direct unobstructed line of sight between the transmitter and the receiver. Strong sunlight will interfere with infra-red signals.

Microwave transmission is used as a method of communication within public telephone services. Many organisations use private installations to transmit data between key sites. Unlike the cellular phone systems which are broadcast systems, microwave transmissions use highly directional transmitters and receivers with dish aerials.

Satellite links are used for international communications by many providers of public telephone services. Unlike satellite broadcast systems, these links use highly directional, narrow beam, two-way transmissions. A single channel is capable of simultaneously carrying a very large number of separate transmissions.

Wire connector

including: copper cable, coaxial cable, twisted pair (TP), unshielded twisted pair (UTP)

is a standard form of wire cable used to provide the connections in a network. *Copper cables* are commonly used as connectors for local area networks, since they are readily available and have suitable electrical characteristics. Various types of copper cable are used, including:

Coaxial cable, which is made to a variety of specifications, is the same kind of cable that is used for connecting a television aerial to a television set. It has two conductors. One is a wire down the centre of the cable, which may be a single strand, insulated from the second, which is made up of many strands braided around the insulation for the inner wire.

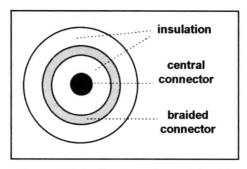

Figure B7.2: Section of coaxial cable

Twisted Pair (TP) cable is commonly used for data transmission. In its simplest form it is a pair of insulated copper wires twisted together surrounded by a copper braid and external insulation. Some cables are made up of a number of twisted pairs surrounded by an overall (earthed) braid screen. In another form, stranded copper wires are twisted together in pairs with an earth wire. These pairs may be grouped to form a single multi-connector cable. These cables all have different specifications and, used in the correct situation, provide minimum interference data transmission.

Unshielded Twisted Pair (UTP) is similar to the *twisted pair cables* described above, but have no earthed shield. In suitable circumstances they can be used for data transmission.

Fibre optic cable

also known as: optical fibre

is a very fine glass strand that allows rapid transmission of data, using modulated light beams. It is usual to put many strands together in a single cable, each one capable of carrying one or more data signals. Fibre optic cable provides interference-free, secure data transmission and, unlike metal wires, is not subject to corrosion.

Signal concentrator
also known as: message concentrator, concentrator
is any device, such as a multiplexor, which is used to enable a single channel to be used for carrying multiple communications.

Router
including: bridge, brouter, repeater, multi-part repeater
is a communications device, now nearly always software running on a suitably located computer, which receives data and forwards it to the correct location via an appropriate route.

A *bridge* is a connection between two local area networks. The use of a bridge produces a logical network, which appears to all users as a single network although it may be made up of several physically distinct networks. All users have access to all the resources on the resulting extended network, in particular the various *servers* (see page 157). See also *gateway*, page 158.

A *brouter* is a device which combines the functions and properties of a bridge and a router on a local area network.

A *repeater* is a device used to link two cable segments. Because of the loss of signal strength in network cables, a repeater amplifies the signals it receives before passing them on.

A *multi-part repeater* is a repeater that can be used to create a spur off a network.

Signal level
including: signal amplifier, signal booster
is the measure of the strength of a communications signal. In the same way that sound and light become weaker with distance, electrical signals passing down a wire become weaker as they travel along the wire. For this reason *signal amplifiers* or *boosters* are built into communications networks at appropriate intervals. These increase the signal level before passing the signal on to the next part of the network.

Signal converter
including: analog signal, digital signal, Analog-to-Digital (A-to-D or A/D) converter, digitising, Digital-to-Analog (D-to-A or D/A) converter
is a device which converts serial signals from one form to another. Signals may be *digital*, consisting of discrete bit patterns, or *analog*, consisting of a continuously varying voltage. Both analog and digital signals are used to represent data. Some devices generate analog signals or need to be supplied with data in analog form, while others generate or have to be supplied with data in digital form.

An *Analog-to-Digital (A-to-D) converter* converts analog signals into digital signals for subsequent processing. This conversion is sometimes called *digitising*. For example, the analog output from a microphone has to be digitised before it can be stored or processed by a computer.

A *Digital-to-Analog (D-to-A) converter* converts serial digital signals into analog signals. For example, the digital data for a computer display has to be converted into analog signals if it is to be used as input to a television.

Handshake

is the exchange of signals between devices to establish their readiness to send or receive data, for example the transmission of data from a computer to a printer. Handshaking is one of a number of methods of ensuring that both the sender and receiver are ready before transmission begins.

Baud

including: baud rate, bits per second (bps), bytes per second (bps), bit rate, characters per second (cps)

is the unit used to measure the speed (the *baud rate*) of serial data transmission, for example the transmission of data along a telephone line or the speed of serial transmission to a printer. Generally, one baud is one bit per second, but it is important to note that there is no simple relationship between baud rate and the rate of data transfer between devices. Under any communications protocol additional bits have to be transmitted to provide start and stop bits, error detection and other communications controls. In addition, methods of communication, such as multiphase signalling, and *data compression* (see page 192) can both increase the amount of data that is transmitted in a given time.

Other measures of speed of data transfer are:

Bits per second (bps), sometimes called the *bit rate,* is a measure of the speed with which data moves between various parts of a computer. High bit rates are given in Kbit/s ($2^{10} = 1024$ bps) or Mbits/s ($2^{20} = 1048576$ bps). [Note: sometimes *bps* is taken to mean *bytes per second* which is normally the same as characters per second.]

Characters per second (cps) is a measure of the speed of character data transfer between devices. It is frequently also given as a measure of the speed of printers.

Transducer

is an electronic component which converts one form of energy to another. For example, a thermistor converts a temperature into electrical energy with a varying voltage, a photo cell converts brightness of illumination into a voltage. The term is generally applied to devices which produce electricity rather than those which convert electricity into another form of energy.

Sampler

also known as: digital sampler

is an electronic circuit which takes samples of an electronic signal at intervals and stores them for future processing. In particular, they are used to take frequent measurements of analog signals for converting an analog signal into a digital signal, when it is known as a digital sampler.

Sensor

including: analog sensor, digital sensor, passive device, active device
is a *transducer* (see page 164) which responds to some physical property such as
pressure, rate of flow, humidity, the proximity of ferrous metal. The electrical output
from the sensor may be either analog, an ***analog sensor***, or digital, a ***digital sensor***.
Some sensors, called ***passive devices***, require no external electrical source. Those
which require an external voltage are called ***active devices***.

Servo mechanism

also known as: servo
is a mechanical mechanism for remote control of machines. A simple form is the
motors which operate the control surfaces of a radio-controlled model aircraft, where
the person flying the model plays an active part continuously adjusting the position of
the control levers. Servos can be controlled electronically through computer circuits
which may incorporate feedback to achieve automatic control; in these situations
human participation may be very limited.

Actuator

is any device which can be operated by signals from a computer or control system
causing physical movement. For example, devices for opening windows in a
computer-controlled ventilation system.

Stepper motor

sometimes : stepping motor
is an electric motor which moves in small rotational steps. Suitably controlled and
geared, a stepper motor can provide very small discrete movements, for example the
movement of the paper rollers and the print head in a printer. The control circuits may
well involve the use of *feedback* (see page 54).

Part C
How Computer Systems Work

This part is concerned with those terms which are frequently considered to be associated with Computer Science as opposed to the terms in Part A, which are concerned with the needs of computer system users, and Part B, which provides some technical information which may be helpful to both computer users and to students following courses requiring some knowledge of computer systems and peripherals.

The range of terms covered and the depth of treatment of individual terms has been influenced by knowledge of the difficulties encountered by students, who are studying courses which involve some Computer Science, whatever the name of the course.

C1 Systems Design and Life Cycle

Related topics can be found in A17 User Documentation,
C2 Systems Documentation, C8 Program Documentation and
C9 Developing, Testing and Running Programs.

There is an enormous difference between an individual writing a computer program for their own use and the large-scale commercial production of software. Many stages that can be ignored by an individual become crucially important. There is the need to establish precisely what the customer requires; to organise the design and coding so that teams of people can work together; to keep track of the many changes that will inevitably be necessary; to provide suitable documentation for the future maintenance of the software, and suitable documentation for the user.

For a purpose-built computer system, designed for a single user (a large company, perhaps), the problems will centre around establishing exactly what it is that the customer requires, avoiding the traditional complaints *"Yes – but what I really meant was ..."* and *"Yes – and while you're about it, can you just ..."*. For software that will be marketed in volume, such as word-processors, spreadsheets and so forth, there will be the commercial pressure to ensure that features absent from competing software are on offer, at the same time as ensuring that the software will run with the minimum amount of extra memory or peripherals. It will usually be necessary to ensure that existing users of earlier versions of the software can easily and cheaply upgrade to the new version (rather than being tempted to a competitor's product). At the same time, it will be commercially advantageous to make it easy for users of a competing product to transfer – by offering the ability to read files prepared in other software packages, or by designing the command structure so that it has similarities with competing products.

When commercial software packages are designed to be run under the control of a particular operating system (such as Windows, or UNIX), the designer of the operating system may have defined 'rules' for applications software that ensure that future upgrades to the operating system can be achieved in a way that does not result in existing software ceasing to operate.

It should be clear that the design of computer systems (which may include hardware as well as software) is a task that requires considerable management and discipline. This has been reflected in the relatively recent change of title from simply 'programming' to 'software engineering'. The construction of large, complex systems (on which safety as well as profits may depend) is very similar to the construction of civil engineering projects such as bridges or buildings.

Applications system design

including: systems design, systems analysis, feasibility study, systems specification, functional specification

is the process involved in the design of applications software packages (*systems design*). Typically this begins with an analysis of any existing system and of the requirements of the new system (*systems analysis*). A *feasibility study* of potential computer involvement may be made, estimating costs, effort, effectiveness, reliability and the benefits to be expected from a new system. The desired system will be specified in a *systems specification* setting out hardware and software requirements, and the organisational and human implications. This may include a separate *functional specification* describing exactly how the system will behave. Only when all these stages are complete will work begin on the production of the software.

Audit trail

including: journal file

is an automatic record made (in a *journal file*) of any transactions carried out by a computer system, such as updates to files. This may be required for legal reasons (so that the auditors can confirm the accuracy of the company accounts); for security reasons (so that data maliciously or accidentally deleted can be recovered); or simply to monitor the performance of the system.

Benchmark

is a standard set of computer tasks, designed to allow measurements to be made of computer performance. These tasks can be used to compare the performance of different software or hardware. Examples of tasks are; how long it takes to re-format a 40-page word-processed document, how many pages can be printed in one minute, how long it takes to save 1000 database records to disk. Users seeking to buy software or hardware may be able to obtain some information about the performance of possible purchases.

Benchmarks may also figure in *acceptance testing* (see *Figure C1.1*, page 174) of a computer system, by specifying performance that must be achieved before the system is considered finished. See also s*oftware metric*, page 173, for a description of the theoretical equivalent of the more practical benchmark.

Compatibility

including: backward compatibility, downward compatibility, upward compatibility

describes how well different computer systems work together.

Backward compatible (also known as *downward compatible*) is used to describe a computer system designed to work with older systems. For example programs can load files from older versions of the program or computer hardware will run software designed for older types of computer. Backward compatibility ensures that new software can be acquired without needing to buy new hardware and that the data from the old computer system can continue to be used.

Upward compatible is used to describe a computer system designed to be extended and improved without the need to retrain staff or to alter any stored data.

Configuration management

is the automatic tracking and monitoring of changes to software during development, so that everyone involved is aware of the features of the latest version.

Customise

is to alter a computer system to the specific requirements of the user. This may involve adding extra fields to a database, adding extra functions to a program, altering the keys used to suit a particular user or adding a peripheral such as a bar code reader.

Default

including: default option, default value

is an assumption made by computer software in the absence of explicit instructions to the contrary. This may be a *default option* – your files are listed in alphabetical order, unless you request date or size order – or a *default value* – the computer prints one copy of a document, unless you request multiple copies. The best software is designed so that the most frequently-used options are all available as defaults, so that users are not troubled by the need to continually specify such values. It is often possible for users to customise software, by selecting their own choice of defaults.

Formal methods

including: formal specification

is the name given to the mathematical techniques used to attempt to prove that software works, without having to test every possible route through the programs. With large complex computer systems, it is uneconomic and virtually impossible to test that the system behaves properly under every possible combination of circumstances. Individual parts of the system will have a precise *formal specification* including inputs that they will recognise and outputs that they will produce.

Jackson Structured Development (JSD)

including: Jackson Structured Programming (JSP)

is a method invented by Michael Jackson in 1983 for the analysis and design of data processing and real-time systems. It emphasises the need for orderly structure in the development and design of systems.

Jackson Structured Programming (JSP) is a structured programming technique that uses diagrams as a step to developing programs. *Structured programming* (see page 174) emphasises an orderly approach to program development, breaking down large tasks into smaller sub-tasks. Jackson structured programming is a particular form of this diagrammatic method which enables the design process to be efficiently managed.

Modular design

including: module

is a method of organising a large computer program into self-contained parts, *modules*, which can be developed simultaneously by different programmers or teams of programmers. Modules have clearly defined relationships with the other parts of the system, which enables them to be independently designed, programmed and maintained. Some modules may be independently executable programs, while others may be designed to provide facilities for the suite of programs to which they belong.

Object-oriented programming (OOP)

including: object, message, object-oriented design (OOD), object-oriented language (OOL)

is a type of programming where the programmer defines not only the type of data, but also the allowable operations that can be carried out on that data.

A definition of data and permitted operations, often in tabular form, is known as an *object*. Objects can pass *messages* between each other, with one object making a request of another. This generally results in more reliable software, because each object is 'responsible' for checking that the message it receives is 'sensible'.

Developing programs using *object-oriented design* allows a team of programmers to work simultaneously, and also allows further development of existing programs without jeopardising existing parts of the program. Obviously, object-oriented programming requires an *object-oriented language* such as *Smalltalk* or *C++* (see page 250).

Object linking and embedding

including: embedded object, linked object

is the insertion of data items in one format into data in another format, for example a picture in a text file. Information such as the location of the data and its format may be included as links to the data, or the data may be embedded in the file. A program using the data can load the right program to edit that particular type of data without the user having to *export* the data, edit it and later *import* it back again (see page 10). Each item is an *object* (see above).

Embedded objects are inserted as part of the data and saved with it.

Linked objects are stored separately and only loaded when they are needed; the location (usually a filename) is stored in the main data. Changes made to the linked object automatically apply to the main data.

Developmental testing

including: alpha test, beta test

Commercial software is traditionally developed to an incomplete state, with some questions of design, command sequences, defaults, etc. left unresolved. It is then issued in an *alpha test* version to a restricted audience of testers within the developer's own company. When the results of this in-house testing have been studied and appropriate changes made, a *beta test* version is released to a number of privileged customers in exchange for their constructive comments. Beta test versions are usually close to the finally released product. They are made available to computer magazine reviewers, authors of independent 'how to' instructional manuals and developers of associated software or hardware products, who can work over a period of time with a near-complete package, so that the final launch can be accompanied by valuable and informed publicity.

Operational mode

including: batch processing, transaction processing, multi-access, time-sharing, real-time system, interactive processing, remote access, tele-processing, off-line processing, on-line processing

is the way a computer system is used and operated. Decisions about operational modes are made during systems design. Often the *operating system* (see page 272) manages the functioning of the operational modes in use.

The terms in this section are not necessarily mutually exclusive, and more than one might be applicable to any particular computer system.

In *batch processing* all the data to be input is collected together before being processed as a single efficient operation. This method is also used when computer users submit individual *jobs* (see page 278) which are processed together as a batch.

Transaction processing deals with each set of data from a user as it is submitted. This is normally used in commercial systems where a transaction may be a booking, an order or an invoice. Each transaction is completed before the next is begun.

Multi-access systems allow several users apparently to have individual control of the computer at the same time. One method of implementing a multi-access system is by allocating a period of time to each user; this is called *time-sharing*. See also *time slice*, page 278.

Real-time system is one which can react fast enough to influence behaviour in the outside world; for example, this is necessary in air-traffic control systems and desirable in on-line reservation systems.

Interactive processing provides the user with direct, immediate responses from the system. There is often some kind of dialogue with the system. Examples include the booking of airline tickets, requesting information about a bank account through a cash dispensing machine.

Remote access or *tele-processing* is the use of a geographically remote computer system via communications links. See also *remote job entry*, page 279.

Off-line processing occurs when computer devices are not under the immediate control of the main computer, for example data entry to disk or tape storage.

On-line processing allows the user to interact directly with the main computer.

Thread

including: multi-threading, concurrent thread

is the processing performed on a single set of data in the system.

Multi-threading is the use of a single copy of a program to process several sets of data which are at different stages of processing. This is most useful in a multi-tasking situation where tasks may need to be launched at any time. Only one copy of the program needs to be loaded, which saves memory. The program design ensures that the data for each thread is kept separate and that the appropriate program instructions act on the thread which is being executed.

Concurrent threads are two or more threads being executed at the same time using *multi-tasking* (see page 278).

Implementation

including: parallel running, pilot running, direct changeover, big-bang, phased implementation

is the process of starting to use an information system in a real situation after having designed and developed it. It may enable final testing in a real situation. Four different approaches are used depending on the size of the system and the properties of the data being processed.

Parallel running requires the new system to operate for a short period of time alongside the older system. The results can be compared to ensure that the new system is working correctly.

Pilot running requires the new system to operate alongside the old system but only processing part of the data. The results can be compared to check that the system works correctly but pilot running cannot test how the system will operate with the larger quantities of data of the real situation.

Direct changeover or *big-bang* requires that the new system replaces the old system without any overlap. In some cases the nature of the system prevents parallel or pilot running and a direct changeover is the only option, for example with an emergency control system.

Phased implementation involves replacing part of a system with a new system while some tasks continue to use the old system. This enables training and installation to be spread over a period of time. For example, a supermarket chain might install a new system in a few of its branches to begin with and phase the introduction into its other branches as they are refurbished. This initial phase of the implementation will inevitably involve some parallel running.

Software metric

is a number or other measure that can be associated with a piece of software to describe its efficiency, performance, ease of development, and other properties. *Benchmarks* (see page 169) measure how software actually behaves, while software metrics attempt to describe performance from a study of the code alone. Simple and sometimes not very helpful metrics include the number of lines of code and the space occupied in memory.

SSADM

abbreviation for: Structured Systems Analysis and Design Method

is the standard method of analysis and design of large-scale software packages used within government departments in the UK.

Software life cycle

is the stages in the life history of a large-scale piece of software, produced in a disciplined way. There is disagreement over the precise number and description of the stages, but a fairly typical list is shown in Figure C1.1. Many people add the extra stage *obsolescence* to this list.

SOFTWARE LIFE CYCLE	
Stage	*Description*
System requirements	identifying what the customer wants ...
Software requirements **Overall design**	... and turning this into a software specification specifying the whole system
Detailed design	splitting it into containable modules
Module design	deciding what each part will do ...
Module production	.. and turning this into a computer program
Module testing	making sure each module works alone ...
Integration and system testing	... and together with all the other modules
Acceptance testing	getting the customer to agree that it works
Release	the software is sold, or delivered to the customer
Implementation and operation	it works ... ... or some parts do not and have to be corrected
Maintenance	maintenance usually includes upgrading the software to meet new requirements

Figure C1.1: Software life cycle

Structured programming

including: structured planning technique, top-down programming, stepwise refinement, bottom-up programming
is a methodical approach to the design of a program which emphasises breaking large and complex tasks into smaller sections. This is also referred to as *structured planning technique*.

Top-down programming or *stepwise refinement* is a particular type of structured programming, where the problem is defined very simply and then split into a number of smaller sections. Each of these sections is successively split and refined until they are small enough to be programmed. It is an axiom of this approach that new ideas which were not in the original global design should not be added.

Bottom-up programming involves programming a number of small modules and building them into a larger structure. In practice it is often difficult to ensure that an efficient system is developed by this method. See also *modular design*, page 170.

System development cycle

also known as: system cycle, system life cycle

is the complete cycle of activities involved in the creation of a new or modified computer system, including several activities described elsewhere in this section. There are differences of opinion about the precise number and description of stages, but a typical set is shown in Figure C1.2. Compare this with Figure C1.1: *Software life cycle* (opposite page) which is very similar, but describes only the software components of a computer system.

	SYSTEM DEVELOPMENT CYCLE	
Stage	*Description*	*see also*
Specification	of the user's requirements	*system specification* and *functional specification*, page 169.
Analysis and design	of the system	*systems analysis and systems design*, page 169 *Jackson structured development*, page 170 *object oriented programming*, page 171 *structured systems analysis and design method (SSADM)*, page 173.
Implementation (of the design)	using the design from the previous stage	*modular design*, page 170.
Testing	of the implemented design	*developmental testing*, page 171.
Implementation (of the system)	with the existing system	*implementation*, page 173.
Documentation	of the whole system	*user documentation*, pages 92/4 *systems documentation*, page 176 *program documentation*, pages 225/6.

Each stage involves iterative review until the result is acceptable.

Figure C1.2: System development cycle

C2   Systems Documentation

*This section is concerned with the written comments and graphical
illustrations which form the description of a system. The symbols
and layout conventions referred to are those given in British
Standards BS4058:1973 and BS6224:1982.
Related topics can be found in A17 User Documentation,
C1 Systems Design and Life Cycle, C8 Program Documentation,
C9 Developing, Testing and Running Programs.*

Software systems will require some modification during their lifetime. If this is to be
done satisfactorily, it is vital that good, complete and understandable documentation is
available. Requests to modify software may arise for a number of reasons, which
could include changes in company procedures, requests for improvements, errors in
the software which were not found at the testing stage and changes in government
regulations (for example, new taxation law). The resources required at the
maintenance stage of the **Systems Life Cycle**, which is covered in C1 Systems Design
and Life Cycle, frequently equal and indeed sometimes exceed the initial resources
required to deliver the software in the first instance.

The original team that did the analysis and design, and the implementation, of the
software may well not be available to carry out the maintenance stage. This makes it
all the more important that good, up-to-date documentation is available throughout the
life of the software.

A standard form of documentation may be followed, which may be specified by the
company involved. There are a number of recognised system development
methodologies, for example **SSADM (Structured Systems Analysis and Design
Method)**. These specify, at various levels of detail, what documentation should be
produced and in what form. Software tools also exist, such as CASE (Computer
Aided Software Engineering) tools, which can help to produce consistent
documentation of changes.

Documentation produced at the design and analysis stage will include the
requirements specification, which is sometimes 'signed off' as a formal agreement
between the customer and the software group. As the design develops, a range of
diagrams will be produced; these will include:

- diagrams showing the relationships between the data (**entity-
relationships** or **entity-relation diagrams**);
- diagrams showing the relationships between the data and the processes
or programs that manipulate and transform the data (**data flow
diagrams** or **system diagrams**).

The design task will be tackled in a hierarchical way, gradually breaking it down
into smaller parts (sub-tasks), using methods such as **JSD (Jackson Structured
Development)**. Often diagrams, such as those used by Jackson System Development,

use different shapes to indicate the use of a particular device or medium, in the same kind of way that icons are often used in a graphical user interface.

As the programs are designed and developed there will be other documentation for the programs. These have particular forms and are covered in *C8 Program Documentation*.

Maintenance documentation
including: technical documentation
is written for the computer professional rather than the user. It will include both *systems documentation* (see the introduction to this section, page 176) and *program documentation* (see page 225). Some parts will be highly technical, for example the specifications of peripherals and their configuration. The reader of this *technical documentation* will need to have expert knowledge.

Undocumented feature
is a facility included as part of a computer system which is not described in the official specification or documentation. The feature may not be fully tested or may be provided to help engineers diagnose faults. The user cannot rely on the feature since it may be altered or removed at a later date.

Requirements specification
is that part of the system documentation which sets out the customer's requirements for the system. It may be drafted as a formal, contractual agreement between the customer and the software system developers. In some respects, it will provide measures against which the performance of the implemented system will be assessed.

Flowchart
including: flow line
is a graphical representation of the operations involved in a process or system. *System flowchart symbols* (see page 179) are used to represent particular operations or data, and *flow lines*, which connect the flowchart symbols, indicate the sequence of operations or the flow of data. Flow lines may use arrows to indicate sequence, or a top-down, left-right convention may apply if there are no arrows.

System flowchart
also called: data flow diagram (DFD), data flowchart, system flowchart diagram, system diagram
is a diagram used to describe a complete data processing system. The flow of data through the operations is diagrammatically described, down to the level of the individual programs needed to achieve the system requirements. The details of programs are not included, since these are covered in the *program documentation* (see page 225).

Entity-relationship diagram

including: entity-relationship

is a diagram used to show how data (entities) are related to each other. For example, how the different layers of data in a database are related and how access to one layer of data will automatically achieve access to related data items and related layers. An *entity-relationship* is a formal statement of the way in which one data item is related to another, or of the way in which a class of data items is related to items in another class. See also *data model*, page 20.

Figure C2.1 illustrates two different classes of entity-relationships, many:many and 1:many.

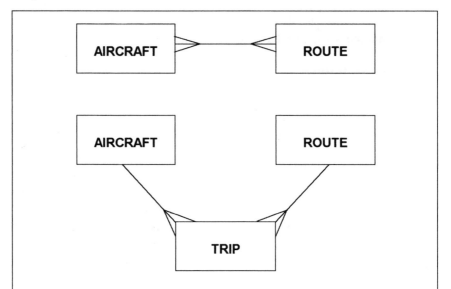

*In the top diagram, two entities, **aircraft** and **route**, are identified. Attributes are not shown, but might include the plane number, its type, passenger capacity and so on, for the aircraft, and the starting point and destination for the route. There is a relation between these entities: an aircraft can be used on many routes, and a route can be travelled by many aircraft. Such 'many-many' relations are not easy to implement in a database, so the designer breaks this relation, invents a new entity called **trip** which represents one specific journey over that route by one specific aircraft. One aircraft now makes many trips, but each trip is only made by one aircraft. Similarly, one route has many trips over it, but each trip is over just one route. Two such one-many relations are more efficient to implement.*

Figure C2.1: *Entity-relationship diagram used in designing a database*

System flowchart symbol

is a symbol used in a system flowchart diagram. Different shapes indicate the various kinds of activity described by the diagram. Sometimes highly formalised shapes are used, each having a specific meaning; in other situations very simple boxes with words are used. Provided the meaning is clear, either method is an equally acceptable way of representing a process or system. Examples of how these symbols might be used are given in Figure C2.9 (page 181), where rectangles are used for all processes, and Figures C2.10 and C2.11 (pages 182 and 183), which use more formal shapes.

Input/output symbol

also known as: data input/output symbol
also used as: output symbol, input symbol
is used for any input or output of data however achieved.

Figure C2.2: *Input/output symbol*

Interactive input symbol

is used to indicate data input by keyboard or other operator-controlled input system such as a bar-code reader. It may also be used for on-line interrogation.

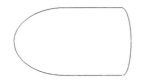

Figure C2.3: *Interactive input symbol*

Document output symbol

also known as: output document symbol
is used to indicate that data is to be printed.

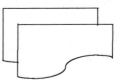

Small document   Large document

Figure C2.4: *Document output symbol*

Process symbol

also known as: data processing symbol
is used for the processing of data, for example by a computer program.

Figure C2.5: Process symbol

File symbol

sometimes called: data symbol
including: on-line data file symbol, (magnetic) disk file symbol, (magnetic) tape file symbol
A number of different symbols are used when processing data files. In most instances the symbol shapes make it easier to recognise the process defined within the symbol .
On-line data file symbol is used for data held on any on-line file, whatever the purpose.

Figure C2.6: On-line data file symbol

The ***(magnetic) disk file symbol*** is used whenever the data is held on a disk .

Figure C2.7: (magnetic) Disk file symbol

The ***(magnetic) tape file symbol*** is used whenever the data is held on a tape.

Figure C2.8: (magnetic) Tape file symbol

Flowcharts of a payroll system.

The flowcharts in Figures C2.9, C2.10 and C2.11 describe the part of a payroll process where the wages information for each employee is processed. The transactions are validated, sorted and then used to update the wages master file.

The descriptions (printer, disk, etc.) may be altered, according to the particular medium being used; alternatively, the descriptions may be omitted completely, if a less specific flowchart is required.

System flowchart (using simplified symbols)

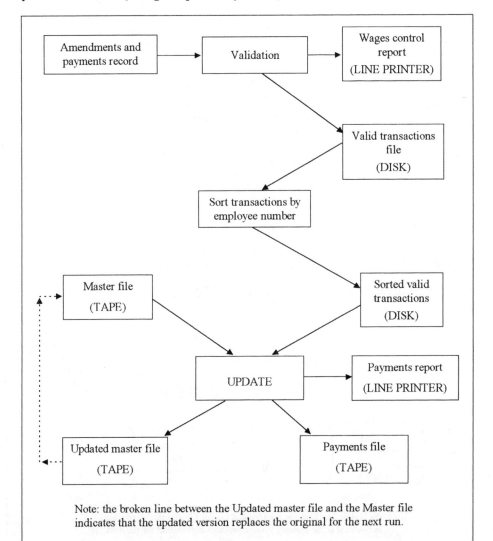

Note: the broken line between the Updated master file and the Master file indicates that the updated version replaces the original for the next run.

Figure C2.9: Flowchart of payroll process, using simple symbols

System flowchart (using British Standard symbols)

This flowchart (Figure C2.10) uses British Standard symbols to show the process described on the previous page. The annotation on the right of the flowcharts in Figures C2.10 and C2.11 have been used to describe the function of the symbols. A similar annotation method can be used to provide an explanatory commentary on the algorithm or process represented by the flowchart diagram.

An alternative set of symbols is used in Figure C2.11.

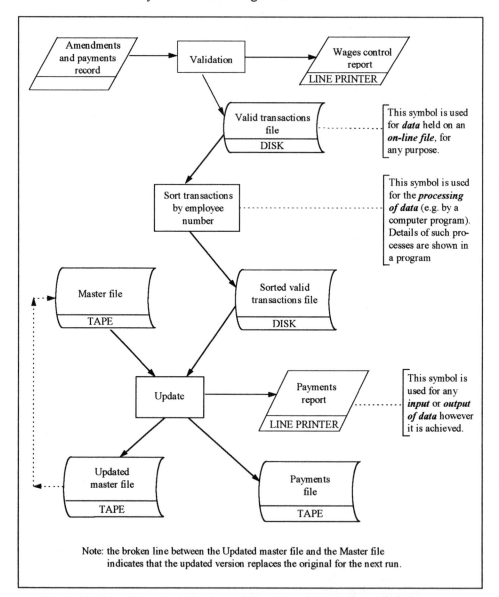

Figure C2.10: Flowchart of payroll process, using British Standard symbols

System flowchart (using British Standard alternative symbols)

This flowchart (Figure C2.11) uses alternative symbols to describe the process shown in Figure C2.10. There are also other, less commonly used, symbols. The document symbols can also be used for the input of data to a system by means of documents (e.g. written orders).

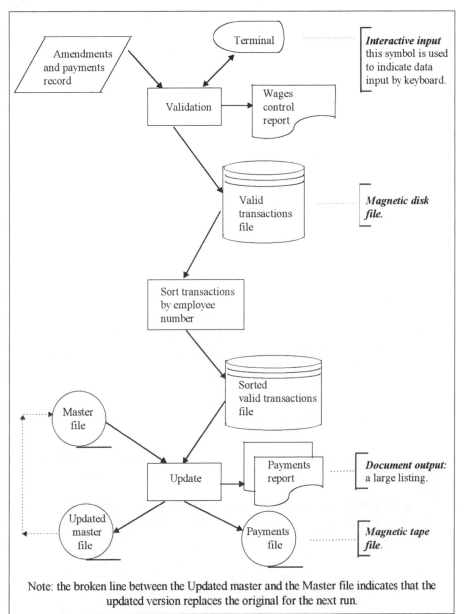

Figure C2.11: Flowchart of payroll process, using alternative symbols

Structure diagram

is a means of representing the design of a program or system. It consists of a number of levels, each of which describes the whole design, but at increasing levels of detail.

The structure diagram, Figure C2.12 (page 184), shows another way of representing the payroll process shown in Figures C2.9, C2.10 and C2.11. This is based on the *JSD (Jackson structured development) notation* (see page 170). The hierarchical structure diagram is displayed in a top-down, left-to-right manner. At each successive level (labelled 1,2,3,...) the tasks are described in greater detail. The lower boxes expand the description of the task defined in the box in the level above to which they are connected. This process of expansion is continued to varying depths in different parts of the diagram until it is judged that sufficient detail is given.

The numbers are used to identify the boxes uniquely. The actual numbers are not significant although they can be used to indicate levels; in this case the first digit indicates the level, for example 3.59 would indicate a box at level 3.

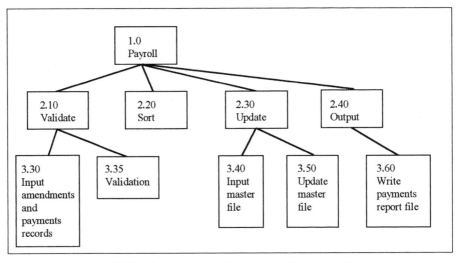

Figure C2.12: *A structure diagram for the payroll process*

At greater levels of detail it can be helpful to draw the expanded version of a section in the structure diagram, in this case the validation section, as a separate diagram, Figure C2.13.

In this example horizontal and vertical connecting lines are used. It is of no importance which type of connecting line is drawn although it is normal to be consistent.

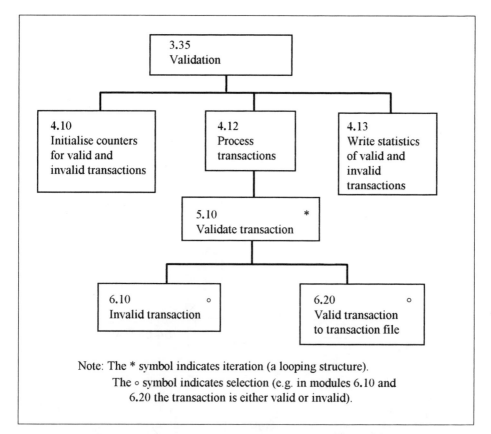

Figure C2.13: *Expansion of process 3.35 in figure C2.12*

Block diagram

is a diagram made up of boxes labelled to represent different hardware or software components and lines showing their interconnections.

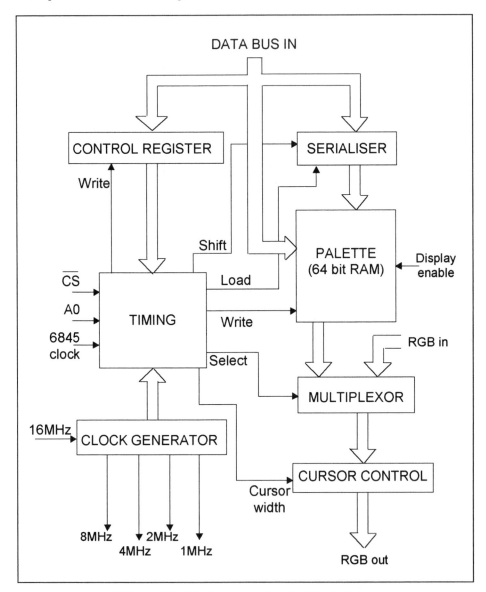

Figure C2.14: An example of a block diagram
(courtesy Acorn Computers)

C3　Management and Manipulation of Data

Related topics can be found in A1 Data Processing, A2 Word Processing, A3 Spreadsheets, A4 Databases and Information Retrieval, B3 Memory, C11 Data Representation and C12 Numeric Data Representation.

Computer users tend to keep their programs separate from the data they operate on. The data is usually held as one or more *files* on backing storage, and the systems software encourages the user to believe that the file is held here (for example, on a disk) all the time. In fact, when a program wishes to use the data in a file, it is necessary for the portion of the file being worked on to be copied into primary storage in order to work on individual items of data. The systems software is responsible for copying between backing and primary storage, ensuring that the correct portion is readily available, without explicit action by the user. Because of this automatic management, it is necessary for users to access files in a formal way.

If the file is a new one, it must first be *created*, and this might include specifying how large the file will become, and how it will be organised. Before any use of an existing file, it is necessary to *open* the file, when a section will be copied to primary storage, and other programs will be notified that the file is in use. Any changes will be made to the copy, and when access is requested to a part of the file not currently in primary storage, the systems software is responsible for making the changes to the permanent version, and loading a fresh copy of the required portion.

When access to the file is no longer needed, it must be *closed* so that any remaining changes are written back to the permanent version, and other programs can be notified that the file is no longer in use.

A file may be *deleted* from backing store, but it is usual for the systems software simply to mark the file in some way, so that the space it occupies may be used for other files, rather than physically erase the contents.

File

including: file name extension

is a collection of related data. It is traditional to think of files as being structured as a collection of identically structured *records* (see page 258) made up of *fields* (see page 259).

To be accessed, a file has to have a name which is recognised by the system. Disk operating systems determine the conventions for file names. All file names carry some kind of extension, *file name extension*, which may or may not be user controlled. The file name extension identifies the kind of data in the file, for example graphic data, word-processed document. See also *file type*, page 262.

Random file

including: address-generating algorithm

is a file in which each record is stored and accessed using the physical address of its location. Usually the file uses the whole of a single storage device.

Random files are usually stored on disc and the address of each record is the sector and track number where the data is located. The algorithm for working out what address to use to store or retrieve data is called an ***address-generating algorithm***. Unlike most other file structures, there is no concept of storing data in a linear structure. See also *blocking factor*, page 258.

Sequential file

sometimes called: serial file

is a file in which the records are stored in a specified order. For example, in a student record system this could be in alphabetic order of the surname or in numerical order of reference number.

Random access file

is a file where the records are stored sequentially, that is one after another, but which can be directly accessed, as in a *random file* (see above). This is done by using the position of the data in the file as its address. See also, *file access*, page 190.

Record number

is a unique number which identifies the position of a record in a datafile. This means that record number one identifies the first physical position and the data in that position. The concept of a record number is not used in some file structures such as *random files* (see above) and in some *relational database* systems (see page 23).

Many datafiles can be processed serially by working through the file one record at a time and, in this situation, the record number identifies the position of the record currently being processed. A record number may serve as a *pointer* (see page 190). See also *file access*, page 190.

Archive file

is one containing data no longer in use, but held for historical purposes, perhaps for auditors. It is often stored away from the computer system, in a secure location.

Backup file

is a copy of a current file kept as a security measure in case the original is corrupted in any way. As with an *archive file* (see above), it is often kept in a secure location away from the computer system.

Reference file

is a special type of *master file* (see page 189) which is not updated during the job being processed. It contains fixed data that does not change. When changes are necessary, this will be achieved by a separate program.

Master file

including: transaction file

is the principal source of data for an application. It holds data which is mostly static but which can be added to or amended by updating as necessary during processing. In a traditional commercial batch-processing application, such as a payroll, the master file (of all employees) is updated by reference to a *transaction file* of hours worked in the current month, leave, sickness, promotions, etc.

Grandfather, father, son files

are the three most recent versions of a file that is periodically updated, for example the *master file* (see above) in a batch-processing application such as a payroll. The most recent, the '*son*' file, is used for the next run of the program; if an error occurs that corrupts this copy of the master file, the '*father*' version is still available, and can be used with an archive copy of the *transaction file* (see above) from the previous run, to re-create the damaged 'son' version. The '*grandfather*' version provides an additional level of security.

Index file

is a file used to access a large datafile quickly. It contains key field data from the file that the index is for. The key data is in a format which can be searched quickly and the attached addresses are used to access the data.

File operations

including: read, write, update, insert, append, read-only

are those activities that can be performed on an existing data file.

Reading is the operation of taking a copy of a data item from a file.
Writing is the operation of saving any changes to a file.
Updating is altering an existing data item already written in the file.
Inserting is adding a new data item to an existing file. This implies moving all later
     items to make space.
Appending is adding a new item at the end of an existing file.

In multi-user systems problems can arise if more than one user is allowed to access a file at any one time. Only the first user who requests access to a file will be allowed to update it or append to it. Until the first user has released the file, subsequent requests for access may be denied or allowed *read-only access* to the file or individual records.

File access

*including: serial access, sequential access, direct access, random access, index
sequential access method (ISAM)*
The way in which a file is to be accessed by users influences how it is stored, and the
information the systems software needs to hold in order to allow for efficient reading
and writing.

Serial access is where the items are read, one at a time, from the physical start of the
file, in the order in which they are stored. Items may vary in length, provided
there is some marker to signal the end of one item and the start of the next.

Sequential access is where the items are read, one at a time, from the logical start of
the file, in key value order. Because the records in a file held on a *serial access
device* (see *magnetic tape*, page 125) need to be sorted into the order in which
they are to be processed, serial access is sometimes referred to as sequential
access.

Direct access is where any item can be retrieved immediately, provided its position in
the file is known. This often means that items must have a known length, so that
software can calculate where in the file the required item is located. Direct
access files are commonly called *random access* files because they are usually
held in storage that has random access. See also *magnetic disk*, page 122, and
random access memory, page 128.

Index Sequential Access Methods (*ISAM*) index the records of a sequential file.
This allows both sequential and index approaches to be used. For example to
search an index-sequential file of surnames. To locate 'Smith' an index is first
consulted to discover the first item beginning with 'S', after which the file is
searched sequentially. For this to work both the file and the index must be in
alphabetic order.

Pointer

is the address or reference of a data element which allows it to be retrieved without
further searching.

For example a database, which stores information about students, may use pointers
to identify students in a particular class. It may use one pointer to locate the first
student and further pointers between the students. In this way, to find the students in a
class, the pointers allow the next student in the class to be accessed without searching
other parts of the database.

Pointers allow fast access to data because little searching is required. When used on
data stored in the computer's memory the pointer is usually the address of the data in
the memory. However in a database system the pointer may be the *primary key* (see
page 260) or the reference number of the related record

Merge

is to combine two or more ordered data structures, such as files, into a single ordered
one.

Sorting

is the process of arranging data items in a pre-determined order (such as alphabetical or numerical). When the data items are themselves structured – a record in a file, for example – one particular part of the structure must be specified as the item to be used in determining the ordering: this item is known as the *key* (see page 260). In a file of names and addresses, for example, the 'surname' might be used as the key.

Search

including: hit, hit rate, serial (or linear) search, binary search
is the process of examining a file to see if a given data item occurs in it. A successful location of an item is called a *hit*, and the success rate the *hit rate*. Unless the file is in some useful order, searching may involve examining every entry in the file until the item is found or the end of the file is reached, a *serial* or *linear search*. Efficient *sorting* methods (see above) are important in searching. If the file is in alphabetic order, a particularly efficient search method is the *binary search* (Figure C3.1).

BINARY SEARCH

Archimedes
Aristotle
Armstrong
Arnold
Asquith
Aubrey
Auden
Austen
Austin   <-------- *first comparison – goal is later*
Aytoun
Bacon   <----------------------- *third comparison – later*
Bagehot   <-------------------------------- *successful fourth comparison*
Balfour   <----------------- *second comparison – earlier*
Ball
Barbour
Barker

In searching for the entry associated with 'Bagehot' in this alphabetically-ordered table, a first comparison is made half-way down the list: this indicates that the 'goal' is later in the list. Halving again and again, as many times as necessary, locates 'Bagehot' after 4 comparisons (this number would find any item on a list this length). A serial search would take 12 comparisons.

Figure C3.1: An example of a binary search

Validation

including: data vetting, range check, check digit, batch total, control total, check sum

is computerised checking to detect any data that is unreasonable or incomplete. It is also known as *data vetting*. There are many methods, chosen to suit the data being processed. Some operate on single data items: a *range check* would signal any data items outside a plausible range (a worker's age that was less than 15, or over 75, perhaps); *check digit* is an extra digit added as part of a numeric data item (like a part number): it is derived from the other digits in a way that can be repeated.

Other methods operate on batches of data: a *batch total* of the number of separate records in a batch might be manually calculated and added to the data, as a check that none had been missed; a *control total* formed by adding up some field from each record could accompany the batch as a double-check. Where the data is computer software, a *check sum* formed by simply adding up all the instructions, treated as numbers, is often added to a file to make sure that it has been copied without error. See also *hashing*, below.

Hashing

including: hash total, hash table, collision

is the process of calculating a numeric value from one or more data items. While this value obviously depends on the value of the data item(s), it does not depend on the meaning attached to them. It can be used as a *control total* (see *validation*, above) to check for errors in copying the data, when it is known as a *hash total*.

It is also an important technique in storing values in a data structure known as a *hash table*. The calculated value can be used to mark the position in the table where the data item should be found, enabling it to be accessed directly, rather than forcing a sequential search.

A *collision* occurs when two data items give the same value under hashing, and should therefore be stored in the same place in a hash table.

Corruption

is the introduction of errors into data or programs during storage or copying. It is usually due to physical causes, such as electrical *interference* (see page 310) or faulty equipment.

Data compression

is the technique of reducing the space occupied by a large file. There are many different methods, suited to different types of data.

The first paragraph of the introduction to this section, C3 Management and Manipulation of Data on page 187, contains 747 characters, including spaces. It can be reduced in size, without losing any of the information it contains, by replacing certain common pairs of letters by a single character (we have illustrated this by using numbers). For example, there are 18 occurrences of the pair 'th'. If these are replaced by '0', 18 characters have been saved. Making the changes listed in Figure C3.2, the introduction is reduced to 635 characters, a saving of 112 characters or about 15%. The file must be re-expanded before it can be used, of course, but space has been saved in storage.

DATA COMPRESSION

Comput9 us92te6 to keep 0eir program2separ73from 03d7a 0ey op973on. 03d7a i2usually held82on3or mo1 *file2*o4backi5 storage,86 03system2softwa1 encourage203us9 to believ307 03fil3i2held he1 (for example, o4a disk)8ll 03time. I4fact, whe4a program wishe2to us303d7a i4a file, it i2necessary for 03portio4of 03fil3bei5 worked o4to b3copied into primary storag3i4ord9 to work o4i6ividual item2of d7a. 03system2softwa1 i21sponsibl3for copyi5 betwee4backi586 primary storage, ensuri5 07 03cor1ct portio4i21adily8vailable, wi0out explicit8ctio4by 03us9. Becaus3of 0i2autom7ic management, it i2necessary for us92to8cces2file2i4a formal way.

Replacements:

0 = th	1 = re	2 = s'N'	3 = e'N'	4 = n'N'
5 = ng	6 = nd	7 = at	8 = 'N'a	9 = er

(a space is represented by 'N')

Figure C3.2: A simple example of data compression

Download

including: upload

is the term commonly used to refer to the transfer of a file from one computer to another. This may be from a larger computer to a smaller one, for example from a mainframe to a personal computer, or across a network such as the Internet. Generally, the term is used when the user who starts the process is operating the computer which will eventually receive the file. When the user is sending the file to another site, the term used to describe the operation is *upload*.

Overwriting

is the erasing of a data item by writing another in its place.

Raw data

is data as input to a computer, before any *validation* (see page 192) or processing.

Overflow

including: numeric overflow, stack overflow, underflow

is a general term describing what happens when something becomes too large to be processed satisfactorily. For example, the result of a numeric calculation may become too large to be stored in the space reserved for numbers (*numeric overflow*); or a data structure, such as a stack, may have space reserved for just 100 entries, so that attempting to add a 101st would cause *stack overflow*. *Underflow* is also possible, a number too small to be represented in the computer, or an attempt to remove an item from an empty stack.

Rounding

including: rounding error

is the approximation of a numeric data item by its nearest equivalent, to a given number of significant figures or decimal places. For example, 1.36 rounded to one decimal place is 1.4. *Rounding error* is the error introduced by rounding (+0.04 in the example). See also *truncation*, below.

Truncation

including: truncation error

is the approximation of a numeric data item by ignoring all information beyond a given number of significant figures or decimal places: for example, 1.36 truncated to one decimal place is 1.3. *Truncation error* is the error introduced by truncation (-0.06 in the example). This use of the term 'error' comes from mathematics and is important in situations where numbers are represented in a fixed-length format but should not be confused with other uses of the term. See also *error*, page 238, *floating-point representation*, page 266 and *rounding*, above.

C4   Programming Concepts

The terms defined in this section cover a variety of techniques and concepts used to communicate ideas and algorithms. These terms are used both to communicate ideas before a program is written and to describe the program design so that other programmers can maintain the program at a later date. Related terms can be found in sections C5 Programming (Flow of Execution), C6 Programming (Subprograms), C7 Program Syntax and C9 Developing, Testing and Running Programs.

The construction of any effective computer program is time consuming and complex, requiring the application of a wide range of techniques, skills and processes. The programmer has to work at a very detailed level to make the computer do what is wanted, so that the resulting program works reliably and at a reasonable speed.

The actual computer program run on the computer has to be in the machine-code used by the computer. There are ways of speeding up and simplifying the production of this program, such as using higher-level computer languages, program generators and specialised computer languages designed to produce particular types of programs, for example database managers. Many of the principles used by these various methods involve the same standard techniques that are used in traditional programming and much of the technical language used is of value to anybody involved in developing computer software.

Regardless of the method used to develop computer software, the designer has to balance the properties of cost, speed, ease of use and reliability of the final product. A slow program can be used with a larger computer, but at a greater cost in computer time. Similarly a complicated program will be more expensive to test. But if software is well designed, using a professional approach, then more efficient software can be developed at lower cost.

A computer programmer has to be prepared to choose between alternative programming strategies in order to get a usable program. The obvious method of solving a problem may be inefficient, as the user will not be prepared to wait while the computer carries out some apparently simple task. To avoid this, the programmer may use a variety of strategies (expressed as algorithms), some of which may be complex, but without which it may not be possible to produce a usable program. One skill a programmer must have is the ability to understand and adapt a wide range of existing algorithms to new situations.

The user will expect a program to work reliably and produce no errors. The programmer may use standard algorithms developed and tested by other people as one way of reducing possible errors in a program. The program must be able to deal with any mistakes the user makes without introducing any errors, for example in the input data.

Address

including: memory location, absolute address, base address, offset, relative address
Each piece of data or program instruction is stored separately in the computer's
memory and it is located by its address. The address is the number for the position of
a word of storage in the main memory. This number is used by a program as the
identification of a particular *memory location*, which may contain a data item or the
next instruction, when a machine-code program is branching.

If the address is the real address used by the internal electronics of the computer, it
is known as the *absolute address*. Many machine-code programs and operating
systems use a method of addressing, which allows a program to have its own
(imaginary) addresses and convert these to the real addresses as the program is
executed. The real addresses are worked out from a starting address number, called
the *base address*, by adding another number, called the *offset* or *relative address*, to
it.

One use of relative addressing is storing arrays. The location of any particular
element of the array can be calculated from the element number and the base address
of the (array) variable.

Algebraic notation

including: infix, prefix and postfix notation, reverse Polish notation
is the way mathematical and logical processes are described when writing a computer
program. Infix, prefix and postfix notations are different ways of writing the algebraic
(and logical) expressions used by a program.

Mathematicians normally use *infix notation* (where the operators are placed
between the operands, such as **A+B**). *Prefix notation* places the operator first (such
as **+AB**) while *postfix notation* places the operator last (such as **AB+**). See Figure
C4.1.

Prefix and postfix notations are easier for a computer to execute. Modern
computers are sufficiently powerful that most users do not need to use either prefix or
postfix notation.

EXAMPLES OF DIFFERENT ALGEBRAIC NOTATIONS

What has to be worked out: Work out the perimeter of a rectangle
which is: twice (**Length** plus **Breadth**)

*The formula in **Infix** notation:*   **2*(L+B)**

*The formula in **Prefix** notation:*   ***2+LB**

*The formula in **Postfix** notation:*   **2LB+***
*(also called **Reverse Polish** notation)*

Figure C4.1: Examples of algebraic notation

Reverse Polish notation is a form of postfix notation where brackets are not permitted (and not needed). No rules about precedence are needed for different operations, which are carried out in the order met in the expression.

Reverse Polish notation has the advantage that any algebraic expression can be processed strictly from left to right. It is widely used by compilers which convert the infix notation that a programmer has used into reverse Polish notation. This reverse Polish notation is then easily converted into a machine-code program. It was devised by the Polish mathematician Jan Lukasiewicz.

Program algorithm

is a sequence of steps designed to perform a particular task. An algorithm may be constructed to describe the operation of a complete system or to describe a particular part of it. Standard algorithms have been developed to do specific common tasks, such as a particular method of sorting a set of data. Many have been published and are available for general use.

Algorithms include precise details about the operations to be performed and in what order. An algorithm is a sequence of instructions including information such as when sections are repeated or choices made. See also *algorithm*, page 56.

Algorithms can be written in any suitable form, such as a programming language, *pseudo-code* (see page 226) or as diagrams. Often they are written in pseudo-code, which is easily communicated and easily translated into any suitable programming language, see Figure C4.2.

AN ALGORITHM IN PSEUDO-CODE

To count the number of words in a line of text:

```
begin  count words
    set  words = 1
    set  character = space                      for a space at the start
    while  not end of line
    begin
        make  previous character = character    for unnecessary spaces
        get next character from line
        if  character = space
            and  previous character not space   two spaces together
        then  add 1 to words
    end
    if  character = space  then  subtract 1 from words   space at end of line
end  count words
```

Algorithms become complicated when covering all possibilities.

Figure C4.2: *An example of an algorithm in pseudo-code*

Array (machine-code programming)

The use of arrays is a fundamental technique in machine-code and low-level programming, since they make it possible to handle large amounts of related data efficiently. Each element in an array will be held sequentially in memory and so an index register or relative addressing can be used to access each element in turn. Since the array is stored as a single block of computer memory the programmer has a variety of methods which can be used to manipulate the data easily, for example copying the entire block as one operation. See also *array,* page 256.

Code

including: program code

refers to the actual set of instructions which form a program. This is either the source text of a program, which is later compiled, or the actual instruction codes of a machine-code program.

The term *program* (see page 219) is often applied to a complete software system (including items such as spellchecker dictionaries) but *program code* applies specifically to the instructions which make up a particular part of the overall system. See also *relocatable code* and *absolute code*, page 205.

Coding sheet

is a special form on which program instructions may be written. It has columns to ensure that instructions are presented in the correct format. These are now very rarely used since most programmers now type their programs directly into the computer using a *text editor* (see page 280).

Assignment

is an instruction that gives (assigns) a value, which could be the result of a calculation, to a specified variable. The value is placed in the memory location corresponding to the given variable.

AN ASSIGNMENT STATEMENT

Working out an area in a program:

area:=height*width;

assigns the answer of 'height' *times* 'width' *to the variable* 'area'

Figure C4.3: Example of an assignment statement

Event

is an external change which is notified to the program by the operating system. This may be a key being pressed or a mouse button being clicked.

The term event has a specific connotation related to multi-tasking operating systems used by personal computers. Events are occurrences which may apply to any of the programs running and are put into context by the operating system communicating with the programs. Events should not be confused with normal input which is directed to a particular program nor with *interrupts* (see page 289) which are usually dealt with by the operating system. One effect of an interrupt may however be to generate an event.

Events are an important element in the design of multi-tasking programs where the operating system handles the input (from the keyboard) and output (to the screen). When a new input is received, a message is sent to the program informing it of the event and allowing it to take appropriate action.

Flag

including: set, unset, status word, status byte
is an indicator that has two states, often called *set* or **unset**. It enables the program to record whether a particular event has occurred, for example whether (or not) a list of numbers has been sorted, whether an interrupt has been sensed (or not sensed).

In a high-level language a variable may be used as a flag. If a *Boolean* or *logical data type* (see *data type*, page 261) is used, the two states, true and false, are equivalent to the flag states set and unset. To begin with the flag may be unset (false) and when a particular case is detected it is set (true); when the action has been completed it is unset again (back to false).

Only one bit is needed to store a flag, so a machine code programmer may use the bits in a single word to store several flags, which can be easily manipulated in machine code using a *mask*, (see *mask* page 200 and *masking*, page 292). Most central processors have a **status word** or **status byte** which is the group of flags used in the control of the arithmetic/logic unit. When individual bits are used as flags, the two states are referred to as 0 or 1.

Carry flag

including: overflow flag
is a flag within the *status word* (see *flag*, above) of the central processor that is set to 1 (or true) when a carry condition occurs, otherwise it is set to 0 (or false). These may be tested by the programmer if some special action may be appropriate, such as producing an error at that point.

Similarly the *overflow flag* is set to 1 (or true) when overflow occurs during an arithmetic operation, because the result of a calculation is too big for the computer to store.

Heuristic program

is one that attempts to improve its own performance as a result of learning from previous actions within the program. See also *heuristics*, page 77.

Initialise

including: initial value

is to set counters or variables to zero, or some other starting value, usually at the beginning of a program or subprogram. These values are known as *initial values*. A common programming error is to fail to initialise a variable. In this case the program will execute correctly but will produce wrong results.

Default option

is the action to be taken automatically by the computer if no specific instruction is given. For example, in some versions of BASIC arrays do not need to be declared, in which case they are given bounds 1 to 10. This is the default option.

Look-up table

is a table used to convert one set of values to another set.

The table normally has two columns. The first column holds a list of data items and the second column holds a list of related values. For example, the first column might hold product codes and the second column their prices.

An example is a tax table (for VAT). Each product has a tax code, which is looked up in a look-up table to find the tax rate to be used. Look-up tables are particularly useful for non-linear values and tax rates are often non-linear.

Another example is a SINE table. Values of sine are calculated for a range of values and stored in the memory. Each time a sine is required it is found in the look-up table rather than being worked out again. This speeds up the program because calculating sines is very slow.

Logical operation

including: AND, OR, NOT, XOR operations, mask, shift

is the use of *logic* (see *logical operator*, page 222/3) within a program. Logical operations are frequently used to determine the future progress of a program within selection statements, such as IF statements, REPEAT and WHILE loops.

Logical operations include *AND*, *OR*, *XOR* and *NOT* which, when used with Boolean values, produce the results described in *logic gates* (see page 315). For example when using a simple database of information about birds, a search might be written:

IF "webbed feet" AND "white feathers" THEN show picture ELSE next item

Both the expressions "webbed feet" and "white feathers" can be either true or false; what happens next depends on the truth value derived from 'ANDing' them.

Logical operations can also be performed on *bytes* or *words* (see page 254) when a group of *bits* (see page 265) is processed together. Logical operations simply compare each bit and the result is assigned to the equivalent bit of the result. An example of their use is the manipulation of a *status word* (see *flag,* page 199) by the operating system.

These operations can be performed using a *mask*, which is a user-defined binary pattern, to select which bits are to be changed while the other bits remain unchanged. See Figure C4.4.

The bits in a byte, word or register can also be shifted. A *shift* moves the whole bit pattern one or more places to the left or right. Bits that move out are lost and empty spaces are filled with a '0'. See also *shift*, page 290.

THE MANIPULATION OF A BIT PATTERN

The byte holds colour information:

The intensity of red is held in the colour byte below in the third and fourth bits from the right:

0 0 0 **1 0** 1 1	*The bold digits 1 0 are the red intensity*
0 0 0 0 1 1 0 0	*A mask to select the bits we require*
0 0 0 0 1 **0 0 0**	*The result of an **AND** operation on the mask and the colour byte: unwanted bits are set to 0*
0 0 0 0 0 0 **1 0**	*The result of a **right shift** of two places*
equals 2 (denary)	*The intensity of the colour red is 2.*

Figure C4.4: A logical operation on a bit pattern

Machine-code instruction

including: operation code field, address field, operand (field).
is a binary code which can be directly executed by the computer. Each type of computer has a set of binary codes which are recognised by its processor as instructions, see *instruction set*, page 282.

Each type of processor has a different instruction set. These are the only instructions that can be used to control the computer. Other instructions (such as those written in BASIC or Pascal) must be converted into appropriate machine-code instructions before they can be executed by the computer.

Each instruction is a binary pattern which can be decoded by the control unit. It consists of several fields, including the *operation code field* and usually an *address field* (see *single-address instruction*, page 202).

The *operation code field* is the part of the binary code for the instruction to be carried out (for example 'add' or 'jump').

An *address field* gives the *address* (see page 196) where the data to be used in the operation can be found. It is sometimes called the *operand field*, or simply the *operand*. See also *address calculation*, page 284.

Single-address instruction

also known as: one-address instruction
including: multiple-address instruction, two-address instruction
is the most common format of a *machine-code instruction* (see page 201). It consists
of two fields, the operation code field and the address field.

A *multiple-address instruction* has more than two fields. There is always an
operation code field and at least two address fields (giving several pieces of data which
can be used by a single operation). In particular a *two-address instruction* has three
fields, the operation code field and exactly two address fields.

Other designs of processor may have different structures. For example, stack-based
processors do not need address fields at all, just the operation code. Another example
is microprocessors, which often use several bytes of storage, instead of one word, for
each machine-code instruction. These are loaded separately but then treated as a
single-address instruction.

For general-purpose computers, single-address instructions are more economical
than other formats.

Mnemonic

including: symbolic addressing
is a code for an operation which is easily remembered. The meaning of the instruction
is normally abbreviated into a related alphabetic code.

Mnemonics are particularly used in assembly languages where each binary
operation code (see *machine code*, page 247) is replaced with a mnemonic, for
example ADC could represent the binary instruction for ADD WITH CARRY.
Mnemonics rather than binary numbers make writing programs faster and make errors
easier to find. Assemblers are used to convert the instruction mnemonics into the
binary machine-code instructions (see *assembler*, page 274).

The use of mnemonics or words to specify the address of a store location is called
symbolic addressing. This is used in assembly language programming where the
address of a store location is specified by means of an *identifier* (see page 224),
normally in the form of a word or mnemonic, rather than the numeric value of the
memory address. See also *symbol table*, page 277.

Program maintenance

including: corrective maintenance, adaptive maintenance, perfective maintenance
is the modification of a program or system after its implementation has been
completed. This may be needed to correct errors found in the system, *corrective
maintenance*. Maintenance may be necessary to adapt the system to changes within
the organisation using it, to external changes such as new legislation or to allow the
system to operate with new hardware, *adaptive maintenance*. Additionally, it may be
advantageous to make changes which will enhance the performance of the system,
perfective maintenance.

Maintenance cannot normally be carried out by the user and specialist staff are
employed, often the team that designed and wrote the original system.

Maintenance is much easier if the program is well designed, well structured and well documented (see *structured programming*, page 174). *Ease of maintenance* (see below) is a desirable characteristic of a computer system.

Program characteristics

including: ease of use, robustness, flexibility, reliability, portability, port, (hardware) platform, ease of maintenance

are the general properties (which may be good or bad) of programs or systems, which determine how successful the program may be in general use. The good properties that programmers will attempt to produce are:

Ease of use means that users will be able to operate the program with limited training and support.

Robustness is the ability of a program or system to cope with errors and mishaps during program execution without producing wrong results or stopping. Events (such as a jammed printer) should not make the computer system fail. If failures do occur, errors can be introduced and customer dissatisfaction will be caused.

Flexibility is the ability of a program or system to be easily reconfigured by the user or adapted for use in a different situation. This may enable a program or system to be sold more widely or to be adapted to changing circumstances.

Reliability is how well a program or system operates without stopping due to design faults.

Portability is the ability of a program or system to be used on different computer hardware. Many large commercial systems remain in use for much longer than the original hardware and will be adapted or *ported* to new types of computer hardware, thus saving the expense of rewriting the system. Most software packages will only work on particular combinations of hardware and operating system, which are sometimes referred to as *(hardware) platforms*.

Ease of maintenance allows modifications that have to be made during the life of a system to be carried out easily and cheaply. *Program maintenance* (see page 202) is a major expense in the use of a computer system. *Structured programming* (see page 174) enables software to be designed in a way that enables ease of maintenance.

Overlay

including: overlays

is the process by which only parts (the *overlays*) of a large program are brought from backing store for processing, as needed. Only those overlays currently requiring processing are held in main store. The major part of the program (which also manages the overlays) is always held in the main store.

The use of overlays is a technique which enables programmers to reduce the amount of memory needed by a program. Similar techniques are *segmentation* (see page 279) and *paging* (see page 285) which is used by operating systems to make efficient use of available memory.

Pretty printer

including: printf, PRINT USING, format
is a subroutine which displays a line of text (on the screen or on paper) in a neat way. This may mean splitting the line between words, justifying it and displaying numeric variables to a defined number of decimal places.

Many operating systems provide pretty printers as machine-code subroutines for use by programmers and some programming languages have predefined functions or procedures (such as the function *printf* in C and *PRINT USING* in some versions of BASIC). See Figure C4.5.

DISPLAY AND PRINT FORMATTING

*Using the **writeln**, **PRINT USING** and **printf** functions*

If the variables a, b and c have the following values:

$$a:=3.14159 \qquad b:=1.5 \qquad c:=1.5$$

*In **Pascal**:*

writeln('Answers   ',a:4:2,b:4:2,c:4:2);

will display: Answers   3.14   1.50   1.50

*In **BASIC**:*

PRINT USING "Answers   #.##   #.##   #.00",a,b,c

will display: Answers   3.14   1.5   1.50

*In **C**:*

printf("Answers   %0.2f   %0.2f   %0.2f",a,b,c)

will display: Answers   3.14   1.50   1.50

The examples display variables

	a	rounded to 2 decimal places, as	3.14
and	c	padded to 2 decimal places, as	1.50
but	b	has the trailing 0 discarded by the PRINT USING statement, a facility not available as standard in the equivalent C and Pascal statements.	

Figure C4.5: *Examples of display and print format statements*

A pattern, known as a *format*, is used to determine features such as total width and the number of decimal places (Figure C4.6).

DISPLAY FORMATS

#.##	Numbers will be displayed rounded to 2 decimal places.	2.52
#.00	Numbers will be displayed to 2 decimal places with trailing zeros if needed.	2.50
00000	Numbers will be displayed as a 5 digit integer with leading zeros if needed.	00123
#.##e+00	Numbers will be displayed to 3 significant figures using scientific format.	2.56e+02
(£#,##0)	Numbers will be displayed as a currency with brackets for negatives.	(£3,250)
dd/mm/yy	Date in European form with obliques:	02/05/95
mm.dd.yy	Date in American form:	05.02.95
Mmmm d, yyyy	Date in American form with month in words:	May 2, 1998

(the formats used vary between software - these are from a typical spreadsheet)

Figure C4.6: *Examples of formatting numeric and date data*

Relocation

including: relocatable code, absolute code, position independent code
is the moving of a program from one area of memory to another by the operating system. This allows the operating system to make best use of memory, for example during compilation. Code which can be moved in this way is known as *relocatable code*, whereas *absolute code* must reside in a particular area of memory.

When a program is relocated, any memory addresses must be suitably altered, in particular any addresses in *jump* instructions (see page 210). This means that programs may need to be written in a special way to be relocatable. See also *relative address*, in *address*, page 196.

Ideally, when we relocate a program we would not want to alter it, which will take time. It is possible, using special techniques, to write a program that will operate correctly wherever it is loaded into memory. Such a program has *position independent code*.

Packing

is the compression of data in order to make the best use of storage space. If a computer has a large word length, much space can be wasted when occupied by small pieces of data. For example a character may only need 6 bits to store it, so a computer with a word length of 24 bits could pack 4 such characters into one word of storage which would otherwise only store 1 character. Packing is sometimes done automatically by the operating system.

Self-documented program

is where the program code describes the operations being carried out. This can be done by the use of comments, statements with meaningful variable names, formatting and clearly visible structures.

These features are in addition to the normal program documentation but are valuable because they help to avoid mistakes being made when a programmer modifies the program. Modifications should always be based on the full program design documentation, otherwise the other effects of introducing changes cannot be predicted.

The use of a fourth-generation language helps this process, because these languages describe the underlying design of a system rather than the detail of its implementation. They rely on powerful compilers to convert the design into an executable system. See also *fourth-generation language*, page 246.

Terminator

also known as: rogue terminator, data terminator
including: rogue value
is a specified value, not normally expected in the data, that is used to mark the end of a list of data items. The program can process the data in order until it reaches the terminator. The number of data items can vary and the number of data items does not have to be known in advance.

The term *rogue value* often implies a *numeric* value (see *numeric data type,* page 270). It may also describe a special value, at some point in the data, used to indicate a particular situation, for example a deleted record.

Common values used as rogue terminators are 0, -1 and 9999. If the data is being entered from a keyboard then simply pressing the enter key can be the terminator (a blank input). When data is stored as a datafile a special terminator, called the *end of file marker* (see page 259), is used to show where the data finishes.

C5   Programming (Flow of Execution)

*Concepts and terms to do with programs in general are in
C4 Programming Concepts, other related terms can be found in
C6 Programming (Subprograms) , C7 Program Syntax and
C8 Program documentation.*

Computers derive much of their power from their ability to repeat groups of
instructions within a computer program and to choose which instructions to execute.
The effect is that the programmer can control the flow (or order) of execution
depending on the data being processed.

The instructions which enable a programmer to do this are known as **control
structures**. When using a high-level language, specific instructions are provided for
control structures. However when using assembly languages the control structures
have to be constructed from combinations of simpler instructions and in particular,
jump instructions.

The main control structures are **loops** and **conditional statements**. However they
are often referred to by the statements commonly used in programming languages such
as **if..then, for loop, repeat..until loop, while loop** and **case statement**.

Control structure

is the general term for the different ways in which a group of instructions can be
executed.

Control structures allow the group of instructions to be repeated a variable or fixed
number of times, or to be selectively executed depending on the data currently being
processed.

Loop

including: nested loop, iteration

is a group of instructions which is repeatedly executed. For example, to produce
payslips for several workers, the instructions for one payslip are repeated many times
with different data.

The instructions may be repeated a fixed number of times (as in a *for loop*, see page
208) or a variable number of times, with the instructions being repeated until some
specified condition is satisfied (as in a *while..do* or *repeat..until loop*, see page 209).

A *nested loop* is a loop contained within another loop. The inside loop will be
executed a number of times for each single execution of the outer loop.

Iteration is the process of repeating a sequence of steps. Iteration will involve a
loop which is repeated (iterated) until the required answer is achieved. The first time
the instructions in the loop are executed is the first iteration. For an example of how
iteration is used in numerical processing, see *iteration (mathematical)*, page 58.

Count-controlled loop

including: for loop, do loop

is a type of *loop* (see page 207) which is executed a fixed number of times. This may be a constant (if the number of repetitions is known when the program is written) or may depend on the data being processed (but the number of repetitions is still fixed at the start of the loop).

With a high-level language this is often called a *for loop* (*for....next loop*) or *do loop*; names derived from the program statements used to implement it. Traditionally the variables i, j and k are used as the control variables which record the number of repetitions executed. See Figure C5.1.

A COUNT-CONTROLLED LOOP

a *For loop*

In Pascal:
```
for i:=1 to 10 do
begin
...
end;
```
i *is a variable which holds the number of the current repetition.*

In BASIC:
```
FOR i=1 TO 10
...
NEXT i
```
... indicates an instruction (or several instructions).

In C:
```
for (I=1, I= =11, I+ +)
{...
}
```

Figure C5.1: *Syntax examples: for loop*

Infinite loop

including: breaking, escaping

An infinite loop is a *loop* (see page 207) from which there is no exit and the instructions in the loop will continue to be repeated for ever. This may sometimes be useful, for example in a program controlling a set of traffic lights, which does continuously repeat the same instructions.

In most cases an infinite loop prevents any other use of the computer. Interrupting an infinite loop may mean having to switch the computer off to reset it, but in a multi-user computer system, the operator should be able to terminate the program without affecting other users. This is called *breaking* out of the program or *escaping* from the program. Control will return to the operating system and the user can issue further commands.

An infinite loop which cannot be interrupted results in a *hung* computer (see page 242).

Condition-controlled loop

including: repeat..until loop, while loop

is a type of *loop* (see page 207) which is executed continuously and only finishes when particular conditions are met. This enables loops to be written where the number of repetitions is unknown. The advantages of this approach include:

- the amount of data being processed need not be known in advance;
- mathematical algorithms can continue until an answer is found;
- more than one exit condition can be used, for example the loop could continue until the result is obtained or an error is found.

Two forms of condition-controlled loops are usually provided by high-level languages. These are often called *repeat..until loops* and *while loops*, names derived from the program statements used to implement them.

Both repeat..until loops and while loops act in a similar way. The repeat..until loop tests for its exit after executing the instructions; while loops test for exiting before any instructions are executed, thus allowing for situations where no action needs to be taken. See Figure C5.2.

CONDITION-CONTROLLED LOOP

	as a Repeat loop	*as a While loop*

In Pascal:	i:=1;
	repeat
	   ...
	  i:=i+1;
	until (i=10) or (flag=true);
	end;
		i:=1;
		while (i<10) and (flag=false) do
		begin
		   ...
		  i:=i+1;

In BASIC:	i=1
	REPEAT
	   ...
	  i=i+1
	UNTIL i=10 OR flag=TRUE
		i=1
		WHILE i<10 AND flag=FALSE
		   ...
		  i=i+1
		ENDWHILE

In C:	i=1
	do
	{
	   ...
	  i++
	}
	while i==10 || flag==1
		i=1
		while i<10 && flag==0
		{
		   ...
		  i++
		}

... indicates an instruction (or several instructions).

Figure C5.2: *Syntax examples: repeat and while loops*

If statement

including: else

is the name for a statement allowing selection within a program. A group of statements may be executed or ignored, depending on the data being processed at the time. The name is derived from the program statement used to implement this control structure. See Figure C5.3.

It is possible for the program to choose between two alternative groups of statements by using an additional keyword *else*.

SELECTION

if..then..else statement

In Pascal:
```
if k=1 then
begin
  ...
end
else
begin
  ...
end;
```
k *is a variable that holds the data on which the current selection depends*

In BASIC:
```
IF k=1 THEN
...
ELSE
...
ENDIF
```
... indicates an instruction (or several instructions).

In C:
```
if (k==1)
{...}
else
{...}
```

Figure C5.3: Syntax examples: if statement

Jump

also known as: branch

including: conditional jump, unconditional jump

allows the order of execution of the statements in a computer program to be changed. Normally instructions are executed in the sequence they are stored but this can be changed by a jump instruction which enables a program to choose which instruction to execute next.

Machine code program instructions are stored consecutively in memory and the control unit works through them sequentially using the *program counter* (see page 283). A jump alters the program counter and thus changes the next instruction to be executed.

Jumps are not normally used with high-level programming languages because they make the program harder to write without causing *logical errors* (see page 238). However, compilers change instructions such as for, while.., and repeat..until loops into suitable combinations of jump instructions.

A jump may be either *conditional* or *unconditional*. An unconditional jump is always executed. A conditional jump is only executed if required by the result of a test, for example 'is a certain variable zero?' or 'has the loop been executed ten times?'.

Case statement

is the name for a statement allowing multiple selection within a program. One of several groups of statements may be executed depending on the data being processed at the time. The other groups of statements are not executed. This enables complex selections to be programmed easily and more reliably than using combinations of *if statements* (see page 210). The name is derived from the program statement used to implement this control structure. See Figure C5.4.

MULTIPLE SELECTION

case statement

In Pascal:
```
case k of
   1:...;
   4:...;
   9:...;
   otherwise ...;
end;
```
k is a variable that holds the data on which the current. selection depends

In BASIC:
```
CASE k OF
   WHEN 1:...
   WHEN 4:...
   WHEN 9:...
   OTHERWISE ...
ENDCASE
```
labels such as 1:, 4: are matched against the control variable data to determine which group of instructions is executed

In C:
```
switch(k) {
   case 1:...;
   case 4:...;
   case 9:...;
   default:...;
}
```
... indicates an instruction (or several instructions).

Figure C5.4: Syntax examples: case statement

C6   Programming (Subprograms)

Concepts and terms to do with programs in general are in
C4 Programming Concepts, other related terms can be found in
C5 Programming (Flow of Execution), C7 Program Syntax,
C8 Program Documentation, and C9 Developing, Testing and
Running Programs.

One of the most powerful techniques available to a programmer is the use of subprograms. Subprograms enable a program to be split into a number of smaller and more manageable sections. Because they can be called in any order, any number of times, the use of subprograms is very flexible.

The design technique of splitting a program into subprograms, each designed and programmed separately, has certain advantages:

- each subprogram is more easily understood, so reducing errors;
- each subprogram may be small enough to be assigned to one programmer, rather than a programming team;
- the subprograms can be tested separately and more thoroughly than a single large program;
- the subprogram can (and should) be written so that it cannot cause errors in other parts of the system.

Another benefit of subprograms is to avoid having to write the same routines many times. The same piece of program code can be used by different parts of the program, which means it only has to be written and tested once. Routines that perform general tasks, such as controlling the screen display, can be re-used in different programs thus saving programming time, testing effort and expense.

When using high-level languages, subprograms are usually implemented by defining **functions** and **procedures**. In machine-code or assembly language programming, subprograms are often called **subroutines**.

The supplier of the operating system will provide subroutines which allow access to the basic operation of the computer - such as displaying a character on the screen or reading data from a file. Operating systems often provide more sophisticated facilities, such as complex screen drawing routines, loading and saving complete files to backing store and spooling printout. These are all accessed as machine-code subroutines, which enables them to be shared between programs. They are effectively a library of subroutines always available to the user through the operating system.

Subprograms generally require data. With functions and procedures, the data is normally passed using **parameters**. Ideally these parameters and any other variables will be **local** to the subprogram, so that the operation of the subprogram cannot affect variables in any other part of the program. If the results from a subprogram are required by the program, then the variables will be passed **by reference**. It is possible for a subprogram to act on **global variables** but this is generally an unwise process, since it could produce adverse effects in other parts of a large program.

Function

is similar to a *procedure* (see below) but returns a single value. The name of the function is used as a variable having that value. Every time the name is used in the program, the function will be executed and the result will appear like any other variable.

A FUNCTION

In Pascal:

The function **square** *is defined like this:*

```
function square(number:integer):integer;
begin
   square:=number*number;                    number is the parameter
end;
```

then it could be used as follows:

```
answer:=square(5);
```

     or   if **square**(x)=25   then ...

Figure C6.1: Example of a function

Procedure

is a *subprogram* (see page 214) which is generally written using a precise formal definition. The procedure is defined and given an identifier (or name). This identifier can be used subsequently just like any other program instruction.

A procedure receives data from the program, manipulates it in some way and makes the results available to the program.

Such procedures are usually associated with high-level languages, although sophisticated assembly languages also allow procedure definitions.

Standard function

is a function provided by a compiler or an interpreter which is so common that it is worth providing as part of the language. For example, almost all languages provide standard functions to work out mathematical results such as log, sine and square root.

Routine

is a part of a program to do a specific task. It may simply be a section of the main program or might be formalised as a procedure, function or subroutine.

Machine-code subroutine

is a subprogram stored in machine code. It may be called from another machine-code program, from an assembly language program or from a high-level language program. The operating system often provides machine-code subroutines for common tasks, such as screen updating and printing, which can be called from any user program in any language.

Usually, when a subroutine is called, the current machine status is stored on the system *stack* (see page 257) and when the subroutine is finished, the previous machine status is restored and the computer can continue running the program from where it left off.

When writing a machine-code subroutine, the programmer is directly manipulating the memory and there is no concept of local variables. If appropriate, the programmer could reserve a section of memory for use by the subroutine.

Common machine-code subroutines are often stored as a *subroutine library* (see below). These machine-code subroutines are often designed as *modules* (see page 170) and are frequently described as machine-code modules.

Subprogram

including: subroutine, call, return, exit, subroutine library, closed subroutine, open subroutine

is a set of program instructions performing a specific task, but which is not a complete program. It must be incorporated into a program in order to be used. Different types of subprogram are known as *procedure, function, routine* (see page 213) or *machine-code subroutine* (see above).

The terms *subprogram* and **subroutine** are generally interchangeable, but sometimes each of these terms could mean something more precise, such as implying a machine-code routine.

A program that uses a subprogram must have an instruction to transfer control to the subprogram. This instruction is known as a *call* to a subprogram. When a subroutine, procedure or function is called the computer will start executing it.

When the subprogram has completed its task it must transfer control back to the calling program, which can only continue from its calling position. This is generally done by a **return** (or **exit**) statement in the subprogram. A subprogram may have more than one return instruction.

Commonly used subprograms are stored in a **subroutine library**. This contains a number of prewritten and pretested subprograms, available to a programmer, which perform common tasks such as display a window, sort a set of numbers or save a file.

Subprograms can be used as either *open* or *closed* subroutines depending on which is more efficient.

In a **closed subroutine**, separate calls to the subroutine use the same piece of program code. A closed subroutine should make the program shorter, although the program could be slower because of the extra instructions required to call the subprogram and return from it.

In an *open subroutine*, the instructions become part of the main program. The skeleton code of the subroutine is modified by the parameters passed to it and the resulting code is copied into the program where required. In some situations open subroutines may have advantages, for example avoiding the extra time taken to call closed subprograms.

Recursive subprogram
including: stopping condition
is one that includes, among the statements making up the subprogram, a call to the same subprogram. The subprogram will continue calling itself recursively, so it must have a means of finishing and continuing the calling program. This is done by a *stopping condition* which causes the subprogram to exit rather than call itself again.

Some mathematical techniques involve repeating a process an indefinite number of times using the results of the previous calculations. See *iteration (mathematical)*, page 58. One method of managing this is the use of recursion where the same subprogram is called repeatedly (with the revised data). When the result is found, the automatic way in which the computer handles the return from the subprogram ensures that execution will continue from the calling point. See Figure C6.2.

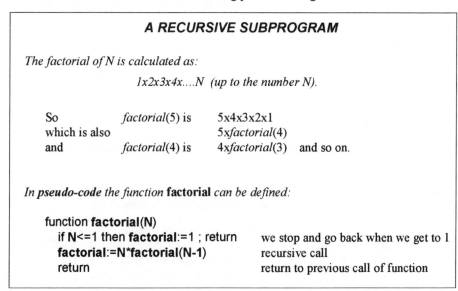

A RECURSIVE SUBPROGRAM

The factorial of N is calculated as:

$$1x2x3x4x....N \quad (up \ to \ the \ number \ N).$$

So	*factorial*(5) is	5x4x3x2x1
which is also		5x*factorial*(4)
and	*factorial*(4) is	4x*factorial*(3) and so on.

In pseudo-code the function **factorial** *can be defined:*

```
function factorial(N)
    if N<=1 then factorial:=1 ; return      we stop and go back when we get to 1
    factorial:=N*factorial(N-1)             recursive call
    return                                  return to previous call of function
```

Figure C6.2: A recursive subprogram

Parameter

including: parameter passing, formal parameter, actual parameter, argument, by value, by reference

is information about a data item being supplied to a function or procedure when it is called.

With a high-level language the parameters are generally enclosed in brackets after the procedure or function name. The data can be a constant or the contents of a variable. See Figure C6.3.

When a function or procedure is defined, a formal parameter, which is a *local variable* (see page 221), is declared and this can be used in the program code for the function or procedure.

PARAMETERS

In Pascal:

when the function **length(side)** is called,

the **parameter** is the variable **side**.

when the function **length('Fred')** is called,

the **parameter** has the value **'Fred'**

when the function **SIN(60)** is called,

the **parameter** has the value **60**

Figure C6.3: Examples of parameters

When the function or procedure is used, the calling program must pass parameters to it (*parameter passing*). The *formal parameter* links the data in the calling program (which will change) to its use in the function or procedure. The data item supplied, known as an *actual parameter* or *argument*, is passed to the local variable. See Figure C6.4.

Actual parameters can be passed to functions and procedures either *by value* or *by reference*. If a data item is passed by value, a (local) copy of the data is used, which is discarded when the subprogram exits. If the data is passed by reference, the location (in memory) of the data is used. This means that any changes are retained after the procedure or function has been completed. Effectively, a single variable has two identifiers, with the subprogram using a pseudonym for the data item involved.

PARAMETER PASSING TO A FUNCTION

function definition:

```
function increment(number);   local variable is number
begin
    number:=number+1;         adds 1 to number
    increment:=number;        function returns the value assigned
end;                          to increment
```

main program:

```
begin
    fred:=2;                  variable fred starts at 2
    bill:=increment(fred);    fred is the parameter - its argument is 2
    write(bill);              variable bill is now 3
end;
```

*Note that the value of **fred** after execution of the function will be different depending on whether the **parameter fred** is passed **by value** or **by reference**. The variable **fred** will still be 2 if passed **by value**, but will be 3 if passed **by reference** (an example of the unplanned effects of using global variables).*

Figure C6.4: An example of parameter passing

Re-entrant program

or: re-entrant subroutine, re-entrant subprogram

is one where the same physical copy of the program code can be used by several different tasks. The program must be written so that data about different tasks does not get mixed up. This is particularly important with systems software, where the computer can be executing the subroutine and an interrupt transfers control to a different program which may then use the same subroutine. If this subroutine is not re-entrant then data may be corrupted and errors may occur.

One example is an interrupt handling routine, which may still be handling one type of interrupt when a different type of interrupt is received.

Another example is the use of a high-level language interpreter on a time-shared system, where a single copy of the interpreter is used by the different users with different data depending on whose time slot is currently being executed .

Macro

including: programmed by example, macro instruction

is a sequence of instructions which are defined as a single element. When a macro is *called* (see *call*, page 214) the sequence of instructions is used. A commonly used routine can be defined as a macro with an identifier and the user can then simply call the macro, using the identifier, to save time and reduce errors.

Macros are used to provide a limited degree of programmability to applications software. They allow the user to customise the application and make it more efficient for their environment (see *human computer interface*, page 80). For example, when using a word processor, a macro could be used to format and print a document quickly in house style. A macro will usually consist of a sequence of commands used by the software, although some software may provide additional commands to make the macros more useful. Sometimes a macro will be ***programmed by example***, storing the user's operations as they occur. See also *macro recording*, page 86.

In a low-level language a macro is also known as a ***macro instruction***. Calling a macro (instruction) would insert the set of instructions into the program at that point, so that the program may include the same set of instructions several times. This is different from a subroutine, where the program jumps to the code to be used, although a macro is sometimes incorrectly called an *open subroutine* (see page 214).

C7   Program Syntax

*This section considers the various elements which make up a
computer program rather than how they are used. Related material
can be found in C4 Programming Concepts, C5 Programming (Flow
of Execution), C6 Programming (Subprograms) and
C10 Programming Languages.*

A computer program, which must be written in a very precise way, is written in a
programming language. Programming languages have a vocabulary of only a limited
number of words with precise rules describing how they may be combined.

Unless a program is written in machine code (which is very rare) it needs to be
translated into some form of machine code before it can be executed. A program can
be **assembled**, **interpreted** or **compiled**, which are all forms of **translation**.

Program
including: program suite
is a complete set of program statements that can be executed by the computer to
perform some task. The program statements may be written in assembly language or
in a high-level language. In order to be executed, the program will need to be
translated by a translator program into machine code.

If a program is not complete, it will not work successfully. A correctly written
program can be thought of as a specification of the algorithm that the design process
has produced. Large software systems are normally *suites* of several programs to do
all the tasks required.

Syntax
is the precise way program statements must be written to be understood by the
computer. It is the set of rules for combining the elements of a programming language
(such as characters and reserved words) into forms that the compiler, interpreter or
assembler can understand. The set of rules does not define meaning, nor the use of the
final construction. But it does allow programmers to know if a statement they are
making is a correctly structured statement.

Semantics
is the meaning of the individual elements which make up a computer language
statement, such as the words, symbols and punctuation. The overall meaning of any
statement, which is made by combining these individual elements, is uniquely
determined by the semantics of the programming language.

Program statement

is any one of the instructions within a program. Program statement is usually taken to mean a statement in a source language instruction, which is human readable, rather than a binary code instruction. When a program statement is translated it often generates several machine-code instructions.

Block

including: block structured language

is a group of program statements which are treated as a single unit. Special *reserved words* (see page 224) or symbols are used to show which statements form a block. Blocks enable complex programs to be constructed from simple elements without any confusion about how statements will be executed. See Figure C7.1.

Programming languages which encourage the use of blocks are called *block structured languages*.

SYNTAX FOR A BLOCK

In Pascal: begin
                    ...   *... indicates the statements which*
                end;   *form the block*

In C: {

                    ...

                }

Figure C7.1: Examples of block structure

Declaration

is a statement in a program which gives the translator information it needs. It is not an operation carried out as the program is executed but is needed for the correct translation of the program. For example, in Pascal the declaration:

var area : integer;

informs the translator that whenever the program uses the variable 'area' it must be treated as an integer (a whole number) rather than as a real number, a string or other data type. Declarations provide information about such things as array sizes, variable types, constants, functions, procedures, library routines and memory allocations. See also *directive*, page 224, and Figure C11.4, page 257.

Label

is an identifier (normally a name) which identifies a particular statement in a program. Labels are normally only needed to indicate the destination of a *jump* (see page 210), which is the next instruction to be used after the jump instruction.

Variable

including: global variable, local variable, strongly typed languages, dynamic variables, static variables

is the identifier (or name) associated with a particular memory location used to store data. By using a name the programmer can store, retrieve and manipulate data without knowing what the data will be.

Global variables can be used anywhere in the program but *local variables* are defined only for use in one part of the program (normally a function or procedure). They come into existence when that part of the program is entered and the data they contain is lost when execution of that part of the program is completed. Using local variables reduces the unplanned effects of a variable being used in another part of the program and accidentally being changed. In a large system, global variables should only be used for data that needs to be shared between sections and should be clearly documented at the design stage.

The data that is identified by a variable can be a number (such as integer or real), a character, a string, a date, a set, a file, an array, a sound sample or any other kind of data. This is called the *variable type* or *data type* (see page 261). In a high-level language, the type may need to be declared when the variable is first used, so that adequate storage space is provided. In a machine-code program, the programmer has to manage the different types of data although they still need to be identified and defined in the design process.

The special features of the data types provided in many high-level languages enable a programmer to write better programs (see *program characteristics*, page 203). These features include:

Strongly typed languages which *validate* (see *validation*, page 192) the data and prevent the wrong kind of data being assigned to a variable.

Dynamic variables which store the data in the most efficient way, often by using a pointer to locate the data which is held in a different location. The programmer has limited control over how or where the data is stored.

Static variables are stored in a known format in a known location allowing the programmer to use unorthodox methods to manipulate the data. Static variables can also be used to preserve local data between the calls to a subprogram.

Scope

is the range of statements for which a *variable* (see above) is valid. This will normally be the subprogram in which it is declared and any other subprograms embedded within that subprogram. A variable cannot be used outside its scope as it appears not to exist.

This concept enables the same identifier to be used in different parts of the program for different purposes without conflict. This concept defines which variable will apply in any given situation during compilation. In a large software project several programmers may be used but this characteristic of variables means they will not have to co-ordinate their use of identifiers.

Dummy variable

is a variable (or identifier) that appears within a program but which is not actually used. This may be because the syntax of the programming language requires a variable but the data contained is not needed.

One use of a dummy variable is illustrated in Figure C7.2. An assignment statement is used to produce an outcome which is desirable and a dummy variable has to be present to accept the (unwanted) result of the assignment.

A DUMMY VARIABLE

In BBC BASIC:

```
110  PRINT "Press any key to continue"
120  dum = GET
130  CLS
```

In line **120** *the statement* **GET** *provides the code of the key being pressed and this is stored in the variable* **dum**. *This value is not needed and is ignored.*

Figure C7.2: *Example of the use of a dummy variable*

The identifiers used in the definition of a *procedure* or a *function* (see page 213) have sometimes been called dummy variables because they will be replaced by other identifiers when the program is executed. Better descriptions for these would be *parameters* (see page 216) or *local variables* (see page 221).

Operator

including: binary operator, unary operator, arithmetic operator, string operator, relational operator, Boolean operator, logical operator

is a symbol used to indicate that a particular operation is to be performed and gives a shorthand method of indicating in a computer program how data is to be manipulated. An obvious example is the '+' sign to mean 'add', but most programming languages now provide a wide variety of operators for different contexts.

OPERATORS

Two different uses of the '**+**' *operator:*

$5 + 7$ means 12

         in the context of the addition of numbers.

But   'Fred' **+** 'Smith' means 'FredSmith'

         in the context of the concatenation of strings.

Figure C7.3: *Example of* '**+**' *operator*

The important distinction between an operator and a program instruction is that an operator manipulates one or more pieces of data. Most operators are *binary operators*, which combine two pieces of data, although *unary operators*, which act on a single piece of data, are commonly used.

UNARY AND BINARY OPERATORS

In Pascal: *operators are in **bold***

unary operators: **not** end_of _file

                             −5

binary operators: result **and** end_of_file

                             length **+** width

Figure C7.4: Examples of unary and binary operators

Arithmetic operators manipulate numbers by carrying out normal arithmetic tasks such as addition or subtraction.

String operators combine or manipulate strings by performing such tasks as concatenation (joining strings) or replication (replacing part or all of a string).

Relational operators compare data and produce an answer of *true* or *false* (see *truth value*, page 312). This answer can control the flow of a program using IF, WHILE or REPEAT UNTIL statements. Examples of relational operators include equals '=' and less than '<'.

Boolean (or *logical*) *operators* combine Boolean values using operators such as AND, OR, NOT to produce a Boolean result, *true* or *false*. This result can control the flow of a program using IF, WHILE or REPEAT UNTIL statements. See *logical operation*, page 200.

RELATIONAL OPERATORS

In these examples, the operators **=** *and* **>** *are shown:*

are two numbers equal ?

           maybe   if number = 5 then ...

is a string alphabetically after another string?

           maybe   repeat ...
                                              until word > 'FRED'

Figure C7.5: Examples of relational operators

Identifier

is a name or label chosen by the programmer to represent an object within a program. The object could be a variable, a function, a procedure, a data type or any other element defined within a program. It is wise to make identifiers as meaningful as possible by using longer, more descriptive words (such as 'sales' rather than 'S'). See also *variable*, page 221.

Constant

is a data item with a fixed value. In a high-level language it is assigned to a variable which cannot be changed when the program is executed. For example if the following declaration is used:

const **pi** = 3.14159265;

then the programmer can use the variable name **pi** which will make writing the program easier.

Similarly the declaration:

const **tax_rate** = 17.5;

allows the programmer to use the variable name **tax_rate** which is also easy to change the value of at a later date if circumstances change. However the program would need recompiling. Only one *declaration* (see page 220) would need altering and not the many occurrences throughout the program.

Machine-code programs also use constants in the form either of a directive assigning a value to a particular mnemonic, or of a data item stored when the program is assembled, which makes it part of the program rather than its data.

It is generally more efficient to use constants, because the data is inserted directly into the program code, rather than variables, which the computer will have to retrieve from memory every time they are required.

Reserved word

also known as: keyword

is any word in the vocabulary of a programming language which can only have the meaning which is defined in the language.

For example, many programming languages have an instruction FOR which is a reserved word and a variable or other identifier cannot be named FOR.

Directive

is a statement in a program that influences the translation process; examples include, controlling the use of memory, production of a program dump, producing debugging information or the use of declarations. While a declaration provides information for the program, a directive affects the environment of the translation process. See also *declaration*, page 220.

C8 Program Documentation

This section is concerned with the written comments and graphical illustrations accompanying a program. The symbols and layout conventions referred to are those given in British Standards BS 4058:1973 and BS 6224:1982.
Related topics can be found in A17 User Documentation, C1 Systems Design and Life Cycle, C2 Systems Documentation and C9 Developing, Testing and Running Programs.

Program documentation is the documentation that is produced for those stages of the **software life cycle** which are concerned with module development and integration. Program documentation is particularly important at the maintenance stage of the system life cycle.

Software will need to be modified during its lifetime and the original programming team is unlikely to be fully available to assist with modifications, hence the team making the modifications will need to rely heavily on the original program and system documentation.

Each module will need to be documented individually at various levels of detail, depending upon its size and complexity. Some of this will be within the programs, using comment facilities to describe, for example, the data used and the processes carried out. This notion of a **self-documenting program** is an important element in program documentation. As well as the use of comment facilities, there are other functions, which can improve the readability of code; these include the use of indentation (for example, for the body of a loop) and the choice of meaningful names for identifiers.

The history of a module is important, for example who wrote it, where and when it was written, when it was modified and by whom, details of modifications made, testing history including some test data and the results obtained. As with other information about a module, some of this can be included in the module listing, often as a standard header of comments.

Diagrams, such as a set of **program flowcharts** or **JSP (Jackson structured programming)** structure diagrams, help to show the flow of a module and can be particularly valuable for showing how modules are integrated into sub-systems and then into the fully integrated software as it is to be delivered.

Another tool which is also helpful at the module design stage is **pseudo-code**, which is a formalised English-like way of describing the steps involved in a program routine.

Program documentation

is the complete description of a program, intended for use in program maintenance. It should include a statement of the purpose of the program, any restrictions on the use of the program, the format for input data, flowcharts, program listing(s), *test data* (see page 237) with expected results, and any generally helpful notes to assist in future modifications. Some parts of program documentation may also be included in *user documentation* (see pages 92, 94).

Program flowchart diagram

also known as: program flowchart
including: flow line
is a graphical representation of the operations involved in a computer program. Symbols are used to represent particular operations and *flow lines* indicate the sequence of operations. Arrows on flow lines may be omitted if the flow is from top to bottom or from left to right.

A program flowchart forms part of the permanent record of a finished program; it is needed for maintenance purposes. Examples of *program flowcharts* are given in Figures C8.9, C8.10, C8.12 and C8.13, pages 231 to 234. See also *design structure diagram*, page 227.

ECMA (European Computer Manufacturers Association) symbols

are standard symbols used in system and program flowcharts. Examples of the use of some ECMA symbols in *system flowcharts* are shown in Figures C2.9 and C2.10 (see pages 181 and 182). Their use in *program flowcharts* is shown in Figures C8.9 and C8.10, pages 231, 232. In addition there are British Standards for flowcharts.

Pseudo-code

is a method of describing a program or system design. It uses control structures and keywords similar to those found in programming languages, but without the strict rules of programming languages. It may be presented in a form which looks like a combination of English and a programming language. (See the example of pseudo-code, Figure C8.11, page 232.)

Decision table

is a table which specifies the actions to be taken when certain conditions arise.

The example, in Figure C8.1, illustrates possible decisions in the problem of how to go to work. N and Y indicate the values of the condition (Yes and No). X indicates that the action is possible. Blank entries indicate that the action is not possible or that no action decision is needed. For example, column three indicates that on a weekday, after 8.00am (which is also after 7.00am) the decision has to be to go by bus without having breakfast.

Condition	Value of condition			
Action	Value of action			
Weekday	N	Y	Y	Y
Before 7.00am		Y	N	N
After 7.00am		N	Y	Y
After 8.00am		N	N	Y
Breakfast		X	X	
Walk		X		
Go by bus			X	X

Figure C8.1: A decision table

Listing

also known as: program listing
is the printed sequence of program statements. This may also include lists of the data required for the program.

Design structure diagram

also known as: structure diagram
is a means of representing the design of a program or system. The British Standards Institution, in its document BS 6224, uses the term to refer to any flowchart and defines standards for drawing them. Examples of the use of BS 6224 symbols are given in Figure C8.12, page 233.

Usually, a structure diagram consists of a number of levels, each of which describes the whole design, but at increasing levels of detail. Examples of Jackson Structure Programming (JSP) notation are given in Figures C2.12 and C2.13 (see pages 184 and 185).

Program flowchart symbol

is a formalised symbol used in a program flowchart diagram. Different shapes indicate the various kinds of activity described by the flowchart. Sometimes highly formalised shapes are used, each having a specific meaning; in other situations very simple boxes with words are used. Provided the meaning is clear, either method is an equally acceptable way of representing a process or system.

Examples of program flowcharts showing how these symbols might be used are given on pages 231 to 234. In Figure C8.13 (page 234) rectangles are used for all processes whilst more formal shapes are used in Figures C8.9 (page 231), C8.10 (page 232) and C8.12 (page 233).

Connector symbol

also known as: continuation symbol

is used to indicate that the flowchart is continued elsewhere at an identically labelled connector point. To simplify layouts, connector symbols may be used to replace lengthy flow lines, or to indicate that the flowchart continues on another page.

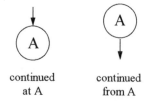

Figure C8.2: Connector or continuation symbol

Input/output symbol

also known as: input symbol, output symbol

is the program flowchart symbol used for any input or output operation. The description in the box may include the device or medium for the process.

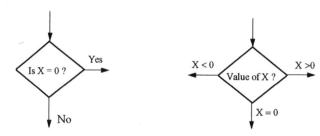

Figure C8.3: Input/output symbol

Decision box

also known as: decision symbol

is the flowchart symbol used to indicate points in a program where decisions are made. There are a number of different ways of representing decisions diagramatically. One set uses the diamond shape in a variety of ways. A decision box may have more than two exits. Four forms are shown in Figure C8.4. Other versions of decisions are shown in Figure C8.5.

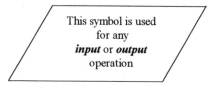

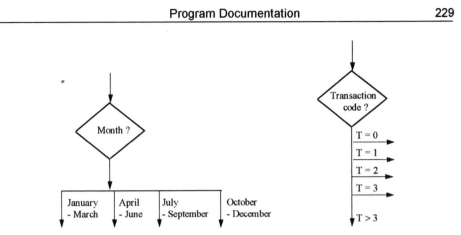

Figure C8.4: *Alternative forms of decision box*

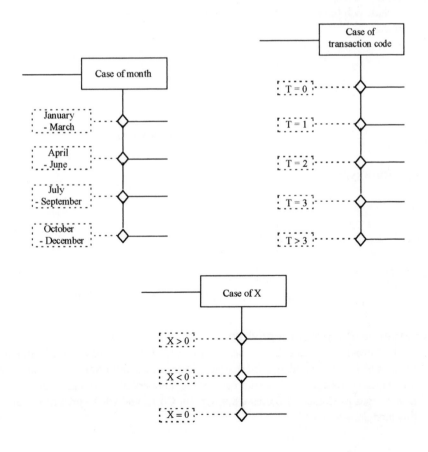

Figure C8.5: *Alternative forms of decision defined in BS 6224*

Process box

also called: operation box, process symbol, operation symbol

is a box used as a flowchart symbol for any operation or sequence of instructions that does not involve a decision. The box can be any suitable size.

This box can be used for
any *operation*
or *sequence of instructions*
not involving a decision

Figure C8.6: *Process box or symbol*

Start/stop symbol

is the flowchart symbol used for both starting and stopping points in a flowchart. A flowchart will have only one start point but there may be more than one stop in a flowchart.

This symbol is used for
both *start* and *stop*

Figure C8.7: *Start/stop box or symbol*

Subroutine symbol

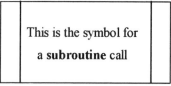

This is the symbol for

a **subroutine** call

Figure C8.8: *Subroutine box or symbol*

An example of a program module

This program module reads a series of records from a transaction file and uses the valid transactions to update a master file. Details of invalid transactions are output on a line printer, together with a summary of the numbers of valid and invalid transactions processed. Figures C8.9, C8.10, C8.12 and C8.13 give flowcharts for this module.

1) Program module flowchart (in traditional notation)

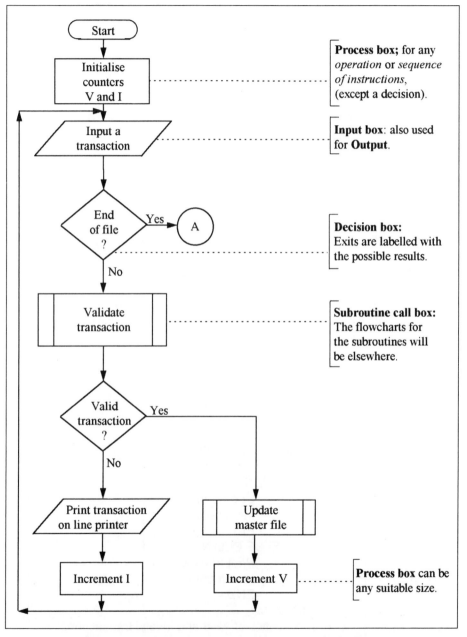

Figure C8.9: Program module flowchart in traditional form

The flowchart continues on the next page.

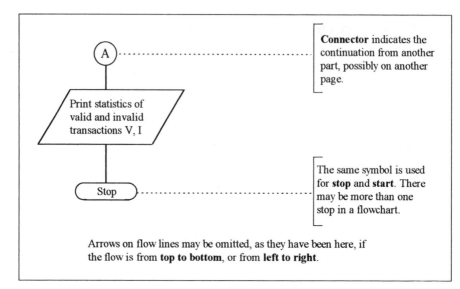

Figure C8.10: Program module flowchart (continuation)

2) Pseudo-code version of program module

In this method of presenting the program module, an English-like approach is combined with the use of a structured layout, which is closely akin to some computer languages.

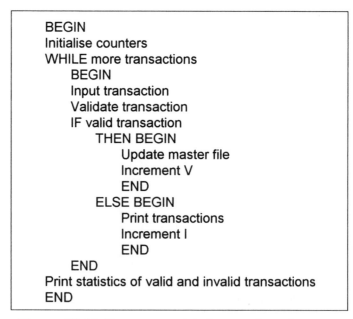

```
BEGIN
Initialise counters
WHILE more transactions
    BEGIN
    Input transaction
    Validate transaction
    IF valid transaction
        THEN BEGIN
            Update master file
            Increment V
            END
        ELSE BEGIN
            Print transactions
            Increment I
            END
    END
Print statistics of valid and invalid transactions
END
```

Figure C8.11: Program module in pseudo-code

3) Program module flowchart (in BS 6224 notation)

The British Standard for flowcharts, or *design structure diagrams* as they are called
in the British Standards Institution document BS 6224, does not generally use arrows.

Since the flow is from *top to bottom*, and from *left to right* at each junction, when
the end of an intermediate structure is reached, a 'fall back' to the original junction
takes place.

At a decision junction a small diamond shape is drawn.

If the condition is **true**, flow is from **left to right**.

If the condition is **false**, flow is from **top to bottom**.

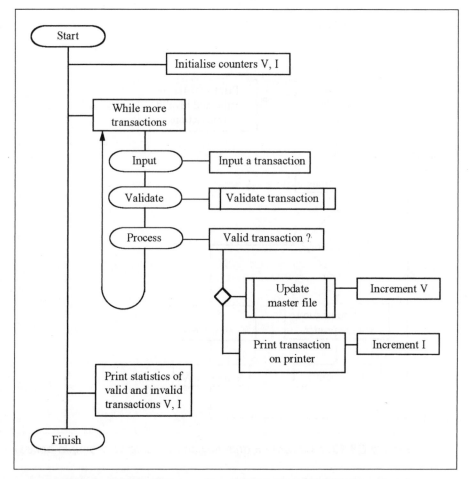

Figure C8.12: *Program flowchart (using BS 6224 symbols)*

An alternative version is shown overleaf in Figure C8.13.

4) Program module flowchart (simplified notation)

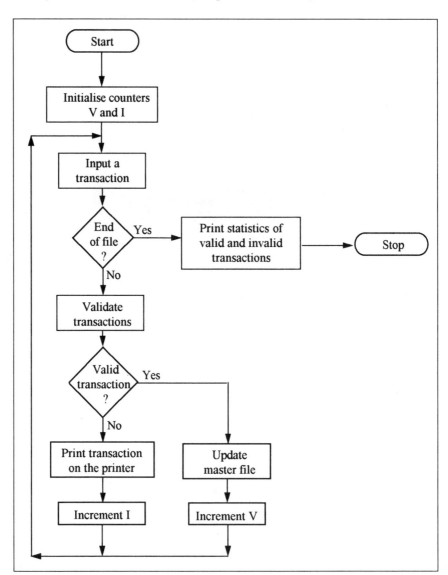

Figure C8.13: *Program module flowchart (using very simple boxes)*

C9   Developing, Testing and Running Programs

*Other related material can be found in C1 Systems Design and Life
Cycle, C4 Programming Concepts, C5 Programming (Flow of
Execution), C6 Programming (Subprograms) and C7 Program
Syntax.*

With so many personal computers in use in everyday life it is easy to think of
computers only being used interactively, in which the computer is given an instruction
and there is an immediate effect or result. There are a number of other ways of using
a computer system which are often more efficient.

With larger computerised systems it may be much more efficient to collect the data
and process it later as a batch (**batch processing**). The data required is collected and
passed to the computer in a single collection (a batch) that the computer works
through from beginning to end. For example, a payroll system often uses batch
processing because salaries and wages are paid on a regular basis and involve large
amounts of data. Batch processing avoids wasting computer time on manual data
input during processing.

Some situations require an almost immediate response (**interactive processing**).
For example, booking an airline ticket from one travel agent would need a fast
response to ensure that other customers were not unduly delayed looking for the same
flight at another agent.

Other situations may require the computer to respond without any effective delay
(called **real-time processing**) such as controlling a chemical plant or an air traffic
control system.

Since data is valuable, it is unwise to allow users unrestricted access either to the
computer system or to the data on the system. If a user modifies an information
system, then other users will be hindered when they try to use it and the modification
may also introduce faults into the system. Unrestricted access to data gives
opportunities for mistakes, conflict between users, fraud and the infringement of data
protection legislation. A good reason for tight management control over a large
project is to ensure that the work of various individuals does not conflict, which could
possibly result in the introduction of errors.

Even with personal computer systems, such as a word processing package, a long
process of development and testing is undertaken to ensure that the system works well
for the customer.

These issues mainly affect the design of a complete computerised system. But of
course much of the effort is directed at the program or programs which produce the
results. In many cases the development of an information system is, in fact, the
development of the software, consisting of the set of computer programs which make
up the system.

The development process for a program involves a cycle of compilation and execution of the program to test for errors, investigation of these errors (**debugging**), modification of the program, and repetition of the testing cycle. The resulting system is then supplied in a way that should be easy to install and run.

The testing process is carried out with a **test plan**, designed to test the widest range of possible situations, which can be used repeatedly until no more faults are found, which ought to mean that there are no faults. The program will normally have to be **compiled** to produce an **object program** which can be **executed**.

Various types of error might be detected. Some, such as **syntax errors**, can be easily identified and corrected. Others, such as **logical errors**, will require much more investigation. These can be investigated using techniques such as **dry runs**, program **traces**, **breakpoints**, **dumps** and **variable checks**, and special software called **debugging tools**.

When the system has passed these tests it can be made available to customers who will run it on their computer system. The user has to be aware that problems may still occur in the **operation** of a computerised system, due to the specific hardware configuration or the interaction between several systems in use at the time.

Source program

including: object program, source language

is the program as written by the programmer using a programming language. It is normally written using a *text editor* (see page 280) and is an understandable document rather than consisting of binary codes. It must be assembled, compiled or interpreted before it can be executed.

When a source program is compiled or assembled a new program is generated called the *object program*. This is the program that is executed. The source program is kept in case any changes have to be made, in which case the modified source program would be recompiled. It is not generally possible to modify the object program if the source program is lost. It is the object code which is sold and this cannot be modified by the user.

The object program is normally in the machine code of the computer being used. There are some exceptions to this, where *intermediate code* (see page 246) is produced. When the program is executed, the intermediate code is easily translated into machine code.

The programming language in which the source program is written is known as the *source language.*

Execution

sometimes: program execution

is the operation of a computer program. Unless the program is being interpreted (see *interpreter*, page 276), it must be in machine-code. If the machine-code is produced by compiling a high-level language program, it is the *object program* (see above) that is executed. If the machine-code is produced from an assembly language program it is the assembled program (see *assembler*, page 274) that is executed.

Test plan

including: test data

is the schedule for testing a program or a system. It is usually a table showing each
item which needs to be tested. The test plan should cover every possible type of input
including those which may be made by mistake, such as values that are too large, too
small or just silly. It should also work in the case of too much data being supplied too
fast. The data used, when following a test plan, is called *test data.* Both the test plan
and the test data need to be available as part of the documentation of the program or
system. For a program the test data will show the inputs to the program and specify
what the results should be, if the program works correctly.

Debugging

including: diagnostic aid, debugging tool, diagnostic program, debugger, cross-
referencer, trace, variable check, step mode, single stepping, post mortem routine

is the detection, location and correction of faults (or bugs) causing errors in a
program. The errors are detected by observing *error messages* (see page 238) or by
finding unexpected results in the test output. The location of the faults may be
obvious (identified by the error message) or may require extensive investigation.
Tools are available to help in this process, particularly with assembly language
programs, where comprehensive error reporting may not exist. These *diagnostic aids*
and *debugging tools* include:

Diagnostic programs attempt to detect and locate faults in another program or a
     system by supervising its operation and providing additional information about
     possible errors.

Debuggers are programs which provide a range of facilities enabling the programmer
     to investigate the conditions when errors occur.

Cross-referencers are programs which identify where variables are used in a
     program. This allows errors such as unplanned use of duplicate names to be
     identified.

Traces are printouts which show the statements executed as the program is being run
     and may include the values of variables. The program flow can be compared
     with the *trace table* (see page 238) to identify where an error has occurred.

Variable checks list the contents of variables at specific points in the program. This
     allows their contents to be compared with the expected values, perhaps from a
     dry run (see page 238). *Breakpoints* (see page 240) provide a way of stopping
     the program to look at the contents of variables.

Step mode or (*single stepping*) is the execution of a program one statement at a time
     under user control. It allows the user to observe the effects of each statement
     after it has been executed.

Post mortem routines display or print the values of variables at the point when a
     program failed. In some systems it is a list which indicates where the program
     failure occurred and gives the latest values of registers, stacks and other
     variables. See *register*, page 283 and *stack*, page 257.

Error

including: bug, error message, listing file, execution error, run-time error, compilation error, linking error, syntax error, statement syntax error, program syntax error, structure error, logical error

is a fault or mistake in a program or information system causing it to produce wrong results or not to work. A *bug* is a fault in a program which causes errors. Most computers attempt to indicate the likely source of an error by producing *error messages*. Usually these messages are produced either on the user's screen if the error is attributed to the user, or on the operator's console for more serious errors.

When a program is being developed, many simple errors will be detected during the compilation process. A *listing file* can be generated during compilation; this will contain the source program with error messages and other diagnostic information.

The many types of error can be classified as follows:

Execution errors or *run-time errors* are errors detected during program execution. These errors, such as overflow and division by zero, can occur if a mistake is made in the processing algorithm or as a result of external effects not catered for by the program, such as lack of memory or unusual data.

Compilation errors are errors detected during compilation and are usually *syntax errors* (see below).

Linking errors occur when a compiled program is linked to library routines. For example, if a particular subroutine is not present in the library or the number of parameters provided is wrong.

Syntax errors occur either when program statements cannot be understood because they do not follow the rules laid down by the programming language, *statement syntax errors*, or when program structures are incorrectly nested, *program syntax errors* or *structure errors*. Examples of statement syntax errors include wrong punctuation and misspelling of reserved words and variables. Examples of program syntax errors include control structures incorrectly nested or incorrectly terminated.

Logical errors are mistakes in the design of a program, such as a branch to a wrong statement, or the use of an inappropriate mathematical formula. A logical error will be recognised because the program produces wrong results or an incorrect display. It is unlikely to generate an error message because the error is in the program design.

Dry run

including: trace table

is working through a section of a program manually. This is useful for locating errors, particularly run-time errors. A dry run can be performed on a section of an assembler program or on a high-level language program. A dry run would usually be carried out on parts of a program rather than on a whole program.

Working from the listing of a section of a program, a *trace table* is constructed with a column to identify the instruction executed and columns for the contents of each variable.

TRACE TABLES

*Example of a **trace table** for a very simple program in an asembler language:*

Current Address	Instruction	Accumulator	&98FF	&9800	&9801	Display
&8001	INP &98FF		5			
&8002	INP &9800			15		
&8003	LND &9800	15				
&8004						

*Example of a **trace table** for a very simple program in a high-level language:*

Line number	Height	Width	Area	Display	
1	5				
2		15			
3			75		
4				75	

*An alternative form of **trace table** for the simple program in a high-level language:*

(Showing the position after line 3 of the program)

Many programmers simply use a box for each variable, making changes to the boxes as instructed by the program but without constructing a formal trace table.

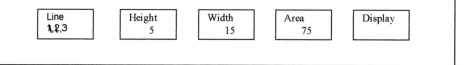

Figure C9.1: *Examples of trace tables*

The programmer follows the instructions from the listing, adding a new line to the trace table each time an instruction is executed. The new line of the trace table should indicate the instruction, either by its machine address or by its line number, and show any changes to the variables. See Figure C9.1.

Run

including: run-time

is putting a program or information system into action so that it can perform the data processing is was designed to do.

Run-time is the time during which a program or information system is in operation. Often data has to be provided during run-time and some effects, such as *run-time errors* (see page 238), can only be detected when the system is operating.

Breakpoint

is a position within the program where the program is halted as an aid to debugging. Whilst the program is halted, the programmer can investigate the values of variables, memory locations and registers. This provides additional information to help locate errors, particularly run-time errors.

This facility is often used with assembly language programs and may be incorporated into the operating system or provided by a *debugger* (see page 237). The machine-code addresses of breakpoints can be set, the progress of the program can be monitored and the program will halt when the instruction at a breakpoint address is reached. A debugger allows the contents of computer memory to be displayed. It may be possible to resume execution after stopping the program at a breakpoint.

A programmer may insert breakpoints in a program as part of a testing strategy. These will be deleted when the tests are successful.

Similar facilities have been developed for use with high-level languages, in particular interpreted languages, but these are less commonly available.

Dump

including: screen dump

is to copy the contents of a file, or the contents of part of immediate access store, to backing store or to an output device. The output is known as the dump, and may be used to test the integrity of a data file, or to assist in program error detection. A dump may also be made as part of a backup process.

A *screen dump* is a representation of the screen stored as a data file or produced as a print-out. A screen dump is an easy way of printing data collected together on the screen and produces a copy of the current screen display.

Patch

is a small fragment of code provided by a software supplier, to enable a user to modify or correct their copy of software without requiring a complete replacement.

Run-time system

is the complete set of software, including any *library programs* or *library routines* (see page 274), that must be present in a computer before a particular program can be executed.

Process state

including: ready, running, blocked, suspended, stopped, completed, deadly embrace

is the status of a program submitted to a computer system for *running* (see *run*, page 239).

The concept is particularly useful with *multiprogramming* systems (see page 278) where several programs may be being processed at the same time. This includes multi-user computer systems which will be operating using some form of multiprogramming.

Programs submitted to a computer, either for batch or interactive processing, are added to a job queue and are then in one of a number of process states:

Ready: a program waiting to continue execution by the central processor. Several programs may be ready at any one time, waiting for execution.

Running: a program being executed by the central processor. A central processor can only execute one program at a time, so only one program will be running (except in a computer with several processors). Execution may be interrupted, in which case the program will be either suspended or blocked.

Blocked: a program waiting for a peripheral. The peripheral may be in use by another program or already committed to a task for this program. When the peripheral becomes available, the status returns to *Ready*, allowing the central processor to continue executing the program when it can.

Suspended: the operating system decides that a program has to be interrupted, perhaps because it is taking up too much time. The program status will be returned to *Ready* to await a further time allocation.

Stopped: a program has been *aborted* (see *abort*, page 242).

Completed: a program has run to a proper conclusion. It will then be deleted from the job queue.

Deadly embrace: a condition in which no processing takes place at all and the system appears to be *hung* (see page 242); this could be the result of a number of situations, for example process A is waiting for process B to complete, which it cannot do until process C is complete, which it cannot do until process A is complete..., the chain could, of course, be even longer.

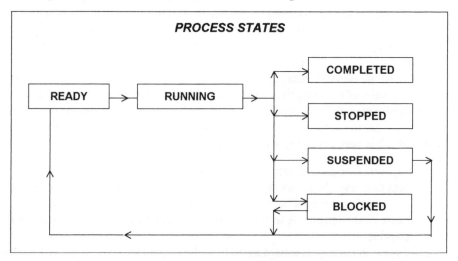

Figure C9.2: Program process states

Down time

is the time when a computer system is not available (*down*) to the user. This may be because the computer is being maintained, it has broken down, there is a failure in the operating system or there is a communications failure.

Abort

is stopping the execution of a program or system before it has reached its normal conclusion. The run may be aborted by the program itself, the operating system or an operator.

A program may be aborted if an error is detected or if the operator requests it. An error such as a missing file will cause a program to be aborted. If the program appears to be working incorrectly, the operator may request that it is aborted. Sometimes the operating system may not be able to abort a run; in this case the computer will not respond and will have to be reset. See also, *hung*, below.

Crash

also known as: bomb

including: system crash, hung

is the term used to describe the situation when a computer system unexpectedly stops working correctly. This could be caused by a hardware failure, an error causing the program to *abort* (see above) or an error causing the computer to be hung.

A *system crash* is a major failure of a computer leaving it inoperable and all users unable to continue.

A computer is *hung* if it does not produce any output, and appears to have ceased to operate. This is often caused by an *infinite loop* (see page 208). The operator will then attempt *recovery* (see below) and if that is not possible, the computer will need to be *reset* (see below).

If a crash occurs on a personal computer, it is possible that any recent unsaved alterations to work or data will be lost.

Recovery

including: warm start, cold start, reset

is the process of returning the system to normal operation after an error. The procedures may differ, depending on the type of program in use and the type of error (whether due to hardware, software or data). Recovery will include identifying any data that has been corrupted and deciding on the restart process.

Warm start: execution is continued from the point at which the error occurred, using data that may already have been processed and stored in memory. Because the computer's memory is not initialised, there is a risk that corrupted data may cause further errors. A warm start enables a fast recovery of the system, if it is possible.

Cold start: the system is started again from the beginning. The computer's memory is initialised and the system should now work as expected. This can be a slow recovery, since the system may have to repeat processing already performed. See also *crash*, above.

Reset: the system is returned to its initial state, as if it had just been switched on or started. This is often used after a program has caused a computer to crash or behave erratically, when the computer may continue to work, but corruption of the contents of critical areas of memory may lead to erratic behaviour and loss of data.

Immediate mode

is the use of a command or program language statement outside a program. The instruction is executed and the results are produced before the next instruction can be entered.

Usually, immediate mode is only available with interpreted systems. Examples include, using a command line interpreter, **DOS** commands and checking the values of variables when using a language such as **BASIC** or **LOGO**.

Screen echo

also known as: echo

is to show on the computer display the instruction being executed at a particular instant or a message indicating the progress of a process. For example, when a document is being printed, a message may appear on the screen which says "printing in progress".

C10 Programming Languages

Other related material can be found in C13 Systems Software.

A program within the computer is a sequence of instructions, held as electronic patterns in memory, consisting of **machine code**. The programmer starts with a design, or algorithm, of what the program is intended to do, but needs a means of expressing this idea in terms that can be understood by the computer. This expression is usually called the **program**, but needs to be translated into the electronic patterns. The written program is known as the **source code** and is translated (by a **translator** program) into the machine code (or **object code**).

Programming languages are obviously not the same as human languages - most obviously because (at present) they are only written and never spoken. But the term 'language' is a very appropriate one. Languages have a **grammar** (or **syntax**) which states the rules of the language. This makes it possible to recognise 'wrong', ungrammatical uses of language, and avoid spending time and effort trying to understand something which has no meaning. The syntax of a language is not simply a collection of 'correct' uses - it is a set of rules that allow programmers to know if a statement they are making is a correct statement, *even if the statement has never been used before*. Languages also have meanings (or **semantics**). One important difference between human and computer languages is that computer languages are never ambiguous - a statement always has just one meaning (even if it isn't the meaning that was intended).

Historically, the first languages were attempts to simplify the process of programming the electronic patterns directly, which was accomplished by entering these patterns as 1s and 0s - binary digits, or bits. If the pattern 101010 was the code for 'ADD', it was easier to allow the programmer to write ADD and let the computer substitute the appropriate code. Because they 'assembled' instructions that could have been coded directly as bits, these languages are known as **assembly languages** and were translated into instructions by **assembler** programs.

Assembly languages are very close to the actual machine code of a computer. A different assembly language is needed for each type of computer. Because of this close link, such languages are known as **machine-oriented** or **low-level**.

As programming became more sophisticated, **translators** were written which allowed programmers to write instructions that were closer to the way they thought about the problem. A mathematical computation could be expressed in mathematical symbols, and the translator would turn this into the (often quite lengthy) sequence of machine-code instructions to perform that computation. This also allowed the programmer to use a single language for different computers, provided that the language was translated by a translator appropriate for the computer in use.

Because such languages were at a different level from the details of how the machine worked, and because they expressed programming steps in a way more suited to the problem than the computer, such languages are known as **problem-oriented** or **high-level** languages.

Writing a program takes a long time, compared to carrying out the instructions in the program. This means that the translation process need not be very fast, provided that the machine code that is produced is efficient. There are several ways of organising the translation. Some translators take in a written program and produce working machine code; others translate into assembly language, and use an existing assembler for the last stage of translation. A third way is to produce an **intermediate code** which is a sort of language (written by the computer) that is easier to translate into machine code, because it is at a lower level.

Translators which produce another program at a lower level (machine-code, assembly language, intermediate code) which could, with more difficulty, have been written by a programmer, are called **compilers**. Compiled programs can be executed without needing the original translator any more. So, after compilation, a user's program need consist of no more than the translated version.

There is also another way of organising the translation. Some translators are designed to recognise that there are many tasks that will be repeated often in a single program (such as printing to the screen): such translators, called **interpreters**, keep a very efficient version of this frequently-used code ready in the translator, and arrange that it is **this** that is used whenever the task is needed. Interpreters have a speed advantage (the code for common tasks does not need to be generated, as it is already there), but a corresponding disadvantage is that all of the translator program needs to be present when the program is executed. So even a quite small program will need a lot of space in the computer when it is running.

Interpreters often translate and execute the program line-by-line, converting a program statement into a sequence of instructions branching to the appropriate routines in the translator software, and execute these routines without retaining the translated version. In a program with a loop, this means that the same statement will be translated each time it is encountered. For this and similar reasons, interpreted programs are usually slower in execution than compiled ones. Because they need the interpreter always present, they are also usually larger. Both disadvantages are outweighed by their ease of use.

Interpreters begin execution of a program immediately and they can work on an incomplete program, hence they are commonly used for interactive languages, like BASIC, where it is important for beginners to see their results as soon as possible after completing their program. Compilers are best used for languages designed for writing software that will be used many times without change - such as systems software and applications packages.

A translator is just a program itself. For efficiency, the version in use is usually a machine-code version, but it was originally written in a higher-level language, and was itself translated.

New languages are designed when existing ones no longer provide adequate facilities - specialist graphics and statistics languages have emerged, for instance. At present, their translators are often written in a particular high-level language called **C** which has its own specialised features to allow the easy design of such systems software.

A table giving comparative information about some significant computer languages appears as Table C10.1 (see pages 250 and 251).

Assembly language

is one very close to the computer's own machine code. Instead of writing actual machine-code instructions (which would typically need to be entered in binary or hexadecimal), the assembly language programmer is able to make use of symbolic variable names and labels. These are then assembled (by software known as an assembler) into the appropriate machine-code instructions. See also *machine code*, page 247 and *assembler*, page 274.

Fourth-Generation Language (4GL)

Although the 'generations' of computers are not precisely defined, it was inevitable that software designers would advertise their software by attaching an appropriate up-to-date descriptive label. Fourth-generation languages are thus those that were being invented around the time of the development of *fourth-generation computers* (see page 112). This is slightly more than an advertising label, however: a characteristic of these languages was the recognition that computing power was becoming more freely and more cheaply available, and that popular software would be that which could reduce the time taken to *develop* users' programs. Thus RPG, the Report Program Generator, was a fourth-generation language that attempted to make the production of printed reports easier – not necessarily making it quicker to print out the report, but making it much faster to specify the format for the report.

High-level language

including: problem-oriented language

is one designed to help a programmer express a computer program in a way that reflects the problem that is being solved, rather than the precise details of how the computer will produce the solution. These languages are often described as ***problem-oriented languages***. The programmer will certainly be allowed to use long descriptive names for the variables, and to structure the program into subroutines or functions to help keep the logic of the solution clearly visible. Mathematical notation will be permitted, allowing calculations to be specified in the same way as in written mathematics. When the language is translated, the *compiler* (see page 275) or *interpreter* (see page 276) will take care of the details of the many machine-code instructions necessary to cause the computer to execute the program. Compare this with the definition of *low-level language*, page 247.

A table giving some comparative information about some significant high-level languages appears as Table C10.1 (see pages 250 and 251).

Intermediate code

Computer programs are generally translated into instructions for the computer to follow in one of two distinct ways, compilation or interpretation. There is also a possible 'mixed' approach, in which the program is first compiled into an intermediate code made up of simpler instructions, which are then interpreted when the program is executed. One advantage of this approach, which has not been as fully exploited as might be hoped, is to reduce the number of translation programs that are necessary: to fully implement (say) 10 different computer languages on 15 machines would normally require 150 translator programs to be written – 15 for each language. Using an agreed intermediate code, 10 translators would be required to get from a language to the intermediate code, and a further 15 translators to get from the intermediate code to the machine code of the computers – a total of only 25 pieces of software. See also *compiler*, page 275 and *interpreter*, page 276.

Low-level language
including: machine-oriented language
Some programming languages are necessarily close to the design of the machine; the available instructions reflect the way the machine is built. *Assembly language* (see page 246) and *machine code* (see below) are good examples. Such languages are necessary for programming tasks connected with the running of the computer, such as driving displays and printers, or for writing translator programs. For this reason they are described as ***machine-oriented languages***. They are not generally good for problem-solving, for which *high-level languages* (see page 246) are necessary.

Machine code
is the set of all possible instructions available from the electronic design of a particular computer. These instructions usually reflect the hardware design of the computer, and operate on very basic items of data, such as bytes or even single bits. These instructions may be given memorable names in the associated documentation, but can only be understood by the computer when expressed in binary notation. Hence machine code is very difficult to write without mistakes. In practice, machine-code programming is achieved by the programmer writing in *assembly language* (see page 246), which is close to machine code.

Query language
including: Structured Query Language (SQL), Query By Example (QBE)
Large databases must allow the user – who may not be a skilled programmer – to ask for information to be extracted: for example, "How many invoices more than 3 months old are recorded in the database that have not yet been paid?" Query languages are simplified programming languages, restricted to querying a database.

A few keywords are used to link the names of fields in the database, and to specify values for comparison:

SELECT invoices WHERE date-sent < 16-04-98 AND total-owing > 0

Popular query languages that you might come across include ***Structured Query Language (SQL)*** or ***Query By Example (QBE)***. See also *database*, page 19.

Report generator

including: RPG (Report Program Generator)

is a piece of software that allows a business user, who is not necessarily a skilled computer programmer, to specify a printed report that draws on values from a database, or the results of calculations performed by the computer. Such software is closer to an applications package than most items considered 'languages', but is generally included in listings of available computer programming languages. The structure of the software allows the user to design the report using statements that are very similar in appearance to programming language statements. The table of computer languages, Table C10.1 (pages 250 and 251), includes **RPG**, the **Report Program Generator**, as the commonest example of such a report generator.

Data manipulation language (DML)

is a form of high-level language, usually part of a *database management system* (see page 20) which is designed to allow the user to access (query), store (insert) and change (update) data in a *database* (see page 19).

Authoring language

including: authoring tool

is a language designed to assist in the preparation of materials that are to be presented on a computer. These materials may be learning material for computer managed learning, web pages or any other situation for which computer presentation is desirable or appropriate. These authoring languages are sometimes referred to as *authoring tools*.

An authoring language for computer managed learning allows the author to specify what material will be displayed (this might include the use of sound or video) and what questions are to be asked of the student. Answers to these questions will be listed, together with the action to be taken in response to each one, and the section of the teaching that follows; in this way, remedial lessons can be offered to students who score badly, while students giving correct answers can be directed along a faster route through the material. See also *computer aided learning*, page 74.

Other specific authoring languages include, *virtual reality mark-up language* (see page 45) and *HyperText mark-up language* (see page 40).

PROLOG

is an unusual high-level programming language. It does not fit traditional classifications, as used in the table of programming languages, Table C10.1. 'Programming' in PROLOG involves adding a large number of 'facts' and 'rules' to the system, using mathematical logic notation, and asking the PROLOG system to deduce conclusions from these. The name comes from 'PROgramming with LOGic'.

FORTH

is an unusual low-level programming language, well suited to control applications. The language consists of a number of pre-defined 'words' at a level very close to machine code: the programmer then defines new words, which are added to the language, just as if they were part of the original definition. Because speed of execution is important, the language uses *reverse Polish notation* (see page 196), in which to add 1 to 2 you would write: 1 2 **ADD**

Backus-Naur form (BNF)

including: replacement rules

is a way of describing the syntax of a computer language. The name comes from its two inventors, although it is sometimes held to be 'Backus *normal* form'. A BNF description is expressed as a series of ***replacement rules*** that describe how some element of the language is built up from choices of simpler elements. See Figure C10.1 for an example.

BACKUS-NAUR FORM

Part of a possible definition of the LET assignment statement in the BASIC language:

    <LET-statement> := [LET] <numeric-variable> = <numeric-expression>|

                     [LET] <string-variable> = <string-expression>

This says that the 'LET statement' *can take either of two forms, shown by the vertical bar, which represents alternatives.*

The first form is

        the word LET (which is optional, because it is shown in square brackets),

        followed by a numeric variable,
        followed by the equals sign '=',
        followed by a numeric expression.

Items shown in angle brackets '<' and '>' have definitions elsewhere in the full language specification.

For example, it is likely that elsewhere you would find the line:

        <string-variable> := <numeric-variable>$

showing that a string variable obeys the same rules as a numeric variable, but is followed by a dollar sign '$'

Items shown in curly brackets '{' and '}' may occur any number of times, including none.

For example the definition of a numeric variable may be:

        <numeric-variable> := <letter>{alphanumeric}

showing that the variable name must start with a letter, but that following characters, if any, may be either letters or numbers.

Figure C10.1: *Example of Backus-Naur form*

Language	Date	derivation of name	translation	structure
Ada	1975-83	after Countess Lovelace	compiled	imperative
ALGOL	1958-68	*ALGO*rithmic *L*anguage	compiled	imperative
APL	1957-68	*A P*rogramming *L*anguage	interpreted	functional
BASIC	1964	*B*eginners *A*ll-purpose *S*ymbolic *I*nstruction *C*ode	interpreted	imperative
C	1972	see notes	compiled	imperative
C++	1979-83	*C plus a bit more*	compiled	object-oriented
COBOL	1959-60	*CO*mmon *B*usiness *O*riented *L*anguage	compiled	imperative
FORTH	late 1960's	pun on 'Fourth'	compiled	unique
FORTRAN	1954-57	*FOR*mula *TRAN*slation	compiled	imperative
Java	1991-95	*Its 'exotic, exciting, adrenaline-pumping connotations'*	compiled	object-oriented
Lisp	1959	*Lis*t Processing	interpreted	functional
LOGO	1966-68	Greek for 'thought'	interpreted	functional
Pascal	1968-71	after Blaise Pascal	compiled	imperative
PL/1	1963-64	*P*rogramming *L*anguage 1	compiled	imperative
POP-2	late 1960's	author: Dr. R. J. Popplestone	interpreted	functional
PROLOG	1972	*PRO*gramming in *LOG*ic	interpreted	logical
RPG	1964	*R*eport *P*rogram *G*enerator	compiled	imperative
Simula	1965	from *simulation*	compiled	object-oriented
Smalltalk	1972-80	to emphasise nature of language interface	compiled	object-oriented
SNOBOL	1962-68	*Stri*N*g O*riented *S*ym*B*olic *L*anguage	compiled	functional
Visual BASIC	early 1990's	*screen based extension of BASIC*	interpreted or compiled	imperative

NOTES:

The **date** is that of initial development; most languages have been continuously improved since invention.

translation indicates the most usual method, not necessarily the *only* one.

structure indicates:

whether the language is used by giving instructions on how to solve the problem (an algorithm, or conventional program) – *'imperative'*;

whether it is based on functions or procedures applied to sets of data – *'functional'*;

or whether its basic structure is that of an *object-oriented* programming language.

Table C10.1: Programming languages

notes	Language
mainly used for large military systems, sponsored by US Dept of Defense	Ada
originally for (paper) description of algorithms – an influential language with several distinct versions (Algol-60, Algol-68)	ALGOL
easier to write than to read; it uses symbols not always found on regular keyboards – requires large memory	APL
easy to learn and (in modernised versions) the world's most frequently encountered programming language, especially on micro-computers	BASIC
systems programming language, derived from 'B' which derived in turn from BCPL, which derived from CPL	C
object-oriented features added to C	C++
easier to read than to write; large memory requirements, hence a mainframe language; highly structured data suited to business use	COBOL
very different from other languages: used in control and graphics applications – see separate description in this section	FORTH
mainstream scientific programming language; language still reflects punched-card input – too early to be a structured programming language	FORTRAN
platform-independent extension of C for the Internet	Java
artificial intelligence uses – an influential language, in that many other languages have been derived from it	Lisp
based on Lisp, but noted for its 'turtle graphics' subset; popular in education, as it 'teaches' thinking as well as programming	LOGO
mainstream general-purpose structured language of the 1970s and 1980s	Pascal
introduced new simple concepts but never gained popularity	PL/1
artificial intelligence uses	POP-2
artificial intelligence uses – a very different language	PROLOG
almost an applications package for business reports	RPG
simulation	Simula
forerunner of most graphics interfaces	Smalltalk
string manipulation language	SNOBOL
provides quick and easy means of creating interface applications for MS Windows™	Visual BASIC

FORTH and **PROLOG** are both rather unusual languages and are described on page 248. **Java**, and some other languages, may be encoded into an intermediate code which can then be interpreted on other systems.

Table C10.1: Programming languages

C11 Data Representation

Related material, particularly about numbers and their
representation, can be found in C12 Numeric Data Representation.

The essence of any computer is its ability to store and manipulate data. The data is stored electronically and this section looks at the principles used to interpret the stored data as understandable information.

Within the computer all information is represented as some combinations of physical properties. What these properties mean depends on how we interpret them. Indeed a particular set of these properties could represent a number, a letter, a word, an instruction or a variety of other things. What a particular set of properties is taken to mean depends on the context it is in when interpreted by the computer's central processor.

In a digital computer these properties are made up of individual elements which can have one of two values (often voltages). It is convenient for us to think of this element as a binary digit (a **bit**) which can be written as either 0 or 1. Binary digits can then be grouped to form patterns which are used as **codes**. These codes provide a way of thinking about how the computer works internally but the technology actually used can vary from computer to computer.

The codes allow us to describe how data is stored and manipulated in a way which is common between computer systems. We can also consider the codes as binary numbers which allows us to use mathematical theory to manipulate the data.

Data representation is about the way in which binary digits are grouped to provide codes, how these are interpreted and how larger groupings, such as arrays, stacks and lists, are used for sets of data.

Data

is information coded and structured for subsequent processing, generally by a computer system. The resulting codes are meaningless until they are placed in the correct context. The subtle difference between data and information is that information is in context, data is not.

Character set

including: character, character code, control character, internal character code,
EBCDIC (Extended Binary Coded Decimal Interchange Code), ASCII (American
Standard Code for Information Interchange), ISO 8859, Code page, ANSI
(American National Standards Institute) character set, teletext character set
is the set of symbols that may be represented by a computer at a particular time. These symbols are called *characters* and can be letters, digits, spaces, punctuation marks and include non-printing, control characters.

Individual characters are represented by a single code number (the *character code*) stored as a binary integer. Any textual data will be stored as a sequence of these codes. When the data is displayed or printed the code is converted into the appropriate shape.

The shape assigned to a particular code number can be changed and the resulting display will be different. In particular, this occurs when the screen display character set is different from the printer character set, in which case the printout will be different from the screen display.

Many character sets also have codes for *control characters*. These non-printing characters are used for special purposes. Examples of control characters are, end of record and end of file markers in a file, carriage return and line feed for a printer, begin and end transmission with a modem and cursor movement on a screen.

All the symbols available form a character set which could be specific to a particular computer or application. A microcomputer system will usually use *internal character codes*, which are the code numbers produced by pressing the keys on the keyboard. These internal character codes will usually be converted into standard codes for use by applications software.

Many computer systems now have the flexibility to use several character sets as required, for example to provide foreign language characters or for compatibility with earlier systems. In practice most computers use internationally agreed character sets such as:

EBCDIC (Extended Binary Coded Decimal Interchange Code) is an older character set used by large computer systems for internal communication and data storage.

ASCII (American Standard Code for Information Interchange) was devised for use with early telecommunication systems but proved to be ideal for computer systems and forms the basis for almost all other character sets.

ISO 8859 is the current international standard for computer character sets and has several variations for use in different cultures. The variations are more usually known by their names such as *Latin1 alphabet, Latin2 alphabet* and *Greek alphabet.*

Code page is the name for optional character sets defined for use with IBM-compatible microcomputers.

ANSI (American National Standards Institute) character set provides various lines and shapes as additional characters. These simplify the production of screen displays involving lines and shapes.

Teletext character set enables screen displays involving simple graphics to be constructed. These are very compact and can be economically transmitted.

The ASCII code uses 7 bits giving 32 control codes and 96 displayable characters (an eighth bit could be used for error checking). Most modern character sets are extensions of the ASCII code, using 8 bits, which provides the possibility for more characters, but letters, digits and common punctuation characters retain the same code numbers. The most noticeable effect of character set variations is that some characters appear to change, for example a '£' may appear as a '$' or as a '#'.

Word

including: word length

is a group of bits which can be addressed, transferred and manipulated as a single unit by the central processor. The size of a word, the *word length*, is determined by the width of the data pathways within the computer and is usually larger than a *byte* (see below) possibly consisting of 16, 24, 36 or even 64 bits. Large word sizes may mean that a computer can work faster than a computer with a smaller word size, but is less efficient when the data does not need to use the full word length.

Byte

is a group of bits, typically 8, representing a single character. This is normally the smallest grouping used by a computer. A byte may also be used to represent a small number, either less than 256 or between -127 and + 128.

Collating sequence

is the order in which a computer will sort character data. This could be the order in which a particular application sorts data, but it is often the sequence of characters in the order of their character codes. Obviously letters such as A to Z will be in the usual alphabetic order, but various computer systems may differ in whether 'A' comes before 'a' or whether '1' comes before 'A' depending on the codes used in the system. The use of a standard code such as ASCII avoids such differences between computer systems.

Data structure

is a group of related data items organised in the computer. A data structure allows a large number of pieces of data to be managed as a single set. Each type of data structure makes it easy for the programmer to find and process the data in particular ways. Each type of structure has its own strengths and weaknesses. Examples of data structures are *arrays*, *lists*, *tables* (see page 256), *trees* (see below), *strings* (see *string data*, page 261) and *files* (see page 187).

Tree

including: node, branch, leaf node, terminal node, parent node, root node, binary tree

is a non-linear data structure where the data items can be thought of as occurring at different levels. There are links between items at one level and their descendants at the next. Each data item has data which relates it to its unique parent node. See Figure C11.1.

The data items are usually called *nodes* with the links known as **branches**. A node may have any number of descendants but itself may only be the descendant of one other node. This data structure is often encountered in a directory of files, where directory nodes are linked to sub-directories. It is usual in computing to draw a tree diagram 'upside down' with the root at the top, unlike a natural tree.

Data can be added to the tree (by creating a new node) or removed from a tree (by deleting a node). The tree can be traversed using a variety of algorithms but only by following the links between nodes.

Some nodes in a tree have particular characteristics. Of particular importance are leaf nodes, parent nodes and root nodes.

Leaf nodes or *terminal nodes* are nodes in a tree without any branches further down the tree. In the conventional way of drawing trees (upside-down), the leaves occur at the bottom.

Parent node is the node immediately above a given node, at the next level up. There can only be one parent node for each node, but different nodes may share the same parent.

Root node is the entry node where we would start before moving around the tree. It is the only node in a tree without a parent node. In the conventional way of drawing trees (upside-down) the root occurs at the top. A tree has exactly one root node. If the data suggests that there should be two or more root nodes, the data structure has to be viewed as several trees.

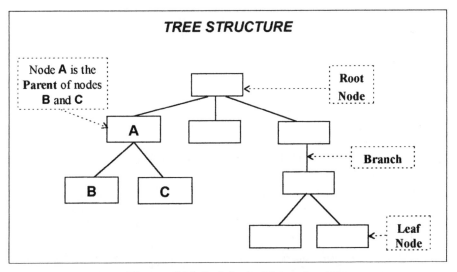

Figure C11.1: A typical tree structure

One particular form of tree is the **binary tree** where nodes have at most two branches down the tree. Binary trees are easier to implement on a computer than other forms of tree. Some of the advantages of a binary tree are:

- there is a way of representing all trees as binary trees;
- a fixed amount of space can be reserved for its branches;
- efficient algorithms exist for adding items to the tree and searching it.

Array

including: list, one-dimensional array, dimension, subscript, two-dimensional array, table, array bound, subscripted variable

is a set of data items of the same type grouped together using a single identifier. Each of the data items is addressed by the variable name and a *subscript*, for example in Figure C11.2, **NAME(4)** is the fourth element of the array **NAME**.

A column of data like this is called a *list* or a *one-dimensional array*.

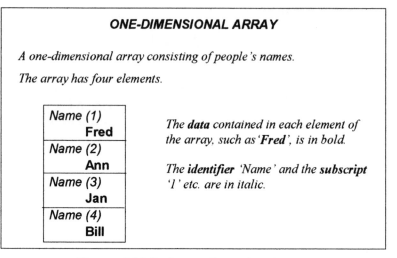

Figure C11.2: A one-dimensional array

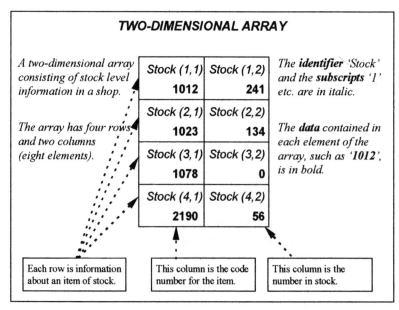

Figure C11.3: A two-dimensional array

Arrays may have many *dimensions*, and have a *subscript* for each dimension. So in Figure C11.3, **STOCK(3,2)** is an element in the *two-dimensional array* called **STOCK.** On paper two-dimensional arrays are the same as tables (with rows and columns) and are sometimes called *tables* in the computing context.

Before an array can be used in a program, it must be *declared* (see *declaration*, page 220) and its size defined, so that the computer can allocate a part of memory for the array. Examples of array declarations are given in Figure C11.4. The limits of the array are known as the *array bounds* and it is usual to declare the array by stating its name and giving the maximum values of each dimension.

A *subscripted variable* refers to an individual element of an array, for example **AGE(20)** or **STOCK(3,2)**.

ARRAY DECLARATION

Two-dimensional array of stock items	*One-dimensional array of the results of throwing two dice*
In Pascal:	
var **stock** : array [1..10,1..5] of real;	var **dice_score** : array [2..12] of integer;
In BASIC:	
DIM **STOCK**(10,5)	DIM **DICESCORE**(12)
In C:	
float **stock** [10][5]	int **dice_score** [12]
This example defines an array (of real numbers) which has two dimensions, with upper bounds of 10 'rows' (the first subscript) and 5 'columns (the second subscript).	This example defines an array (of integers) for a problem using subscripts 2 to 12. Pascal allows the lower bound to be set at 2, rather than the more normal lower bound of 0 or 1.

Figure C11.4: Declaring array dimensions

Stack

including: Last In First Out (LIFO), push, pull, pop

is a list where items are added or deleted from the same end. The operation of a stack is *Last In First Out (LIFO)*. The most recent item to arrive is dealt with first.

Push is the term used for adding an item to the stack. *Pull* and *pop* are terms used for taking an item from the stack. Taking an item from the stack makes the next item in the stack available. Items in other positions in the stack cannot be accessed.

Stacks are often represented by an array with a pointer to the top of the stack where the elements are added and removed.

Linked list

is a list where each item contains the data together with a pointer to the next item. There may be an additional pointer to the previous item. This means the items can be accessed in order even if they are not stored in order; they do not have to be stored in adjacent memory locations.

Queue

including: First In First Out (FIFO), circular queue, circular buffer
is a list where any new item is added to one end, and items are deleted from the other. The operation of a queue is *First In First Out (FIFO)*. Items are dealt with in the order they arrived.

Queues are often represented using an array with pointers to the first and last elements of the queue.

A *circular queue* is a queue in which the storage area is fixed and the first item is held in a location which is logically next to the storage location for the last item of the queue. Data items can be thought of as being arranged in a circle; for this reason it is sometimes called a *circular buffer*.

Record

including: record format, logical record, physical record, blocking factor
is the basic unit of data stored in a datafile. It is a collection of items, which may be of different data types, all relating to the individual or object the record describes and is treated as a unit for processing. Most datafiles contain records which have the same types of information but about different individuals or objects.

The contents of a record are described by the *record format* which specifies the record in terms of its *fields* (see page 259).

Where it is necessary to distinguish between the content of a record and the computer-stored record, the terms *logical record* and *physical record* are used. Logical record is used to refer to the information held in a record, but a physical record is a *block* (see page 131) of memory in backing store, which can hold one or more logical records.

The number of logical records in each physical record, which will depend on the size of the logical record and the structure of records and blocks on the backing store, is called the *blocking factor*.

Variable-length record

is a record where the number of bits (or characters) is not predetermined but is governed by the amount of data to be stored. This is useful where textual data is to be stored, which would leave a lot of wasted space in *fixed-length records* (see page 259). However fixed-length records are more easily processed.

Fixed-length record

or fixed-format record

is a record where the number of bits in a record is decided in advance at the design stage. This length is constant and cannot be changed later. The length of a fixed-length record is often thought of in terms of bytes or characters.

EOF marker (End Of File marker)

is a marker written to a file by the operating system immediately after the last record to signal the end of that file to the controlling program. A programmer can use this to process a variable amount of data in a file, processing records until the end of file marker is found. This is similar to using a *rogue terminator* (see page 206).

Field

including: field name

is part of a *record* (see page 258) designed to hold a single data item of a specified type. Most datafiles contain records which have the same fields of information but about different individuals or objects. Each field is referred to by a *field name*, which identifies the data in the field and makes it possible to generalise about the data being processed.

FIELDS AND RECORDS

A **datafile** *holding details of club membership.*

Each **record** *would contain* **fields** *of a member's data:*

name, initials, date of birth and membership number.

The **field names:**

Name, Initials, Date_Of_Birth and Membership_Number

identify the data present, rather than being the actual data, which may be:

Smith, F, 12/3/78, 458923

Each **record** *would have the name, initials, date of birth and membership number of a different member.*

Figure C11.5: *Fields and records in a datafile*

Key

including: key field, sort key, primary key, key field order, secondary key, composite key

is the field (the *key field*) within a record used to identify the record, for example a bank account number identifies a customer's account. The key can be used for finding the record within a file or as the *sort key* for sorting a file into order.

Most datafiles will have a *primary key*, which is unique and used to identify the record. If the records in a datafile can be accessed *sequentially* (see *sequential access*, page 190) the records will be accessed in *key field order*, which is the order they will be in when they have been sorted using the key field.

Datafiles may also have *secondary keys*, which enable the file to be accessed in a different order. *Composite keys*, made up of more than one field, can be used to sort a file. The use of composite keys is shown in Figure C11.6.

KEY FIELDS

In the example (Figure C11.5) of a datafile holding details of club membership containing **fields** *for:*

Name, Initials, Date_Of_Birth *and* **Membership_Number**

the **Membership_Number** *could be the* **primary key** field *because it is unique and identifies who the record is about.*

Name *could be a* **secondary key.**

Date_Of_Birth *or* **Initials** *could* <u>*not*</u> *be* **key** *fields because without the other fields they are out of context (and the data is unidentifiable and meaningless).*

Date_Of_Birth *could be a* **sort key** *because the resulting list would be in order of age, which is useful.*

Name *and* **Initials** *(i.e.* **SmithF**) *could be a* **composite key.**

If the file is sorted using this as a sort key, *all the* **Smiths** *would be together, in alphabetic order according to* **initial.**

Figure C11.6: *Key fields in a datafile*

Data type

including: variable type, field type, user-defined data type, alphanumeric data, character data, string data, Boolean (or logical) data, sample data, sound data, video data, video clip, date data

is a formal description of the kind of data being stored or manipulated within a program or system, for example alphabetic data, numeric data or logical data.

Variable type in a high-level language describes the kind of data held by a *variable* (see page 221).

Field type describes the kind of data stored as a *field* (see page 259) within a datafile.

The specification of data types is important because:

- It provides a limited validation of data;
- Different operations can be performed on different data types;
- Memory can be efficiently allocated to store data.

Different programming languages provide different data, variable and field types. Many allow programmers to specify their own data types; these are called *user-defined data types* and are often combinations of existing data types.

Some systems provide a wide range of data or field types, such as date, sample (sound recordings) and video (moving pictures). These are particularly useful in database systems.

Data, variable and field types can be specified for any data item that has an identifiable structure. Some of the more important ones are detailed below:

Alphanumeric data is a general term used for textual data which may include letters, digits and, sometimes, punctuation. It includes both character data type and string data type.

Character data is a single character represented by the codes from the character set in use on the computer. See also *character*, in *character set* page 252.

String data is textual data in the form of a list of characters, for example words and punctuation. String data is made up of character data and will usually vary in length.

Boolean data or *logical data* can only have one of two values, *true* or *false* (see *truth value*, page 312. This makes it easy to use the values of Boolean variables to control the flow of a program. See also *C18 Truth Tables and Logic Gates*, page 312.

Sample data (digitally recorded *sound data*) and *video data* (a *video clip*) are large complex data structures containing all the information needed to enable a suitable subroutine to play a sound sample or display a video clip.

Date data is in a form recognised as representing a date, for example 1.2.34 or 1st February 1998. Date data must represent a valid date, for example 11/12/89 is allowed, but 31st April 1995 is not allowed because April only has 30 days.

Numeric data can have a variety of types (see *numeric data type*, page 270).

File type

including: CSV file (Comma Separated Variable files), TSV file (Tab Separated Variable files), SID file (Standard Interchangeable Data files), RTF file (Revisable Text Format files or Rich Text Format files), ASCII file, text file
is the labelling of a file to identify the structure of its contents. This means that the user knows which software can be used with that data and that an applications program knows how to load and interpret the data. In some cases the operating system uses the file type to locate, load and run the application software as well. The file type may be implicit or explicit, where the three characters of the *file name extension* (see page 187) indicate the file type.

Most application programs have their own file types for data stored in their format. Other file types are used to transfer data between applications. Some common file types are detailed below:

CSV files (Comma Separated Variable files) are used to transfer tabular data between applications. Each field is separated by a comma and may be enclosed in quotation marks to avoid ambiguity.

TSV files (Tab Separated Variable files) are also used to transfer tabular data between applications. Each field is separated by a special character (the tab character) to avoid ambiguity.

SID files (Standard Interchangeable Data files) are also used to transfer tabular data between applications. The format also allows other data to be stored. SID files are not common outside the UK education market.

RTF files (Revisable Text Format files or Rich Text Format files) are a complex format used to store data from a word processor, including information about fonts, sizes, colour and styles. This standard format can be used to transfer data between most word processor packages without losing the formatting information.

ASCII files or Text files are used to transfer textual data between programs. The data consists only of individual characters in the standard ASCII code. No formatting information is included and, as a result, ASCII data is a file type acceptable to most programs. This is the most common means of transferring data between application packages. Most packages that allow data to be *imported* (see *import*, page 10) will accept a text file.

C12 Numeric Data Representation

*This section defines terms associated with some of the methods used
to store numbers in ways which can be efficiently processed. Other
related material can be found in C11 Data Representation.*

Much of the data stored in a computer are numbers of some kind. Numbers create
special problems for the computer scientist because they vary in type and size in an
unpredictable way.

A number, such as '123', could be treated as the three separate **characters** '1' '2'
'3', but if it is necessary to store its **value**, 'one hundred and twenty three', then there
are several of ways of doing this. Storing numbers as values has the advantage that it
is easier to perform arithmetic efficiently on numbers that are stored as values rather
than as characters.

A number could be very large or very small, positive or negative, a whole number
or a fraction. Whatever it is, it must be converted to a binary pattern for storage and
manipulation in a computer. For a given number of bits there is a finite number of
patterns available to represent number values and this places limits on the numbers
that can be stored. Figure C12.1 shows the number of patterns available for different
numbers of bits.

**THE NUMBER OF PATTERNS PROVIDED BY DIFFERENT NUMBERS
OF BITS:**

1 bit	example: 1	2 patterns (0 and 1)
2 bits	example: 11	4 patterns (00, 01, 10 and 11)
3 bits	example: 101	8 patterns (000, 001, ... 111)
4 bits	example: 1101	16 patterns (0000, 0001, ... 1111)
7 bits	example: 1101100	128 patterns
8 bits	example: 11011001	256 patterns
....	....	....
16 bits	....	65,536 patterns
....	....	....
32 bits	....	4,294,967,296 patterns
....	....	....

Figure C12.1: Numbers of bit patterns

The way numbers are stored involves a compromise between the **range** of values
needed and the **accuracy** with which these values can be represented.

For a limited range of whole numbers each number can be represented exactly
using one of the available code combinations. As the required range of numbers
increases, eventually there will not be enough codes for each code to represent a single

value. A longer word length (more binary digits) could be used to extend the range of values, but there will always be a limit at some value, and using a very long word length all the time would mean that the computer would be slower and could only run smaller programs.

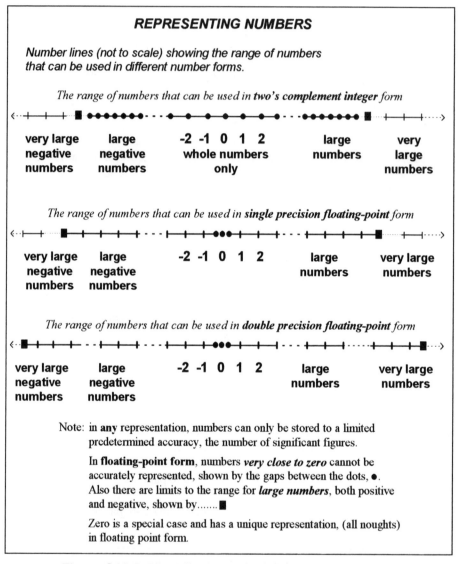

REPRESENTING NUMBERS

Number lines (not to scale) showing the range of numbers that can be used in different number forms.

*The range of numbers that can be used in **two's complement integer** form*

| very large negative numbers | large negative numbers | -2 -1 0 1 2 whole numbers only | large numbers | very large numbers |

*The range of numbers that can be used in **single precision floating-point** form*

| very large negative numbers | large negative numbers | -2 -1 0 1 2 | large numbers | very large numbers |

*The range of numbers that can be used in **double precision floating-point** form*

| very large negative numbers | large negative numbers | -2 -1 0 1 2 | large numbers | very large numbers |

Note: in **any** representation, numbers can only be stored to a limited predetermined accuracy, the number of significant figures.

In **floating-point form**, numbers *very close to zero* cannot be accurately represented, shown by the gaps between the dots, ●. Also there are limits to the range for *large numbers*, both positive and negative, shown by.......■

Zero is a special case and has a unique representation, (all noughts) in floating point form.

Figure C12.2: *Number ranges for different number forms*

To store an even larger range of numbers with the same set of codes, two, or more, numbers close to each other will have to use the same code, which could introduce errors into the results of calculations. Similarly, if provision is made for negative numbers, the largest value that can be stored will be halved, since one of the binary digits is used to indicate the sign.

Even larger numbers require different methods of representation which may also introduce errors into the computer results because similar numbers will share the same codes. To represent very large numbers and fractions, **floating-point representation** is used. This enables a wide range of numbers to be represented to a known accuracy. Figure C12.2 illustrates the range of numbers that can be represented in different forms.

An additional constraint is that the computer has to perform arithmetic with the resultant codes; in particular it has to be able to add and subtract them. The methods used to represent values have to be related to the way the computer does arithmetic, in particular the way it deals with negative numbers.

A programmer normally has control of the types of representation used. A program can be optimised to work as fast as possible, to handle numbers with great accuracy or to handle a wide range of numbers. Some compromise is normally essential since these properties are often mutually exclusive.

Bit (BInary digiT)
including: least significant bit (LSB), most significant bit (MSB)
is a single digit from a binary number, it is either a 0 or a 1. It is the smallest unit of storage since all data is stored as binary codes.

The *least significant bit* (*LSB*) is the bit in a binary number with the least place value and the *most significant bit* (*MSB*) is the bit in a binary number with the greatest place value.

Binary notation
is the number system using base two and the digits 0 and 1. It is a convenient way of representing numbers in an electronic computer. Most computers do arithmetic using binary numbers and other representations need converting into binary form before the computer can do anything with them. For example: 123 (denary) is 1111011 (binary). See *denary notation*, below.

Denary notation
is the familiar number system using base ten and the digits 0 to 9. It is often incorrectly referred to as decimal notation.

Integer
is any whole number, whether positive or negative.

Real number
is any number represented with a fractional part. In most high-level languages, real indicates that *floating-point representation* (see page 266) is to be used when the number is stored or manipulated. This implies that the number may contain a fractional part and that it is processed to a limited number of significant figures.

Fixed-point representation

is the form of representation in which numbers are expressed by a set of digits with the decimal (or binary) point in its correct position. During operations in the computer the position of the decimal (or binary) point is generally maintained by instructions in the program. The size of fixed-point numbers is limited by the construction of the computer, but operations are generally very fast and preferred for most commercial data processing work.

Floating-point representation

including: mantissa, exponent

is a form of representation in which numbers are expressed as a binary or decimal fractional value, called the *mantissa*, which is non-zero, together with an integer *exponent*. The use of floating-point representation increases the range of numbers which can be represented, although the number of significant figures remains constant for any given system. Generally, the advantage of the extra range available when working in floating-point representation is gained at the expense of processing time and precision. Floating-point numbers are often called real numbers in a computing context, although this meaning is different from the strict mathematical use of the term real number.

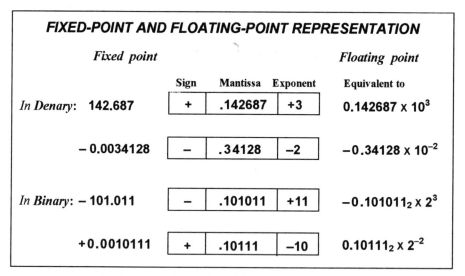

FIXED-POINT AND FLOATING-POINT REPRESENTATION

	Fixed point	Sign	Mantissa	Exponent	Floating point
					Equivalent to
In Denary:	142.687	+	.142687	+3	0.142687×10^3
	− 0.0034128	−	.34128	−2	-0.34128×10^{-2}
In Binary:	− 101.011	−	.101011	+11	$-0.101011_2 \times 2^3$
	+0.0010111	+	.10111	−10	$0.10111_2 \times 2^{-2}$

Figure C12.3: *Fixed-point and floating-point representation*

Negative numbers

including: sign bit, sign and magnitude, sign and modulus, complementation, one's complement, two's complement

are represented within the computer by binary patterns which enable the computer to do arithmetic easily. Generally one bit, called the *sign bit*, is used to indicate the sign of the number. Common methods of representing negative numbers are described below:

Sign and magnitude (or *sign and modulus*) is a method of representing numbers by allocating one bit of a binary word, usually the *most significant bit* (see page 265), to represent the sign of a number whose magnitude is held in the remaining bits of the word.

In the 16 bit number:

1000101010101000

the 1 at the left-hand end is the sign bit,
the remaining 15 bits are the magnitude (or modulus) of the number.
For the sign bit, **0** is usually positive and **1** negative.

Complementation is a method of representing positive and negative numbers. This system requires numbers to be represented by a fixed number of bits. There are two forms of complementation, one's complement and two's complement, which are illustrated below. Two's complement is preferred because subtraction can be performed by adding the two's complement of the number to be subtracted.

43 (denary) is represented as an 8-bit binary number by   **00101011**

One's complement is formed by changing each 1 bit to a 0 and changing each 0 bit to a 1.

the one's complement of   **00101011**   (+ 43) is   **11010100**

and this complement, **11010100** could be used to represent − 43,

but more often the two's complement is used.

Two's complement is one greater than the corresponding one's complement.

the two's complement of   **00101011**   (+ 43) is   **11010101**
                                                             (11010100 + 1)

and this complement, **11010101** is normally used to represent − 43.

Binary Coded Decimal (BCD)

is a coding system in which each decimal digit is represented by a group of 4 binary digits. This is sometimes useful because it maintains the relationship between the place values in decimal and the values stored in the computer. It is not efficient for the computer to store and manipulate numbers in this form but may have advantages in some applications.

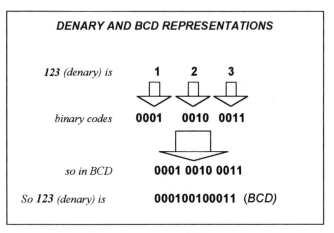

Figure C12.4: Denary to BCD conversion

Octal notation

is the number system using base 8 and the digits 0-7. It has similar advantages to *hexadecimal* (see page 269) in that it is related to the binary pattern (each octal digit represents 3 bits). Most people use hexadecimal in preference to octal.

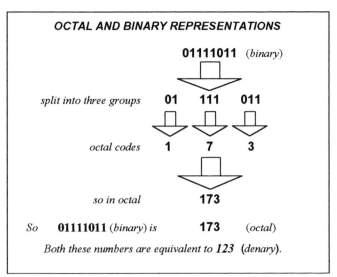

Figure C12.5: Binary to octal conversion

Hexadecimal notation

also known as: HEX

is the number system using base 16 and the digits 0-9 and A B C D E F. It is often used in computing because long binary patterns can be written as short hexadecimal numbers without losing the relationship between the value and the individual bits in the pattern, with each group of 4 bits being represented by one hexadecimal digit. See Figure C12.6.

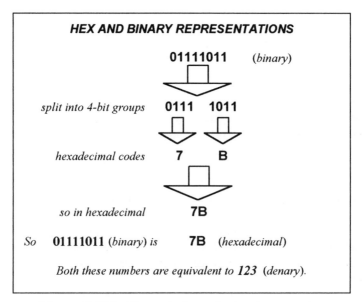

HEX AND BINARY REPRESENTATIONS

01111011   *(binary)*

split into 4-bit groups   **0111   1011**

hexadecimal codes   **7   B**

so in hexadecimal   **7B**

So   **01111011** *(binary) is*   **7B**   *(hexadecimal)*

Both these numbers are equivalent to 123 (denary).

Figure C12.6: *Binary to hexadecimal conversion*

Normalise

is to change a number in floating-point form into standard floating-point representation format. Using a standard format for floating-point representation has some advantages, such as:

- avoiding the problem of having two different binary codes meaning the same thing;
- the form chosen is usually that which provides maximum precision;
- multiplication is performed more accurately.

Numeric data type

including: numeric variable type, numeric field type, integer type, int type, real type, float type, double precision, single precision, complex type

is a formal description of the kind of numeric data being stored or manipulated within a program or system, for example *integers, real numbers* (see page 265), complex numbers.

Numeric variable type or *numeric field type* specify the kind of numeric data held by a *variable* (see page 221) in a high-level language or as *fields* (see page 259) in a file.

In many cases the same numerical value can be stored using any of the representations available; the one that is chosen by the programmer will be the most appropriate to the task being programmed. Some of the more important numeric data types are detailed below:

Integer type data are whole numbers, either positive or negative. Internally the computer will usually store integer type data as binary integers in *two's complement* form (see page 267). Integer type data is sometimes called *int type*.

Real type data are numbers which include a fractional part. Internally the computer will usually store real type data using *floating-point representation* (see page 266). It is sometimes called *float type*.

Double precision type data provides a more accurate representation than the usual *single precision* type data, by using twice the number of bits to store and manipulate the data. Double precision is usually applied to real type data .

Complex type data are complex numbers. Some programming languages allow complex type data, which provides for the direct manipulation of complex numbers.

C13 Systems Software

Other related material can be found in C1 Systems Design and Life Cycle, C2 Systems Documentation and C10 Programming Languages.

A computer system requires a layer of software which enables users to operate it without having to know about the underlying processes that are going on all the time inside. This includes the **operating system** and other forms of **systems software**.

A computer needs separate instructions for even the most elementary tasks. Computer users are interested in solving their problems without having to program every detail into the computer. The systems software is provided by the manufacturer and enables a user to give a few simple instructions which the systems software translates into the millions of minor operations needed for the computer to function in an easy-to-use way.

Every computer is provided with an operating system which controls the vital parts of the computer's operation - using the keyboard, screen display, loading and saving files and printing are some examples.

Additional programs (such as disk formatters and device drivers to control peripherals) are provided which are useful in the operation of the computer. They do not enable the user to get answers to problems (**application programs** do that) but they do make using the computer easier, by allowing resources to be organised and controlled better. They improve efficiency by making the computer easier to use.

Systems software can be classified in a variety of ways depending on whether it:

- is necessary to run the computer (**operating system software**);
- provides other useful functions for operating the computer (**utility programs**);
- provides for frequently required tasks (**library programs**);
- enables software to be produced and maintained (**compilers** and **assemblers**).

Software which is essential to the performance of the computer is usually sold with the computer. Other systems software may be purchased separately to enable the computer to be used for particular types of task.

In brief, systems software is the collection of programs available for the total control of the performance of a computer system.

Systems program

is one of the programs that control the operation of a computer system, enabling the computer system to be developed and to be more efficient. Examples of systems programs are compilers, monitor programs, disk formatters, network software and print spoolers. Many systems programs are part of the *operating system* (see page 272).

Systems programs can be contrasted with *applications programs* (see page 6), which perform some task. These tasks, such as producing a letter, are not part of the actual operation of the computer.

Operating system

including: disk operating system, DOS, MS-DOS, PC-DOS, OS/2, Presentation Manager, Risc-OS, UNIX, Windows, Windows 95

is a program or suite of programs that controls the entire operation of the computer. It is normally provided by the manufacturer and deals with the basic functions of the computer, such as detecting what has been typed in, displaying data on the screen and loading and saving to backing store. Most modern operating systems include *utility programs* (see page 274) which make the operation of the computer easier, such as a program to format a disk. At a technical level the operating system handles the basic and central functions such as *input* and *output* operations (see *BIOS*, page 274) and *interrupts* (see page 289).

The design of the operating system is often modular, allowing new features to be added and new hardware to be accommodated. One part, the portion of the operating system that deals with access to and management of files and programs stored on disk, is often provided separately. This is the *disk operating system* (commonly abbreviated to *DOS*). The *network operating system* (see page 157) provides similar facilities for use with local area networks.

Many modern operating systems also include a *graphical user interface* (*GUI*) (see page 80), either incorporated into the operating system or provided separately.

These are general terms and most manufacturers have their own proprietary names for either the operating system or the disk operating system. Among these are:

MS-DOS is an operating system written by Microsoft originally for the IBM-PC. It is now the most common operating system used with personal computers. It provides an operating system for the Intel 8086, 186, 286, 386, 486 and Pentium microprocessors. A version called *PC-DOS* was supplied as the operating system on the original IBM-manufactured Personal Computers.

OS/2 is a development of the PC-DOS operating system for IBM PCs and compatible microcomputers using more powerful microprocessors than the original Intel 8086. This operating system allows *multi-tasking* (see page 278) which makes it more suitable for use in a complex or network environment.

Presentation Manager is the graphical user interface developed by IBM and Microsoft for use with the OS/2 operating system.

Risc-OS is the operating system and graphical user interface developed by the computer manufacturer Acorn for their computers. The operating system and graphical user interface are integrated, making the system easy to use with all the operations performed using the graphical user interface.

UNIX is an operating system originally written for large machines. Versions are now available for a variety of machines ranging from mainframes to personal computers. It was designed to improve software portability. It has been highly successful as an operating system for minicomputers, because it is particularly suited for running multi-user and networked systems. It is also easily adapted for the specific requirements of each multi-user or networked system.

Windows is the graphical user interface developed by the software producer Microsoft for computers using the MS-DOS and PC-DOS operating systems. It was very successful, with a vast number of personal computers using it.

Windows 95 is a combined graphical user interface and operating system, which is succeeding the earlier combination of windows running under DOS. Many new personal computers are now supplied with Windows software. Users do not need to be aware of what operating system is used, as the Windows interface appears to do most of the required system operations.

Bootstrap

including: booting, system prompt, boot file, config.sys, autoexec.bat, reboot
is a short sequence of machine-code instructions used for loading the program which starts up the computer. It is normally held in read-only memory and activated when the machine is switched on. This process is sometimes referred to as *booting*. It loads or initialises the operating system ready for use. A *system prompt*, indicating for example which drive or directory is current, will be displayed on the screen. See *prompt*, page 89.

The users of a personal computer are often given the opportunity to start it up automatically configured as they want. This is done by placing the required commands in a file, called a *boot file*. This file will be executed automatically by the computer after it has booted the *operating system* (see page 272).

MS-DOS and similar operating systems use two files as part of the start-up sequence. These files must be called *config.sys* and *autoexec.bat*. These files do not have to be present, but if they are then they are automatically used. The file config.sys is a datafile containing values and settings to be used by the operating system; it may include the file names of files to be used by the operating system. The file autoexec.bat is a list of commands (see *batch file*, page 276) which the user wishes to be executed when the computer is started up.

To *reboot* the computer is to restart the system, usually after a hang-up (see *hung*, page 242). All parameters will be reset to their initial values and data which was not saved will be lost. See also *cold start* and *warm start*, page 242.

BIOS (Basic Input Output System)

is the part of the operating system that handles the input and output of the computer. It enables the operating system to use the particular features of the hardware being used. The name specifically refers to a single part of some operating systems which can be easily altered to allow the same operating system to be used by a variety of hardware designs and manufacturers. If the BIOS is altered, the other parts of these operating systems will not need any alteration.

Utility program

including: full backup, incremental backup
is a *systems program* (see page 272) designed to perform a commonplace task, for example the transfer of data from one storage device to another, sorting a set of data, or a disk editor for directly editing the contents of a disk.

Full backup utility creates a backup of all the files on a disk, as opposed to an *incremental backup* which only copies files that have been altered since the last backup.

Software library

also known as: library, program library
is a collection of software held either permanently accessible on backing store or on removable media such as tape or disk. It will include complete software packages, package modules which will only be required occasionally, and machine-code routines for loading into user programs.

Library program

including: library routine
is one available to all users of a multi-user computer system, typically to carry out common tasks (such as file maintenance) required by everyone. Some tasks may be carried out by *library routines* which users can incorporate into their own programs. See also *software library*, above.

Translator

is a computer program used to convert a program from one language to another (for example from a low-level language to machine code). This is a general name for the three types of translation programs, *assemblers* (see below), *compilers* (see page 275) and *interpreters* (see page 276). See also *C10 Programming languages*, page 244.

Assembler

also known as: assembler program
including: assembly language, assembly, macro assembler, cross-assembler
is a program that translates a program written in assembly language into machine code.

An *assembly language* is a special type of programming language where the instructions are closely related to the computer being programmed (rather than a common language which is similar on any type of computer). In general, each assembly language instruction is changed into one machine-code instruction but programming can be simplified by the use of *macro instructions* (see page 218).

The program is written in the assembly language of the computer being used and then translated (assembled) into the machine code of that computer by software called an assembler. This process is called *assembly*

The assembler program is specific to a type of computer and is often provided as part of the systems software, since the assembly process automates the task of producing machine-code software required to operate the computer.

A *macro assembler* is a more complex type of assembler that offers the facility of expanding *macro instructions* (see page 218).

A *cross-assembler* is an assembler that runs on one computer, but that produces machine code for another. It enables software developers to produce programs for computers that are still being designed or to convert software between different types of computer.

Compiler

including: source code, compilation, lexical analysis, syntax analysis, code generation, cross-compiler

is a program that translates a high-level language program, *source code*, into a computer's machine code or some other low-level language. Generally each high-level language instruction generates several machine-code instructions. It produces an independent program which can be run.

This translation process is known as *compilation*. Compilation involves analysing the language structure of the source program, determining if it is valid, and producing suitable machine code. Compilation involves a number of steps:

Lexical analysis: the stage in the compilation of a program which puts each statement into the form best suited to the syntax analyser. The standard components of each statement, such as PRINT, IF, etc., are replaced by their tokens (a unique fixed length code) and programmer-defined names are entered into a *symbol table* (see page 277). The lexical analyser also removes unnecessary characters such as spaces.

Syntax analysis: the stage in the compilation where language statements are checked against the rules of the language, errors being reported if a statement is not valid.

Code generation: produces a machine-code program which is equivalent to the source program.

A *cross-compiler* is a compiler that runs on one computer, but that produces code for another. It enables software producers to develop programs for computers that are still being designed or to convert software between different types of computer.

Interpreter

translates and executes a program one statement at a time. The program may be in a high-level language or an intermediate code.

The interpreter is actually a machine-code program. It is used as an easy, if slightly inefficient, way of executing programs not in the machine code of the computer. For example, when an interpreted program contains a loop, the speed of execution will be slow because the analysis of each statement has to be repeated for each time round the loop; however there are advantages in using interpreted languages. See also C10 *programming languages*, page 244.

Command line interpreter

including: batch file, command file

is the portion of the operating system which analyses a system command typed by the user and performs the appropriate actions. Most operating systems work by asking the user for commands to be typed in, as a line of text after a *prompt* (see page 89), analysing the commands and taking appropriate action. Modern operating systems provide a *graphical user interface* (see page 80), which is often easier to use, but usually the command line interpreter is still available.

Some graphical user interfaces simply convert information from the mouse into an equivalent system command processed by the command line interpreter. Commands may be:

- read from a text file (called a *batch file* or *command file*);
- provided remotely from a peripheral or another computer through an interface;
- provided from within a program.

These commands are all automatically processed by the command line interpreter.

Disassembler

is a program that translates from machine code back to an assembly language. They are generally used to decipher existing machine code by generating equivalent symbolic codes. This is useful for programmers maintaining and modifying machine-code programs.

Loader

including: linking loader, linking, linker, link editor

is a program that copies an *object program* (see page 236) held on backing store into main store ready for execution.

Often common routines are provided already compiled in a *library* (see page 274), and when the program is loaded these routines also have to be loaded and links made to these routines. This is performed by a *linking loader*.

Alternatively, the library routines can be added when the program is compiled or as an additional *linking* operation between compilation and loading. A *linker*, or *link editor*, is the software tool which allows already compiled object code files or modules to be combined with the compiled program and then converted directly into an executable file. This also involves completing address links to the program.

Symbol table

also known as: name table

is the table created and maintained by a compiler or assembler relating programmer-defined names to machine addresses. It may also hold information about properties of data, such as data types.

When translating a program the compiler or assembler works through the program for the first time (the first pass) replacing some parts with tokens and building the symbol table which contains the actual address in memory of each variable, label or subroutine. The program is then processed a second time (the second pass) when each identifier can be replaced with its actual address in memory.

Parsing

is the breaking down of high-level programming language statements into their component parts during the translation process, for example identifying reserved words and variables.

Spooling

is the temporary storage of input or output data on magnetic disk or tape, as a means of compensating for the slow operating speeds of peripheral devices or when queuing output from different programs to one device, such as a printer (see *printer spooler*, below).

Printer spooler

also known as: print spooler
including: print job, print queue

is a program which stores data ready to be printed. Each set of data to be printed is known as a *print job*. When the print job has been received from a program and is complete, the printer spooler can send this data to the printer. Several programs or terminals can send data at the same time for printing, because the data is stored in files by the printer spooler and sent to the printer when appropriate. A printer spooler is normally part of the operating system.

If a printer spooler is used, programs do not have to wait whilst printing is being done (printers work more slowly than computers do). This is particularly important with personal computers and interactive computing, as users do not want to waste time waiting for data to be printed out. See also *printer server*, page 157.

The *print queue* is a list of work waiting to be printed by a printer spooler. Normally it is a list of the files holding data ready for printing. Each file will hold the data from a particular task which will be sent to the printer by the printer spooler when the printer is free. A task could be a single letter or a large batch of commercial documents.

Multiprogramming

including: time slice

is a method of benefiting from the speed of a central processor compared with slower peripheral devices, allowing two or more programs to be processed apparently simultaneously but actually in bursts, controlled by an operating system. For example, while one program is waiting for an input or output operation to be performed or is using a peripheral, another may have access to the central processor. To control this process, priorities may be assigned to jobs.

A *time slice* is the predetermined maximum length of time during which each program is allowed to run in a multiprogramming system.

Executive program

also known as: monitor program, supervisor program

is a control program that schedules the use of the hardware required by the programs being run in a multi-task or multiprogramming situation.

Multi-tasking

including: single-tasking

is a method of organising computer use which allows several different tasks or applications to be available at the same time. The users of a *multi-access system* (see page 172) will be working on different tasks apparently at the same time, although only one program is actually being executed at any one time. Similarly, modern personal computer operating systems allow users to have several tasks apparently running at the same time, with the user switching freely between applications or tasks.

Some operating systems will not support multi-tasking, these are called *single-tasking* systems and only allow one program to be in use at any time.

Processing mode

is the way in which the processing tasks carried out by a computer system are organised to make the most of the potential of the system. Sometimes the choice of mode is given to the user. For example, the user may have a choice between single-tasking or *multi-tasking* (see above) when running a program, or a choice between *foreground* or *background processing* (see page 279).

Different processing modes can also be selected by the central processor for different types of tasks. For example some types of instruction may only be available to the operating system, reducing the possibility of a user program affecting the rest of the computer's operation.

Job

including: job control language (JCL), job queue

is a data processing term for a package of work regarded by the computer as a single unit. Typically, a data processing department will run programs on behalf of its clients. These programs may be small (a single report) or large (a complete payroll). Once started, each program will proceed automatically to completion and from the data processing department's point of view, each is a single task or job to be run.

A specialised language, the *Job Control Language (JCL)*, is used to control the execution of a job in a computer. It enables the operators to specify the requirements of a job (such as which printer to use) when the job is executed. The programmer does not need to deal with these decisions when writing programs. A job control language also enables a series of small jobs to be linked together and executed in one larger and more efficient operation.

In a *multiprogramming* system (see page 278) or a *batch processing* system (see page 172) the jobs wait in a *job queue* until the computer system is ready to execute them. This will normally be in the order they are submitted although in some systems priority levels can be assigned to jobs to ensure some are executed earlier than other less urgent jobs.

Remote Job Entry (RJE)

is the use of a remote terminal to initiate a *job* (see page 278) on a computer within the network to which the terminal is attached. One example is the use of a terminal in a supermarket to transmit the record of the day's transactions to the central computer for the chain and initiate the appropriate funds transfer and ordering routines. Another very simple example is a request for a bank statement from a customer using a cash machine.

Foreground/background processing

including: foreground job, background job

is a method of organising a computer system so that certain important tasks (*foreground jobs*) may claim the sole use of the computer when required, while other less-pressing tasks (*background jobs*) utilise the remaining time.

For example a user can continue typing at a word processor (the foreground job) whilst the computer sends data to a printer (the background job) using processing time which is idle whilst waiting for user input.

The same concept applies to a *multiprogramming system* (see page 278), where the foreground job will have priority, but if the processor is idle (for example, waiting for disk access) then a background job will use that time.

Segmentation

including: segment, interleaving

is splitting a large program into a number of smaller programs or *segments*. Each segment is a complete program that is executed separately. The function of the large program is achieved by running segments consecutively. Segmentation allows a large program to be executed on a computer with insufficient memory to store the whole program.

The segments of several programs can be *interleaved*, which allows several large programs to be run concurrently in parts, to make optimum use of resources. These techniques are not widely used now due to the relatively large memory of modern computers. Similar techniques are *overlays* (see page 203) and *paging* (see page 284/5).

Scheduling
including: round-robin
is the method by which central processor time is allotted in a multi-access system. The scheduling algorithm may be as simple as the *round-robin* which deals with each user equally in turn, or as complex as a scheme of priorities distinguishing between users and between tasks.

Systems Application Architecture (SAA)
including: Common User Access (CUA), Systems Network Architecture (SNA)
is a set of standards for achieving both consistency and compatibility between software running on various types of IBM computer, including a consistent user interface. A number of standards are defined for the various parts of the Systems Application Architecture including:

Common User Access (CUA) which is the set of standards for the screen and keyboard layout, labelling and functions.
Systems Network Architecture (SNA) which is the standard for distributed processing, providing for communication between terminals and a host computer.

Garbage collection
including: fragmentation, defragmentation
is a 'housekeeping' task carried out by software. Many applications packages and systems software programs do not immediately rearrange their immediate access storage when data is deleted and the 'free space' becomes distributed throughout memory. In order to re-use this efficiently software will need to 'collect the space together' and this tidying up is called garbage collection.

A similar problem occurs with some *disk operating systems* (see page 272) where files may be split (and stored on different parts of the disk). This *fragmentation* usually happens when a disk is almost full. The access speed of the disk and hence the performance of the system will be improved if the separate elements of these files are collected together, a process known as *defragmentation*.

Text editor
also known as: editor
including: screen editor, line editor
is a program that enables the user to input, inspect and alter text files, which may be programs or data. Text editors are particularly used by computer programmers who need to produce text files suitable for compilation or assembly. Most text editors have special features which make the programmer's task easier.

In a *screen editor* the user interacts with a file by moving the cursor to the required position in the file, which is displayed on the screen, as in a word processor. In contrast, a *line editor* requires the user to specify a particular line of the file, for example a line number in a BASIC program.

C14 Machine Architecture

Other related terms can be found in B3 Memory, C15 Interfaces and Buses and C16 Physical Components.

The structure of a computer, or more properly the **Central Processing Unit (CPU)**, and how the particular components are related to each other is called Machine Architecture. The working of the computer can still be considered in terms of binary patterns and codes. The physical characteristics of the central processor affect the way the computer is used and also determine the speed, power, cost and suitability of the computer for a particular application.

The choice of integrated circuits and other components can determine how fast the computer will operate. This is important when selecting a computer for a particular application. For example, an important part of the specification of a personal computer is its **microprocessor** (such as a, '386', '486', 'Pentium', '68010' or 'ARM600') since this tells the purchaser something about the complexity of the programs it will run. Other parts of the central processor can affect a computer's performance for particular jobs, for example a **floating-point unit** will make a computer much faster at solving scientific problems, but may be of little value in an office context.

An important factor in the design of the central processor is the selection of the binary patterns used internally. For example the number of bits used as an address affects the maximum size of the main memory and the number of bits used to store a number affects very large and very small numbers.

Ways exist of getting round these problems, but always at the expense of performance and at a price. Various techniques may be employed within the hardware of the central processor to enhance performance, but further development of a type or series of computers will be limited by these technical factors and the initial design decisions.

Central Processing Unit (CPU)
including: central processor, processor
is the main part of the computer, consisting of the registers, arithmetic logic unit and control unit. See *control unit* and *register*, page 283, and *arithmetic logic unit*, page 288. Usually the central processing unit includes the main memory (see *immediate access store*, page 121). It is sometimes called the *central processor* or *processor*. Many computers have more than one processor.

A special form of central processing unit is the *microprocessor* (see page 282) which is used in microcomputers and small computerised devices, for example the control circuits of washing machines.

Microprocessor

including: Complex Instruction Set Computer (CISC), Reduced Instruction Set Computer (RISC), Z80, 6502, 8086, n86, Pentium, ARM, 68000, Transputer

is an integrated circuit where the components of the *central processing unit* (see page 281), excluding the main memory, are combined as a single unit. Microprocessors are manufactured in large numbers for use in microcomputers and small computerised devices. The general user has to obtain software suitable for that type of processor, since software cannot usually be used on different types of central processor.

Two of the main approaches to the design of microprocessors are the *Complex Instruction Set Computer* (*CISC*) and the *Reduced Instruction Set Computer* (*RISC*). A complex instruction set computer design produces a complicated and expensive integrated circuit capable of performing a large variety of complex operations. A reduced instruction set computer design produces a simple, cheap integrated circuit with a basic range of operations. It is however faster and relies on its speed to perform complex operations by using several machine instructions.

There are many types of microprocessor available including:

Z80 microprocessor which was used in many early microcomputers and computerised control systems. It is now obsolete.

6502 microprocessor which was used in some early microcomputers including the BBC microcomputer. It is now obsolete.

8086 microprocessor which was used in the earliest IBM PC and similar computers. It is now obsolete.

186, 286, 386, 486 and *Pentium* microprocessors which are further developments of the original 8086 microprocessor. Each succeeding newer design is much faster than its predecessor but they share a similar *instruction set* (see below) so that most software written for earlier IBM PC compatible computers can still be used without modification. These microprocessors were originally designated 80186, 80286, etc.

ARM2, ARM3, ARM250 and *ARM 600* microprocessors are used in Archimedes and Acorn computers. They are based on *RISC* (see above) design principles and so are fast operating and inexpensive. Their design is modular and variants are produced to control devices such as laser printers and personal organisers.

68000 microprocessor and its variants are used in the Macintosh series of computers.

Transputer is a microprocessor which includes the *immediate access store* (see page 121), hence its nickname 'computer on a chip'. Combining processor and store in the same chip makes it very easy to build parallel processing arrays containing many processors.

Instruction set

is the complete collection of instructions which are used by a particular type of central processor. These are the instructions available for use in machine-code or assembly language programs for that computer. The instruction set is part of the design of a central processor or microprocessor and so the machine code of different types of computer are rarely compatible. See also *machine-code instruction*, page 201.

Control unit

including: fetch-execute cycle, instruction cycle, instruction decoder, fetch phase,
execute phase

is the part of the central processor which manages the execution of instructions. A characteristic of all computers is the ability to follow a set of instructions automatically. The control unit fetches each instruction in sequence, decodes and synchronises it before executing it by sending control signals to other parts of the computer. This is known as the *fetch-execute cycle*. See also *program counter*, below.

The fetch-execute cycle is the complete process of retrieving an instruction from store, decoding it and carrying it out. This is also called the *instruction cycle*. Part of the control unit is the *instruction decoder* which decodes the machine-code instructions during the fetch-execute cycle and determines what actions to take next.

The cycle consists of two phases, the *fetch phase* where the instruction is copied into the control unit and decoded, followed by the *execute phase* in which the instruction is obeyed.

Register

including: program counter, instruction address register (IAR), next instruction
register, sequence control register (SCR), address register, memory address register
(MAR), memory buffer register (MBR), Memory Data Register (MDR)

is a location, normally used for a specific purpose, where data or control information is temporarily stored. Some registers are used in the different parts of the *fetch-execute cycle* (see *control unit*, above) whilst others may be available for use by the program being executed. Registers usually are much faster to access than the immediate access store, since they have to be accessed so often.

The various registers include:

Program counter in the control unit that contains the address of the next machine-code instruction to be executed. *Instruction Address Register (IAR)*, *next instruction register* and *Sequence Control Register (SCR)* are alternative names for the program counter.

Address register in the control unit that holds the address part (see *address field*, page 201) of the instruction being executed.

Memory Address Register (MAR) in the central processor that stores the address of the memory location currently in use. In the fetch phase this would be the address of the instruction being loaded and in the execute phase the address of the data being used. The memory unit has access to the MAR and switches the address selection circuitry to access the appropriate location.

Memory Buffer Register (MBR) in the central processor that stores the data being transferred to and from the immediate access store. It acts as a buffer allowing the central processor and memory unit to act independently without being affected by minor differences in operation. A data item will be copied to the MBR ready for use at the next clock pulse, when it can be either used by the central processor or stored in main memory. *Memory Data Register (MDR)* is another name for the memory buffer register.

Address calculation

including: direct addressing, indirect addressing, vector, immediate addressing, indexed addressing, index register, address modification

is working out which *memory location* (see *address*, page 196) is to be accessed by a machine-code instruction. Part of a machine-code instruction is called the *address field* (see page 201) which contains data about which memory location the instruction is to use. There are a number of alternative methods for determining the address of the memory location, such as:

Direct addressing uses the data in the address field without alteration. This is the simplest method of addressing and also the most common.

Indirect addressing uses the address field to hold the address of a location which contains the required address. The action of a program can easily be changed by altering the data in the location pointed to by the instruction. The location holding the real address is known as a *vector*.

One use of a **vector** is to provide access to library routines. Program control is passed to the address in the vector. The locations of the vectors are defined for other programmers to use. Routines can be changed without all the programs using them also being changed. This is because the address of the vector remains the same, but its contents can be altered to point to the new start address for the routine. See also *vectoring*, page 293.

Immediate addressing uses the data in the address field, not as an address, but as a constant which is needed by the program. An example is a routine counting up to 10, which may have the constant '10' supplied in the address field of an instruction. Although the address field cannot hold numbers as large as those that can be stored as data in a memory location, because space has to be left for the *operation code field* (see page 201), this is a particularly convenient method of loading constants into the accumulator.

Indexed addressing modifies the address (either a direct or an indirect address) in the address field by the addition of a number held in a special-purpose register, called an **index register,** before the address is used. Index registers are quickly and easily altered providing an efficient way of accessing a range of memory locations, such as in an array.

Address modification is changing the address field of a machine-code instruction as the program is running, so that each time the instruction is executed it can refer to a different memory location.

Memory management

including: memory management unit (MMU), bank switching, virtual memory, paging, pages, page turn, page fault, threshing, direct memory access (DMA)

is organising the flexible use of the computer's main memory, the *immediate access store* (see page 121). This can be done by the **Memory Management Unit** (**MMU**), often a single integrated circuit in a microcomputer, which allows the addresses used by the *central processing unit* (see page 281) to be stored at a different physical location. The memory management unit automatically converts the logical address provided by the central processor into the physical address in memory.

This allows programs in a multi-user or multi-tasking computer system apparently to use the same memory locations. The memory management unit places them in different physical parts of the immediate access store. Four memory management techniques which can be used are bank switching, virtual memory, paging and direct memory access:

Bank switching is used for overcoming the limitations of computers that can only address a limited amount of immediate access storage. Several 'banks' of storage are provided, each one occupying the same place in the computer's memory map. Only one bank may be active at any one time, and the required one is selected as needed by the software.

Virtual memory is used when sufficient immediate access store is not available. Part of a disk drive is allocated to be used as if it were main memory. When accessing these memory locations the software has to copy the contents of the relevant disk block into a reserved area of main memory, having first copied its existing contents back onto disk. This is very slow and the software will attempt to use the immediate access store if possible.

Paging is the organisation of memory into fixed size units, called *pages* (for example a page of 32K bytes). The immediate access store is organised as a number of physical pages. The logical pages used by the central processing unit can be assigned, by the memory management unit, to any page in physical memory. A form of *virtual memory* (see above) can be used with less frequently used pages being stored on disk, but when required they are reloaded into the immediate access store as a complete page.

Page turn is the movement of a page to or from backing store. The movement of pages is counted in page turns, which are sometimes confusingly called *page faults*. Monitoring the rate of page turns can lead to improved efficiency by indicating where unnecessary movement is taking place. Rapid up-loading and down-loading of pages is known as *threshing* and can be recognised by a very high rate of disk access. In extreme cases something close to a *deadly embrace* (see page 240/1) may occur, because tasks cannot continue for any effective time before being interrupted and while new pages are loaded.

Direct Memory Access (*DMA*) is the use of part of the immediate access store independently from the operating system or the memory management unit. This is usually used in the design of games for use on microcomputers, where the screen display is accessed directly allowing a faster and more complex display.

Array processor

is a central processor designed to allow any machine instruction to operate simultaneously on a number of data locations (data arrays). This design enables problems involving the same calculations on a range of data to be solved very quickly. Examples of suitable problems are weather forecasting and airflow simulation around a new aircraft. See also *floating-point unit*, page 286.

Floating-point unit

including: maths co-processor, Floating-Point Accelerator (FPA)

is a component that can be added to the central processor to make arithmetical operations faster. It provides registers sufficiently large to handle floating-point representation of numbers as single units. It contains micro-code routines optimised to perform floating-point arithmetic operations very quickly.

Floating-point units are manufactured as a single integrated circuit for use in suitable microcomputers where they are called **maths co-processors** or **Floating-Point Accelerators** (**FPA**).

Floating-point units increase the performance of a computer when carrying out large numbers of calculations. They do not improve performance of text processing nor of peripheral handling. They are widely used in graphics applications to perform the calculations needed to plot screen images, for example in a computer aided design system.

An alternative approach to complex mathematical problems is the *array processor* (see page 285).

Parallel processing

is the simultaneous use of several processors to perform a single job. A job may be split into a number of tasks each of which may be processed by any available processor.

Bit map

including: disk map, screen map

is a pattern of bits describing the organisation of data. For example, the arrangement of data on a disk might be represented to the operating system as a bit map in which each bit represents one sector on disk: a '1' for sectors in use, a '0' for unused sectors.

A bit map for a disk is called a **disk map**. A graphic screen prepared in a painting or drawing package may be held as a bit map, often called a **screen map**, each bit relating to the setting of an individual pixel on the screen.

Bus

including: address bus, data bus, highway

is a common pathway shared by signals to and from several components of a computer. For example, all input and output devices would be connected to the I/O (input/output) bus. In practice each bus has two parts, an **address bus** which carries identification about where the data is being sent, and a **data bus** which carries the actual information. The principle of a bus is that the same wires go to each component in turn. The components watch the address bus until an address which they recognise, by using an address *decoder* (see page 326), is present. When this occurs they take action, either retrieving the data from the data bus or placing new data on the bus for the central processor.

Highway is a rarely used alternative name for a bus.

Buffer

including: buffering, single buffering, double buffering
is an area of computer memory allocated to transferring data between the computer
and a peripheral. Sometimes a buffer is used between components within the
computer (see *memory buffer register*, page 283). Using a buffer provides a barrier
between devices with different working speeds or data organisation.

It is much more efficient to send or receive data as a *block* (see page 131) of many
words or bytes. Magnetic disks and tapes require data to be read or written in such a
way that a block of data is moved in a single operation. The computer and the
peripheral have to be capable of sending or receiving a whole block of data at high
speed when required.

The management of block data transfer is done by *buffering*. An area of memory is
allocated as the buffer, and when information is to be transferred, it is stored in the
buffer until an entire block is compete. This block is then sent, leaving the area it
occupied free for assembling the next block of data. When a block is received into a
buffer, the data is processed before the next block is requested and transferred.

With *single buffering*, one device has to wait for the block to be received before
using the data (and the other device has to wait whilst it is processed). This is
inefficient and slow. An improved method is *double buffering*, where two areas of
memory are allocated, and as one buffer is emptied the other can be filled up. This
reduces the time a device has to stop while waiting for the data transfer.

Some peripherals may communicate with single bytes of data, for example keyboard
input or musical sounds. The buffer for these peripherals may be organised as a
circular queue (see page 258) enabling data to be added or removed as required.

Cycle

*including: cycle time, processor cycle time, machine cycle time, millions of
instructions per second (MIPS), program loop time*
is the sequence of actions to perform a particular hardware operation, which is either
repeated continuously or performed whenever it is required. In many cases the time
taken for an operation is constant and is known as the *cycle time*. Cycle time is useful
when calculating the speed of a particular computer task.

The *processor cycle time* or *machine cycle time* is the cycle time for one
fetch/execute cycle (see page 283) and is governed by the speed of access to the
immediate access store. Processor cycle time gives a rough guide to the speed of a
computer, although other factors, such as word length, are also important. Processing
speed is sometimes expressed in *millions of instructions per second* (**MIPS**), which
is also only a rough guide, and is normally based on the average number of machine-
code instructions executed.

The *program loop time* is the time taken by a single repetition of a *loop* (see page
207) and is useful for calculating the expected speed of a routine.

Arithmetic Logic Unit (ALU)

including: arithmetic unit, accumulator, arithmetic register

is the part of the central processing unit where data is processed and manipulated. It is also called the ***arithmetic unit***. The processing and manipulation of data normally consists of arithmetic operations or logical comparisons allowing a program to take decisions.

Most operations involve the ***accumulator***, a special storage register within the arithmetic logic unit. It is used to hold the data currently being processed by the central processor. Any data to be processed is temporarily stored in the accumulator, the results ending up in the accumulator before being stored in the memory unit.

Most computer calculations are based on addition methods and so the 'accumulator' is where the computer does its 'additions'. A computer performs subtraction by two's complement addition and multiplication by combining addition with shifts for column alignment. See also *two's complement*, page 267, and *shift*, page 290.

The ALU usually includes ***arithmetic registers*** (see *register*, page 283) which are special store locations used to hold operands and results temporarily during calculation.

Adder

including: full adder, half adder, sum bit, carry bit

is part of the arithmetic logic unit (ALU) which has the specialised job of addition within the central processor. Its proper name is ***full adder***, a logic design which takes two binary numbers and adds the equivalent bits, adding in any carrys. Full adders are made from smaller components called ***half adders*** which simply take two bits and add them together producing the answer (called the ***sum bit***) and a ***carry bit*** if the result is greater than one. See also *standard logic networks*, page 324, for *half adder* and *full adder*.

Only some very specialised computers, such as *super-computers* (see page 110/1) or computers using *floating-point units* (see page 286), have specific components to do any arithmetic other than addition. The arithmetic unit can do subtraction by adding complements but has to do multiplication and division using a special program (often written in *micro-code*, see page 289) which uses combinations of addition and subtraction.

Interface

is the hardware and associated software needed for communication between processors and peripheral devices, to compensate for the difference in their operating characteristics (e.g. speeds, voltage and power levels, codes, etc.). A number of internationally accepted standard interfaces (and their associated protocols) have been defined, these include: RS232, IEEE 488, SCSI and Centronics (see *C15 Interfaces and Buses*, page 294).

Micro-code
including: micro-program, micro-instruction
is machine-code instructions which are executed by calling small programs held elsewhere in the computer. To the user a micro-code instruction behaves like a machine-code instruction but the control unit implements it by passing control to the micro-code routine. The micro-code is stored within the central processor for speed of access. Micro-code enables the instruction set of a computer to be expanded without the addition of hardware components, but it will be slower than a machine-code instruction.

Each micro-code routine is a *micro-program* consisting of a sequence of *micro-instructions*, typically defining a machine-code instruction.

Interrupt
including: timer
is a signal, generated by a source such as an input or output device or a systems software routine, which causes a break in the execution of the current routine. Control passes to another routine in such a way that the original routine can be resumed after the interrupt.

This enables peripherals to operate independently, indicating to the operating system, with an interrupt, when they need to communicate with the central processor. An example is a keyboard, which only sends data to the central processor when a key is pressed. The central processor continues with other tasks until, on receiving an interrupt, it *polls* (see *polling*, page 293) the various peripherals to establish the reason for the interrupt. If the interrupt is from the keyboard, the central processor collects the data, the code for the key which has been pressed, and stores it in the keyboard *buffer* (see page 287) before continuing. Timing circuits, called *timers*, are also used to generate interrupts at fixed intervals, for example to refresh the screen display.

Channel
including: channel number
is any physical path followed by data, particularly between a central processing unit and a peripheral device or, by extension, between the user's program and a file on backing store.

Although different peripherals work totally differently, the computer is simply sending or receiving data, but along different physical routes. These routes are all called channels and are normally given a number (a *channel number*) by the operating system. A program can alter the peripheral used simply by altering the channel number and allowing the operating system to redirect the data stream, allowing great flexibility in switching between peripherals and adding peripherals to the system.

An example is a music system, where a generated tune could be saved to a suitable disk, or played by a variety of output devices. Each output device can be linked to a separate output channel of a *MIDI interface* (see page 65) which switches the output to one or more devices simply by setting and altering channel numbers.

Shift

including: shift register, arithmetic shift, logical shift, cyclic shift, rotation
is an operation that moves the bits held in a register, called the ***shift register***, either to the left or to the right.

There are three different types of shift: arithmetic shift, logical shift and cyclic shift (also called a rotation). They are distinguished by what happens to the bits that are shifted out of the register at one end and what is moved in to fill the vacant space at the other end.

Arithmetic shift to the right causes a bit at the right-hand end of the register to be lost at each shift, and a copy of the sign bit is moved in at the left-hand end. This operation preserves the sign of a number and has the effect of dividing a binary number by 2 at each shift, regardless of the representation system or whether the number is negative or positive. The division will be inaccurate because of the truncation caused by the loss of a digit at each shift.

Arithmetic shift to the left causes the bit at the left-hand end of the register, the sign bit, to be lost at each shift. A zero bit is moved in at the right-hand end. If the bit to be moved into the sign bit position is different from the one that was there before the shift, an overflow flag is set.

The use of two's complement representation ensures that shifting left gives correct results for multiplication by 2 until an overflow is flagged, because the number is too large to be represented in this size of register. See also *two's complement*, page 267.

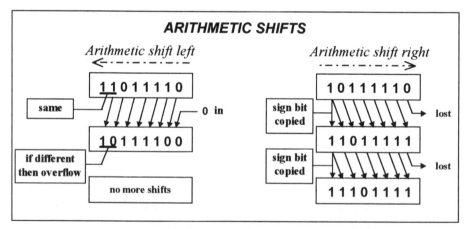

Figure C14.1: *Arithmetic shifts*

Logical shift is where the bits shifted from the end of the register are lost, and zeros are shifted in at the opposite end. It is called a logical shift because it is suitable for *logical operations* (see page 200) rather than for arithmetic.

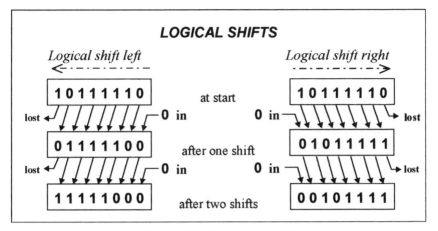

Figure C14.2: Logical shifts

Cyclic shift or *rotation* is where the bits shifted out at one end of the register are re-inserted at the opposite end.

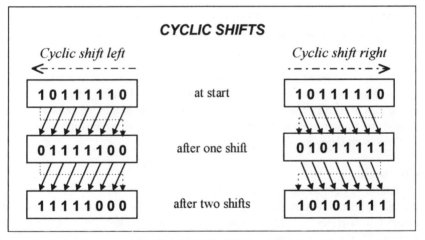

Figure C14.3: Cyclic shifts

Pipelining

is the concurrent decoding of two or more machine instructions. While part of one instruction (for example, an address field) is being decoded, another part of a second instruction (for example, an operation code) may also be decoded, as a means of increasing the speed of execution of a program.

Wait state

is an interval built into some *machine-code instructions* (see page 201), to enable other parts of the computer to complete their actions before the processor moves on to the next instruction. For example, because the processor runs much faster than the RAM, it has to wait for some memory operations to be completed.

Masking

is an operation that selects certain of the bits in a register for subsequent processing. Usually, another register of equal length holds a bit pattern called a mask with each bit set to 1 where a corresponding bit is to be selected and 0 otherwise. For example, if a 16-bit register holds a machine-code instruction divided as follows:

OPERATION CODE							ADDRESS								
1	0	0	0	1	0	1	0	0	1	1	0	1	0	1	1

the operation code can be selected by constructing the following mask:

1	1	1	1	1	1	1	0	0	0	0	0	0	0	0	0

Using the *AND operation* (see page 200) gives a result of:

1	0	0	0	1	0	1	0	0	0	0	0	0	0	0	0

If necessary, the result can then be *shifted* (see *shift*, page 200) to the right by 9 bit places to put the operation code at the right-hand end of the register.

The idea of using a mask in this way is so fundamental that the same words are used to describe similar selections at a much higher level, such as in using a *data manipulation language* (see page 248).

Parity check

including: parity bit, even parity, odd parity

is a test applied to binary data to ensure that it has been stored or transmitted without error. It is possible for technical failures to corrupt (or alter) the data in a computer system. This may be caused by electrical interference, dust or corrosion. Corrupt data can be detected by a parity check and the user alerted to the problem.

A bit in each word or byte of data is reserved to be a *parity bit*. This parity bit is altered to make the number of '1's in the data either even (for *even parity* systems) or odd (for *odd parity* systems). If the data is corrupted, the even (or odd) total is unlikely to apply so that, when the data is checked, the error will be detected.

Parity checking may be used inside the computer (to check the internal workings of the computer), when data is transmitted to a peripheral (such as backing store or a printer) or when data is being transmitted over longer distances using a network or telephone system. Usually when sending data using a serial interface (for example, to a printer or modem) parity checking will be used and the user must ensure that both devices use the same parity check.

Polling

is the sequential checking of a range of possibilities to identify which should be dealt with next. This allows the operating system to manage a range of choices, such as determining what has caused an *interrupt* (see page 289) or which terminal in a multi-user system is waiting for processing. Usually a message is sent to each routine in turn and the routine has to respond positively to claim the attention of the operating system. The routines are polled one after another so that each routine can claim (if required) its full share of the processor.

Vectoring

is the technique for passing control in a computer program through an intermediate address or vector. For example, on detecting an interrupt, instead of the computer passing control directly to a service routine, it may first jump to a location which in turn hands control to the routine. By altering the contents of this intermediate location, alternative service routines may be introduced without affecting programs that have already been written for that system.

Von Neumann architecture

also known as: Von Neumann concept or machine
is the name given to traditional computer architecture which forms the basis of most digital computer systems. A single control unit manages program control following a linear sequence of "fetch-decode-execute-output".

John von Neumann (1903-57), who was a member of a team working on first-generation computers, is credited with the idea that programs and data were indistinguishable, and hence could be stored in the same memory unit. In early computers, programs and data were stored in separate memories and the process of entering or altering programs was very tedious. Treating programs as just one form of data made changing programs easier and opened the way for compilers, whose input was text and whose output was a program in binary code.

Von Neumann is also credited with the introduction of the flowchart and with the concept of 'assertion boxes'. These say *what should be true* before or after a step in a program as opposed to *what should be done* at that point in the program.

C15 Interfaces and Buses

*Related terms can be found in C14 Machine Architecture,
C16 Physical Components, C17 Communications Technology.*

What goes on inside a computer is of little interest to most users. For those who are interested in the basic concepts of the internal workings, machine architecture is covered in the preceding section. It is when they connect peripherals to a microcomputer that most users are affected by the computer's architecture.

All peripherals are connected to a computer through an **interface**, but each type of computer may have to be fitted with slightly different interfaces depending on the computer's internal design. Some peripherals require their own dedicated interface, but in situations where a variety of peripherals may be connected, the interface may provide an **expansion bus**. The expansion bus allows several peripherals (of a suitable type) to be linked in a chain to one computer interface.

Inside a microcomputer all the components are connected together by a bus. Any peripherals have to be connected to this bus. An **interface board** plugs into a special socket connected to the bus. The electronics on this interface board need to be tailored to fit the electrical connections used by that particular computer's bus. So each design of bus requires its own particular interface boards.

Each peripheral is provided with an interface and is connected, generally through a cable, to the equivalent type of interface on the computer. For the computer and the peripheral to communicate with each other, the interface in the peripheral and the interface in the computer need to be of the same type.

Some peripherals use a **bus interface**. Several peripherals attached to the same bus can share one computer interface, making it easy to use many different peripherals and change peripherals as needed. The computer can identify each peripheral by an address which is set when the peripheral is first installed.

Interfaces may be plugged into the main printed circuit board of the computer, called the **motherboard**, or into an extension of the motherboard. The degree to which a microcomputer can be expanded depends on the physical space available in its case, which limits the size of the interface board, and the number of sockets available; these are normally called **slots**.

Motherboard
including: mainboard, daughterboard, carrier board
is the printed circuit board (PCB) that holds the principal components in a microcomputer system. The motherboard contains at least the main bus. The other components, such as the microprocessor and clock chips, will be either plugged into the motherboard or soldered to it. The motherboard is also known as the ***mainboard***.

Some components may be mounted on their own printed circuit board, called a *daughterboard* which will be plugged into the motherboard. Components attached using daughterboards can easily be replaced or upgraded and are not limited by the sockets or circuitry provided by the motherboard. Daughterboards are sometimes called *carrier boards.*

Print buffer

is an area of computer memory where data to be printed is held until the printer is ready to print it. It enables a program to continue operating without waiting for each character to be printed, as it can send its data to the buffer. The buffer is normally managed by the operating system. When a printer, which works much slower than a computer, is ready to print the next data, it can signal this by means of an *interrupt* (see page 289) to the operating system. The operating system will remove the data from the buffer and send it to the printer. See also *buffer*, page 287.

Bus (microcomputer)

including: S100, ISA, EISA, AT and MCA buses

is the common pathway shared by signals between the internal components of the microcomputer. Each design of microcomputer uses different electrical signals and physical layouts. This is important when new components, such as *interface boards* or *cards* (see page 297), are being added, since they will have to be manufactured to fit that type of computer.

Typical designs of standard microcomputer buses are the S100, ISA, AT, EISA and MCA buses. Interfaces designed for one type of bus will not fit another type.

S100 bus is now obsolete but was widely used in small personal microcomputers and was so called because it could link a maximum of 100 components.

ISA (Industry Standard Architecture) bus, *EISA (Extended Industry Standard Architecture)* bus, *AT (Advanced Technology)* bus and *MCA (Micro Channel Architecture)* bus are all standard designs used by various types of IBM-compatible microcomputers.

Local bus

including: video bus, VESA and PCI buses

is an additional bus in a microcomputer normally with a specific function. Some functions of modern microcomputers (such as maintaining the VDU display and sending data to and from the disk drives) can require the computer to move vast amounts of data. This can use between 10% and 50% of the microcomputer's power. One way of cheaply increasing the power of a microcomputer is to provide a special bus for one or both of these functions, so relieving the load on the main bus. This special bus doing a specific function is known as a local bus. If the local bus is simply maintaining the screen display then it is sometimes called a *video bus*.

VESA (Video Electronics Standards Association) and *PCI (Peripheral Component Interconnect)* are both standard designs of local buses used by various types of IBM-compatible microcomputers.

Expansion slot

including: slot, expansion card, card, memory card, PCMCIA card
is a socket which is provided in a computer to allow additional components, such as
additional disk drives and network interfaces, to be added to the computer later. These
sockets are also called *slots*. The more slots that are provided, the greater the number
of extra components that can be added.

Expansion slots allow *expansion cards* (or *cards*) to be added. These expansion
cards are usually *interface boards* (see page 297) but can also provide extra facilities
such as a small hard disk drive or a co-processor. Similarly many computers can
accept *memory cards* which allow the computer's main memory to be increased.

In most microcomputers, the expansion slots are connected directly to the main bus.
This means that the expansion board must be designed for that particular bus design
(or architecture). One important agreed standard is the *PCMCIA* (**Personal
Computer Memory Card International Association**) *card,* which is the size of a
credit card, for fitting into the expansion slots of small portable computers. Although
originally intended for memory expansion cards, a variety of peripheral cards,
including modems and hard disk drives, are now available.

Bus interface

also known as: expansion bus
IEEE bus, SCSI (Small Computer Systems Interface) bus
is an *interface* (see page 288) which provides an additional *bus* (see page 286)
external to the computer to which several peripheral devices can be connected. This
makes it easy to use a range of peripherals or to change the peripherals being used.
Each device has an address, which is set on installation, so that the microcomputer can
distinguish between the various peripherals. The most common bus interfaces are the
SCSI (Small Computer Systems Interface) and the IEEE interface, which are
internationally defined standards. Peripherals fitted with one of these interfaces can be
connected to any microcomputer fitted with the same type of bus interface; this means
that peripherals do not have to be designed for one model of microcomputer but can be
interfaced with many different types of computer. Many different pieces of equipment
can be connected to the computer at the same time via the same bus.

IEEE bus conforms to standards defined by the Institute of Electrical and Electronic
    Engineers (USA). It is used outside the computer to connect scientific equipment
    to a computer. The computer will have an IEEE interface to convert signals on
    the IEEE bus into signals suitable for the main computer bus. As it is a common
    standard, many types of equipment are manufactured with the logic and
    connections needed for the IEEE bus. These pieces of equipment can easily be
    connected to computers with an IEEE bus.
SCSI (Small Computer Systems Interface) bus was designed to connect a wide
    range of devices to microcomputers at minimum cost, in particular disk drives
    and scanners which need a high data transfer rate. It is widely used in general
    microcomputing. Each SCSI interface can connect up to seven peripheral
    devices.

Interface board

also known as: interface card
*including: parallel port, serial port, centronics interface, RS232 interface, V.24
interface, RS432 interface, IDE (intelligent device electronics or integrated drive
electronics) interface*
is the necessary hardware (see *interface*, page 288), mounted on a small printed circuit
board (PCB), needed for a microcomputer to communicate with a peripheral device (or
another computer). Appropriate *interface cards* can easily be plugged into the
expansion slots (see page 296) of the microcomputer .

Some international standard interfaces are used by microcomputers. These include
a *parallel port* and a *serial port*. Although these are general terms, when referring to
microcomputers they refer to particular international standards. The parallel port is
often a Centronics interface and the serial port frequently uses the RS232 interface.
The wide range of interface standards include:

Centronics interface, an interface initially designed for use with printers, is a form of
parallel port. The latest versions have been developed to allow the interface to be
used for both input and output, enabling it to be used for data transfer between
computers or for the easy attachment of a range of peripherals; this is sometimes
called 'the PIO' (parallel input/output) interface.

RS232 interface is a widely used international standard serial interface. The serial
port is often referred to as 'the RS232 port'.

The *V.24 interface* and the *RS432 interface* are almost identical to the RS232
interface.

IDE (integrated device electronics or intelligent device electronics) interface is
another common standard, which is used to control hard disks in a
microcomputer. The IDE interface is built into the hard disk it is controlling,
which reduces the cost of adding hard disks to microcomputers. In high
performance applications, other interfaces such as the *SCSI bus* (see page 296)
are more likely to be used.

One particular type of interface board is the *expansion bus* (see page 296) and
another important standard interface is the *MIDI interface* (see page 65) for sound.

Docking station

is a device containing a range of peripherals and interfaces for use by a portable
computer. For lightness and to reduce power consumption, *portable computers* (see
page 110/1) have few peripherals other than disk drives and use a small LCD screen
rather than a large monitor. One solution to this lack of peripherals is a docking
station which may be part of a network. When plugged into the docking station, the
portable computer has access to a large monitor, printer, extra disk drives and other
peripherals, such as modems. The portable computer can be quickly disconnected and
used elsewhere.

C16 Physical Components

Related terms can be found in section C14 Machine Architecture.

The computer industry has produced a range of electronic components to perform specific functions within a computer system. Some of these components, such as the clock, simply provide the controlling electronics needed by a computer, whilst others allow a particular type of computer to be designed for a specific role.

Many of these components are integrated circuits and are designed to a standard size which makes them easy to incorporate into computer designs.

The development of standardised components means that they can be mass produced rather than being individually constructed. This has the advantage that components are much cheaper and that it becomes economic to design a variety of computers with particular characteristics.

Although computer systems are usually viewed conceptually as a 'black box', it is useful to appreciate the functions of some of the individual components.

Clock

including: clock rate

is the electronic unit that synchronises related components by generating pulses at a constant rate. Clock pulses are used to trigger components to take their next step, so keeping all components in time with each other. The *clock rate* is the frequency at which the clock generates pulses. The higher the clock rate, the faster the computer may work. One limiting factor for machine speed is the manufactured tolerance of the slowest component.

Hard-wired logic

is a function permanently built into the circuitry. Often this is an integrated circuit designed to control the function. Such functions are immediately available when switched on and cannot be altered by the user. This ensures that the device will always be in the same initial state when switched on.

Integrated circuit (IC)

including: chip, Small Scale Integration (SSI), Medium Scale Integration (MSI), Large Scale Integration (LSI) and Very Large Scale Integration (VLSI)

is a solid state micro-circuit in which all the components (such as transistors and capacitors) are formed within a very thin slice of silicon. The popular name for an integrated circuit is a '(silicon) chip'.

Most integrated circuits used in computers are produced using Large Scale Integration (LSI) or Very Large Scale Integration (VLSI) which are techniques for producing integrated circuits of very high density. These have large numbers of components (transistors, diodes etc.) and circuits (decoders, flip-flops etc.) combined as a single integrated circuit.

Small Scale Integration (SSI) has up to 20 logic gates on a chip; typically they are used for (hard) wired logic circuits.

Medium Scale Integration (MSI) has 20 to 100 logic gates or less than 1000 memory bits on a chip; these are also used for (hard) wired logic.

Large Scale Integration (LSI) has 100 to10000 logic gates or up to 16000 memory bits on a chip; used for computer logic or memory.

Very Large Scale Integration (VLSI) has more than 10000 logic gates or more than 16000 memory bits on a chip; used as standard for computer manufacture.

Bistable
including: flip-flop

is a device that has two stable states. Since each state is stable the device effectively forms a memory which can differentiate between two pieces of data. Whatever the technology, which could be electronic, magnetic, liquid or pneumatic, the two states are used to represent the binary digits 0 and 1. This means that mathematical manipulation can be performed on data held in binary form.

The bistable in the integrated circuits used for the main memory of computers is a *flip-flop*, a logic circuit designed to store a single data bit. The receipt of an electrical pulse by the flip-flop will reverse its state, and a series of pulses causes it to flip successively between the two stable states.

Latency
including: propagation delay, access time

is the time delay before a component in the computer responds to an instruction, for example the time between data being requested from a memory device and the time when the answer is returned.

Even a single logic gate has a latency (or *propagation delay*) which will be very small (a fraction of a microsecond) but, with a large number of gates involved, these delays can be significant. The computer cannot work any faster than the limit imposed by latency.

A special case of latency is *access time*, which is the time delay in retrieving data stored either in main memory or on backing store. Access time is relevant when deciding which backing store should be used in any particular context to produce an acceptably fast computer system.

Logic element
including: logic circuit

is a *gate* (see page 312) or combination of gates needed to perform a logical function as part of the circuitry of a computer. It may be a single *AND gate* (see page 316) or a more complex component such as an *adder* (see pages 324/5). Hardware system designers can produce complex circuits using logic elements as modules in the construction of their designs.

A *logic circuit* is designed to perform a more complex function, perhaps specific to the system being built, producing a required set of outputs from a given set of inputs.

Programmable Logic Array (PLA)

also known as: Uncommitted Logic Array (ULA)

is an array of standard logic gates, in which each element is identical, manufactured on a single LSI (large scale integration) chip. The logic circuits required for a particular application are created by 'burning out' unwanted connections.

Real-time clock

is an electronic unit that maintains the time of day in a special register that may be accessed by suitable instructions in a computer program. It is powered by internal batteries, and continues to function even when the computer is switched off. For example, the computer can use this time information to label files with the time and date they were created or to trigger timed events such as collecting a weather satellite broadcast.

ZIF socket

or zero insertion force socket

is a socket on a printed circuit board in the computer into which an *integrated circuit* (see page 298) is plugged. The socket is designed so that no pressure is needed on the component to plug it in (*zero insertion force*) or to remove it. This means that an integrated circuit can be removed and replaced without damage. It also means that a computer can be easily upgraded by having an obsolescent integrated circuit replaced by a new one without risk of damage to the integrated circuits or to the computer itself.

Dual In-Line (DIL) socket

including: Dual In-line Package (DIP)

is a socket which accepts most standard *integrated circuits* (see page 298). These integrated circuits are constructed with two parallel lines of pins, one at each side of the integrated circuit package. This form of package is known as a *Dual In-line Package (DIP)*. There are a number of standard sizes of dual in-line packages, which enable flexible design and interchange of components.

DIN socket

is a plug/socket design adopted by Deutsche Industrienorm (the German Standards Organisation) but which is widely used internationally. There are a variety of types of DIN socket with various numbers of pins and layouts. The most common is the '5 pin DIN', which is also widely used in audio systems.

C17 Communications Technology

This section is concerned with the principles involved in achieving communication between computer systems, and the conventions that determine how such systems communicate with each other. Related terms can be found in A4 Communications, B6 Networks and B7 Communications Devices and Control Devices.

Ways of communicating data between distant places, using electrical energy, have been in use for over 100 years, of which the telegraph was the first. Very quickly, machines replaced people and automatic communications became typical. Telephones, tele-printers, radio, and television were all well developed before computers were combined with them to produce the range of global communications that is now available.

Global communications require that there are the same standards for the equipment used in all the countries of the world. Some of these standards have been set by those countries which initially developed the systems, but most have been worked out and agreed by international bodies, sometimes with the direct authority of the United Nations. Each industrial country has a national organisation that sets standards for all kinds of products. These organisations have been setting standards, and revising them, throughout the last 100 years. Thus there are international standards defined by ISO (the International Standards Organisation) and by ITU (International Telecommunications Union), formerly the CCITT (Committée Consultatif International Téléphonique et Télégraphique) of the United Nations, and other standards of a national origin are accepted through organisations like the General Agreement on Tariffs and Trade (GATT).

The specification of standards is a complex and expensive process. The implications of a particular choice can be very far reaching, both for the industries that make products to those standards, and for the consumers of those products. As far as the consumer is concerned, the acceptance of a single manufacturer's standards for some device or system can have limiting effects, particularly when there is severe competition for sales of the product. However in a situation of rapid technical development, the consumer is likely to benefit from clearly defined standards which help to ensure some measure of compatibility between hardware and software originating from different sources. The most important areas of standards definition for the computer and information technology industries are those of input/output specifications and external communications.

Channel

is a path for a signal. The path may be provided by wires, fibre optic cable or microwave (radio or infra-red) links. The material and design of the means of providing the channel will determine the range of frequencies that the channel can carry. See also *bandwidth*, page 305.

Data transmission

including: duplex, full duplex, half duplex, simplex; synchronous transmission, asynchronous transmission, start bit, stop bit, parallel data transmission, serial data transmission, echo

is the passing of data from one device to another. This may be between parts of a computer system or between computers in a network.

Data transmission may have a number of distinct characteristics:

- it may be synchronised or unsynchronised;
- it may be serial or parallel;
- it may be in both directions at the same time, called *duplex* or *full duplex*; in only one direction at a time, called *half duplex*; or in one direction only, called *simplex*;
- checks may be made on the accuracy of transmission (*parity checks*, see page 292, or the use of echo processes);
- data may be *packeted* (see *packet switching system*, page 303) with the addresses of destinations.

Synchronous transmission is a method of transmitting data between two devices in which all the data transfers are timed to coincide with a clock pulse. Within a computer the timing is provided by the computer's clock. Between computers, the clock in one computer acts as the master clock for the system.

Asynchronous transmission is a method of data transmission, in which a character is sent as soon as it becomes available rather than waiting for a synchronisation signal or a clock pulse. A *start bit* marks the beginning of a character and one or two *stop bits* mark the end of a character.

Parallel data transmission sends the bits for a character simultaneously along separated data lines. This means that an 8-bit code will require a minimum of 9 *channels* (see page 160) for parallel transmission (8 data and at least one ground, return channel).

Serial data transmission sends the bits for a character one after another along the same data line. This means that serial transmission requires only two wires (a data line and the ground, return line), although more may be provided.

Echo is a feature of data transmission in which the data received is returned to the point of origin for comparison with the original data in order to check it.

Signal routing

including: circuit switching, message switching, message queuing

is the choice of route for a particular message through a network. In *ring* and *star networks* (see pages 152 and 153) there is little choice of route. But more complex network topologies provide many possible routes for any message. If the direct connection between two nodes is unavailable, perhaps because of some fault or because the connection is busy, then the intelligence in the *routers* (see page 163) at the nodes sends the message forward in a direction which is available. Since the time for a message to travel between nodes is often nearly the same regardless of the distance apart, this is more efficient than waiting for the direct link to become available. For example, it is possible that a message from London to Manchester may be routed via a satellite to Los Angeles and then on to Manchester. The computer in London which sent the message and the computer in Manchester have no control over the route used, nor has the computer in Los Angeles through which it may have passed. The next part of the message may go by some completely different route. See also Figure A8.1, page 35.

Circuit switching is a method of communication in which a path is set up from sender to receiver immediately before the start of transmission and kept open until the transmission is completed. After the transmission is completed, all parts of the path are released and can be used for other transmissions. See also *packet switching*, below.

Message switching is a method of batching, organising and storing sections of data, so that they can be transmitted economically in a network; it is usually applicable to networks with many computers. Each section of a message is sent from node to node with each node responsible for the choice of route for the next part of the journey. This requires that the nodes are intelligent. A message will be accepted at a node and, if necessary, stored until it can be transmitted onwards. Finally, all the sections of the data are assembled, in the correct order, at their destination.

Message queuing is a method of passing messages in a network in which a host computer stores a message for a terminal until it is ready to receive the message. This is a system appropriate to *star networks* (see page 152/3).

Packet Switching System (PSS)
including: packet, datagram, IP datagram
is a method of sending data over a *wide area network* (see page 151). Packet switching networks are available for general use in most countries .

A *packet* is a group of bits, made up of control signals, error control bits, coded information, and the destination address for the data. In a given situation the size of a packet may be fixed. These packets of information are sometimes called *datagrams*. An *IP datagram* is the basic unit of information which is transferred under TCP/IP.

Since each packet occupies a channel for only a short time, this arrangement provides for very efficient use of the system. Error checking should ensure that errors are detected, and that appropriate recovery procedures are automatically started. If there is an error, it will only be in a small part of the data, and this can be retransmitted quickly. See also TCP/IP, page 45.

Message fragmentation
is the breaking down of IP datagrams into smaller units so that they can be passed to, or through, a particular processor. See also *maximum transmission unit*, below.

Maximum Transmission Unit (MTU)
is the largest unit of data which can be transferred by a particular communications system. See also *message fragmentation*, above.

Open system

including: Open Systems Interconnection (OSI), ISO 7

is a set of protocols allowing computers of different origins to be linked together. The standards relating to open systems are called ***Open Systems Interconnection (OSI)***.

ISO 7 is the seven-layer design for the OSI protocols established by the International Standards Organisation (ISO). It enables manufacturers to design equipment and software for a particular layer. These systems will interconnect with equipment designed for the layer above and the layer below. A brief summary of some of the aspects covered by ISO 7 is given in Table C17.1, below.

The relations between the levels of TCP/IP (Transmission Control Protocol/Internet Protocol) network protocol 'family' and ISO 7 are shown in very simple form in Table C17.2, opposite. See also *TCP/IP*, page 45.

OPEN SYSTEMS INTERCONNECTION (OSI)

7 LAYER NETWORK ORGANISATION MODEL (ISO 7)

level	level name	some functions specified within the level descriptions
Level 7	Applications	specific applications, for example data transfer, messaging, distributed databases; operating system functions and end-user interface
Level 6	Presentation	data transformation, syntax adjustments and formatting for output devices; data encryption and compression
Level 5	Session	establishes and maintains session dialogues; synchronises data exchange; provides access control and protection of higher levels from low-level functions
Level 4	Transport	establishes and maintains communications between users; levels out the data flow; provides greater flow control than the data link layer
Level 3	Network	routing/addressing between open systems; preventing packets from getting lost when crossing networks; multiplexing and physical network access
Level 2	Data Link	error-free connections to networks; error recognition and correction; creating and synchronising data blocks
Level 1	Physical	how bit sequences are to be sent; there is no error correction

Table C17.1: ISO 7 model

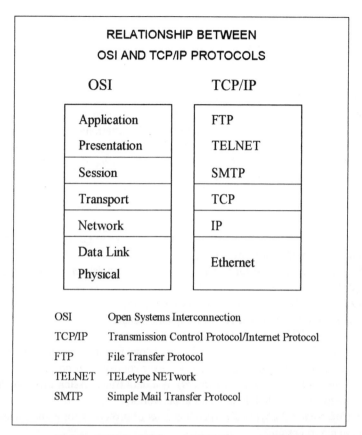

Table C17.2: OSI and TCP/IP equivalents

Bandwidth

including: broadband, narrow band

is a measure of the capacity of a *communications channel* (see page 160). It is the range of frequencies that a channel can handle. Bandwidth may be given as a frequency (range), such as 3 kHz, or as a transmission rate in bits per second (bps), such as 63 Kbps. Transmission rate is often referred to as *line speed* (see page 307). For example, channels might be described as having line speeds of 56K or 64K, meaning 56 Kbps or 64 Kbps.

Broadband is used to describe a transmission channel having a bandwidth in excess of 3 kHz. But for practical network applications it probably needs to exceed 300 MHz.

Narrow band is used to describe bandwidths less than the smallest recognised broadband bandwidth. The term is frequently used to mean fractions of a broadband, since a broadband channel is often divided into a number of narrow band channels.

Communications protocol

including: Z modem, Kermit, X.25, X.400, V.22bis, V.32bis, V.34, ARQ (Automatic Repeat Request), TCP (Transmission Control Protocol), MNP (Microcom Network Protocol)

is a standard set of rules used to ensure the proper transfer of data between devices. Protocols exist which specify the format of the data, and the signals to start, control and end the transfer. Many current protocols have been specified by the United Nations communications committee, the ITU (International Telecommunications Union), formerly the CCITT (Committée Consultatif International Téléphonique et Télégraphique). See also *ITU*, page 43, *Internet protocol*, page 45, and *Open Systems Interconnection (OSI)*, page 304.

Z modem is a file transfer protocol for networks in general, but principally on the Internet.

Kermit is an early file transfer protocol for networks in general, which is simple to implement and is still often used.

X.25 is the ITU standard for public *packet switching system (PSS)* networks(see page 303).

X.400 is the ITU standard for *email* (see page 38).

V.22bis is the ITU standard for 2400 bps modems.

V.32bis is the ITU standard for 14400 bps modems.

V.34 is the ITU standard for 28800 bps modems, formerly called V-fast.

ARQ (Automatic Repeat Request) is an error control protocol used by some modems.

TCP (Transmission Control Protocol) is a data transmission protocol defined for high-speed communications within networks.

MNP (Microcom Network Protocol) is a set of protocols for error correction and data compression.

ISDN (Integrated Services Digital Network)

including: B-channel, D-channel, ISDN service rates (basic, primary, broadband)

is an ITU definition for (global) digital data communications. Its purpose is to ensure that people, computers and other devices can communicate over standardised connection facilities. The criteria include the setting of standards in such a way that users will have access through a limited set of multi-purpose interfaces. This really amounts to the establishment of world-wide digital communications for speech, and other data, with the simplicity of access that current telephone dialling systems provide. ISDN has definitions for the data transmission speeds, or capacities, of channels and the number of channels in each service.

The capacity of channels is set at:

B-Channel is a 64Kbit/s channel which can carry pulse code modulation speech, fax and synchronous or asynchronous data up to a maximum of 64Kbit/s.

D-Channel is a 16Kbit/s channel which carries the control signals to manage B-Channels.

See *pulse code modulation*, page 308/9.

ISDN service rates are:

rate name	number of channels	total capacity
Basic	2 B- and 1 D-	$2 \times 64 + 16 = 144$ Kbps
Primary	30 B- and 1 D-	$30 \times 64 + 16 = 1936$ Kbps
Broadband		more than 34 Mbps

The proposed broadband rates are 150 Mbps and 600 Mbps.

Line speed

including: high-speed links

is the measure of the data capacity of a communications link.

High-speed links are available to provide the opportunities to take advantage of the information available on large networked systems. Transmission capabilities need to be fast enough to handle the large data flows involved. Among the more common transmission capabilities are:

DS0	(Digital Signal Level 0)	64 Kbps
DS1	(Digital Signal Level 1) or **T1**	1.544 Mbps, that is 24 DS0s
DS3	(Digital Signal Level 3) or **T3**	44.736 Mbps, that is 28 T1s
FT1	(Fractional T1)	uses less than 24 DS0s, which is less than 1.536 Mbps

Frame

is a block of data together with its relevant *header* and *trailer* (see page 52).

Signal

including: carrier signal, carrier wave

is electrical or electromagnetic energy transmitted from one point in a circuit to another along the *channels* (see page 160) connecting them. A signal can carry data of either analog or digital origin. A basic *carrier signal* consists of a constant-frequency electromagnetic wave. This wave, the *carrier wave*, is modified by combining it with a representation of the data in a way that can be reversed to extract the data after transmission. This process is called *modulation* (see page 308).

Noise

including: signal-to-noise ratio

is electrical disturbances affecting the transmission of intended signals. The existence of noise generally has the same effect on the accurate transmission of signals that people experience when listening to a person talking in a room with other people who are also talking. This is the basic origin of the term. When the noise level is too high, effective transmission ceases. The comparison of the strength of the signal with the level of noise is called the ***signal-to-noise ratio.***

Modulation

*including: Amplitude Modulation (AM), Frequency Modulation (FM), phase
modulation, Pulse Code Modulation (PCM), demodulation*
is the process of introducing variations into the shape (the waveform) of a *carrier
wave* (see *signal*, page 307). The modulation is used to superimpose data onto the
carrier wave.

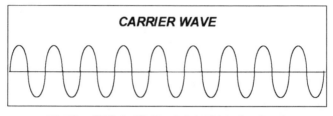

Figure C17.1: *Unmodulated carrier wave*

There are three forms of modulation used for the transmission of digital data,
amplitude modulation, frequency modulation and phase modulation:

Amplitude Modulation (AM), in which the amplitude, that is the height, of the
carrier wave is used to represent 0 and 1. The simplest form of amplitude
modulation is to switch the carrier wave on for a 1 and off for a 0.

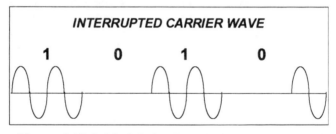

Figure C17.2: *Modulation by switching the wave off*

Other forms involve increasing above a chosen height and decreasing below a chosen
height to represent 1 and 0.

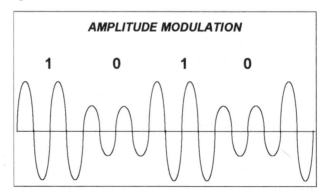

Figure C17.3: *Modulation by changing the amplitude*

Frequency Modulation (*FM*) combines two different frequencies with the carrier wave to produce a waveform which is made up of high and low frequency parts. This is a very common form of modulation for lower speeds of transmission.

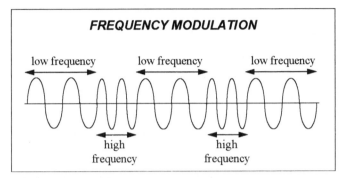

Figure C17.4: Modulation by changing the frequency

Phase modulation combines the carrier wave with an identical wave which is out of phase with it. Two-phase modulation combines two waveforms to provide patterns which are used to represent 0 and 1, shown in Figure C17.5. Four-phase modulation combines four waveforms to provide patterns which are used to represent 00, 01,10 and 11. Four-phase modulation transmits two data bits for each element of the wave, and thus sends data at twice the bit rate of two-phase modulation. Eight-phase modulation provides for three bits (000 to 111) for each wave pattern and sends data at three times the bit rate of two-phase modulation.

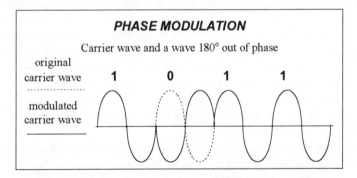

Figure C17.5: Modulation by adding another wave

Pulse Code Modulation (*PCM*) is a method of sampling analog signals to produce an acceptable digital signal which contains sufficient data to allow an acceptable analog reproduction of the original signal. It requires 3 stages: sampling, quantisation and encoding. It was developed for sound transmission and is principally used for voice transmission.

Demodulation is the extraction of the modulating data from the modulated carrier wave signal. The circuits to do this are similar to those used in radio receivers to convert the received signals into sound signals.

Interference

including: Electromagnetic Interference (EMI), Radio Frequency Interference (RFI)
is the introduction of unwanted variations into a transmitted signal. These variations
may be caused by faulty design of communications equipment or by external energy
sources. Interference can sometimes occur inside a computer system, but more
usually affects external communications. At any place there is a large variety of
electromagnetic signals, many of which are unintentionally generated by equipment
such as electric motors. These signals may be picked up by wire conductors carrying
electronic communications and become part of the signal that reaches the receiver. In
addition there is an increasingly high density of intentionally transmitted signals (for
example from portable phones), which may cause interference on equipment for which
these signals are not intended.

Electromagnetic Interference (EMI) is the general term for interference caused by
electromagnetic radiation at any frequency, whether continuous or intermittent.

Radio Frequency Interference (RFI) is interference which is generated at typical
radio frequencies, in the range 10 kHz to 100000 MHz. Radio frequencies are at
the lower end of the electromagnetic frequency spectrum and are more prone to
interference than the higher frequency radiations such as infra red and light.

Collision detection

including: Carrier Sense Multiple Access/Collision Detection (CSMA/CD)
is a method of managing data traffic on a *local area network* (see page 151).
Individual computers are responsible for waiting for the network to be free before
sending a message. If two messages are sent at the same time, a collision occurs. It is
detected and the messages have to be retransmitted when the network is free.

The network interface in each computer is watching all the messages being sent over
the network and waits if it detects a message being transmitted. When no traffic is
detected by the computer, any message awaiting transmission can then be sent. As it
is likely that several computers are waiting to transmit messages and that they will do
so at the same time, message corruption will result. The network interfaces detect this
corruption (or collision) and are designed to wait for a short time before trying again.
This staggers the load on the network.

Carrier Sense Multiple Access/Collision Detection (CSMA/CD) is a protocol for
implementing this process used on Ethernet local area networks. See also *token ring
network*, page 155.

ACK (Acknowledge) signal

is a signal sent back to the sender to confirm that a message has been received by the
next point in the communications link. It normally contains the sequence number from
the header of the message. See *sequence number,* page 311, and *header*, page 52.

Sequence number
including: Initial Sequence Number (ISN)
is a number attached to each part of a multi-part message to ensure that after transmission the message is assembled in the correct order.

Initial Sequence Number (ISN) is the first number used in a particular *TCP* connection (see *communications protocol*, page 306).

Public Telephone Operator (PTO)
is any provider of publicly available telephone service such as BT, Mercury, cable companies and cellular telephone companies.

Public Switched Telephone Network (PSTN)
is the traditional analog telephone network, which is being replaced by digital services which are elements of *ISDN* (integrated services digital network) (see page 306).

Very Small Aperture Terminal (VSAT)
is a satellite communication system using dishes less than 3 m in diameter. It is primarily for down-linking (receiving satellite transmissions), but it can be used for up-linking (transmission to satellites).

High Definition Television (HDTV)
is a proposed form of television transmission which will provide a wider picture of much clearer quality than present standards. HDTV transmission will require much greater bandwidth but data compression techniques will be possible. For the decompression of picture data, considerable computer processing power will be needed in HDTV receivers.

Video data compression
including: JPEG, delta compression, MPEG
is the use of electronic methods to reduce the amount of data that has to be included when video data, either for still or moving pictures, is stored or transmitted. For moving pictures (video), the principles involve identifying those parts of the picture which change from one scan to the next, and sending data only about the changes, which is known as *delta compression*. This alone will save a significant amount of transmission and storage capacity. Periodically a complete new whole picture will need to be sent. The Joint Photographic Expert Group (*JPEG*) has defined standards for still picture compression, and this format for storage or transmission is called JPEG. These standards have been extended by the Motion Picture Expert Group (*MPEG*) to cover moving images. These proposals are currently being used for video compression on CD-ROM, and the system is referred to as MPEG.

C18 Truth Tables and Logic Gates

Binary logic is important in computing because the truth values, True and False, can be represented as the binary digits 1 and 0. All integrated circuits are designed using Boolean logic. They respond to the binary patterns they receive and produce the required outputs as binary patterns. Binary logic influences not only the design of hardware, but also the design of algorithms and programming languages, for example the way a test such as "If the month is February *and* if it is a leap year" is programmed in a high-level language.

Boolean algebra
including: George Boole
is named after the mathematician *George Boole* (1815–1864) and is a set of rules for manipulating truth values according to truth tables.

Gate
is an electronic device to control the flow of signals. The output of a gate will depend on the input signal(s) and the type of gate. The components of a computer system can all be seen as combinations of a number of gates, each with a number of possible inputs and a single output. For details of gates see *logic gates* page 315.

Truth value
also known as: Boolean value
including: true, false
The truth values in Boolean algebra are True and False (abbreviated to T and F), often represented by the binary digits 1 and 0. In electronics, these are usually represented by different voltages.

Truth table
is a notation used in Boolean algebra for defining the output of a logic gate or logic circuit for all possible combinations of inputs. Examples can be found in the *logic gates*, page 315 and *logical equivalence and combination of gates*, page 320.

Logical equivalence
exists when two logic circuits have the same output(s) for given inputs. Two equivalent circuits will do the same thing even though their designs are different. One result of this is that it is possible to construct all logic circuits using only NAND gates or only NOR gates. This is very useful because it allows the use of a single form of component for a variety of purposes. See also *programmable logic array*, page 300. Some examples of logical equivalence are given in *logical equivalence and combination of gates*, page 320.

Karnaugh map

is a method of displaying and manipulating the relationships between Boolean operations. Karnaugh maps are mainly used to reduce logic expressions to their simplest form. They make use of the fact that all logic can be expressed as the 'AND' of 'ORs' or the 'OR' of 'ANDs'.

In the three-input logic table below, the rows for which the output is 1

represent the logic expression $A.B.C + A.B.\overline{C} + \overline{A}.B.\overline{C} + \overline{A}.\overline{B}.\overline{C}$

INPUT (A)	INPUT (B)	INPUT (C)	OUTPUT (P)
1	1	1	1
1	1	0	1
1	0	1	0
1	0	0	0
0	1	1	0
0	1	0	1
0	0	1	0
0	0	0	1

The Karnaugh map contains those elements for which the output is 1.

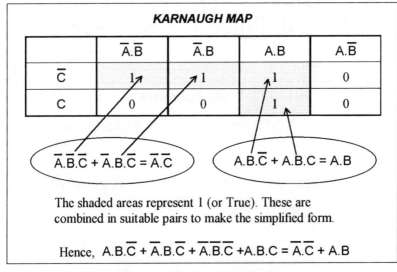

KARNAUGH MAP

	$\overline{A}.\overline{B}$	$\overline{A}.B$	$A.B$	$A.\overline{B}$
$\overline{C}$	1	1	1	0
C	0	0	1	0

$\overline{A}.\overline{B}.\overline{C} + \overline{A}.B.\overline{C} = \overline{A}.\overline{C}$ $A.B.\overline{C} + A.B.C = A.B$

The shaded areas represent 1 (or True). These are combined in suitable pairs to make the simplified form.

Hence, $A.B.\overline{C} + \overline{A}.B.\overline{C} + \overline{A}.\overline{B}.\overline{C} + A.B.C = \overline{A}.\overline{C} + A.B$

Figure C18.1: Karnaugh map

Venn diagram

is a way of representing the relationships between sets in diagrammatic form. There is
a close connection between set operations and logic operations. For example, in Figure
C18.2(a), below, the hatched area represents the set operation corresponding to
'XOR'. When the rules for manipulating Venn diagrams are known, it can be seen that
this diagram also establishes the logical equivalence

A XOR B = (A OR B) AND NOT (A AND B).

Figures C18.2 (b) and (c) illustrate the same relationships between the two sets.

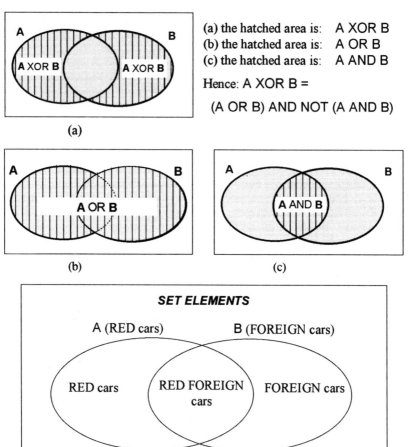

(a) the hatched area is: A XOR B
(b) the hatched area is: A OR B
(c) the hatched area is: A AND B

Hence: A XOR B =

(A OR B) AND NOT (A AND B)

(a)

(b)   (c)

SET ELEMENTS

A (RED cars)   B (FOREIGN cars)

RED cars   RED FOREIGN   FOREIGN cars
                cars

Figure C18.2: Venn diagrams

Logic symbol

is a symbol used to represent a logical operation. In addition to circles with words in
them, there are standard symbols which are conventionally used to denote logic
operations. These symbols are shown in *logic gates*, page 315.

LOGIC GATES

are the components used in making logic circuits. Each gate has one or more inputs and produces a single output which depends upon the input(s).

Some important simple logic gates are described below.

For each, the following information is given:

- the name of the gate
- a brief description of its function
- how it may be written (there are several notations in common use)
- its truth table (showing how the output changes with different inputs)
- how it may be represented in diagrams (there are several methods, some using different shaped boxes for different gates).

NOT gate

including: inverse, inverter

The output of a NOT gate is the *inverse* of its input. If the input is TRUE then the output is FALSE and if the input is FALSE then the output is TRUE.

NOT gates have only one input and one output.

A NOT gate is also known as an *inverter*.

It may be written as: P = NOT A

other notations express this as: P = $\overline{A}$, or P = ˜A

INPUT (A)	OUTPUT (P)
0	1
1	0

Figure C18.3: NOT gate

OR gate

The output of an OR gate is TRUE if any input is TRUE, otherwise the output is FALSE.

OR gates have two or more inputs and one output.

It may be written as: $P = A \text{ OR } B$

in other notations as: $P = A + B$ or $P = A \vee B$

INPUT (A)	INPUT (B)	OUTPUT (P)
0	0	0
0	1	1
1	0	1
1	1	1

Figure C18.4: OR gate

AND gate

The output of an AND gate is TRUE if all inputs are TRUE, otherwise the output is FALSE.

AND gates have two or more inputs and one output.

It may be written as: $P = A \text{ AND } B$

in other notations as: $P = A \cdot B$ or $P = A \wedge B$

INPUT (A)	INPUT (B)	OUTPUT (P)
0	0	0
0	1	0
1	0	0
1	1	1

Figure C18.5: AND gate

NOR gate

The output of a NOR gate is TRUE only if all inputs are FALSE, otherwise the output is FALSE.

NOR gates have two or more inputs and one output. They are important because all logic circuits can be constructed from NOR gates alone.

It may be written as: $P = A \text{ NOR } B$

in other notations as $P = \text{NOT} (A + B)$ or $P = \overline{A + B}$

It is equivalent to: $P = \text{NOT} (A \text{ OR } B)$

INPUT (A)	INPUT (B)	OUTPUT (P)
0	0	1
0	1	0
1	0	0
1	1	0

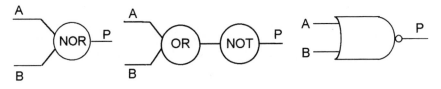

Figure C18.6: NOR gate

NAND gate

The output of a NAND gate is FALSE only if all inputs are TRUE, otherwise the output is TRUE.

NAND gates have two or more inputs and one output. They are important because all logic circuits can be constructed from NAND gates alone.

It may be written as: P = A NAND B

in other notations as   P = NOT (A.B)   or $P = \overline{A.B}$

It is equivalent to: P = NOT (A AND B)

INPUT (A)	INPUT (B)	OUTPUT (P)
0	0	1
0	1	1
1	0	1
1	1	0

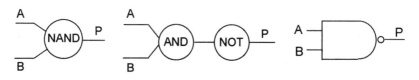

Figure C18.7: NAND gate

XOR (Exclusive-OR) gate

including: EOR gate, NEQ gate, non-equivalence gate

The output of an Exclusive-OR gate is TRUE if the two inputs are different, the output is FALSE if the inputs are alike.

XOR gates have only two inputs and one output.

The Exclusive-OR gate is also known as EOR gate or NEQ (Non-EQuivalence) gate.

It is written as: P = A XOR B   P = A EOR B

                   P = A NEQ B   or   P = A $\oplus$ B

INPUT (A)	INPUT (B)	OUTPUT (P)
0	0	0
0	1	1
1	0	1
1	1	0

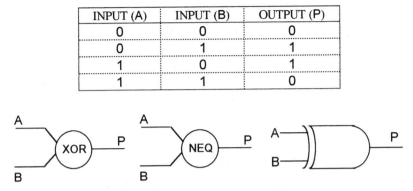

Figure C18.8: XOR or NEQ gate

XNOR (Exclusive-NOR) gate

including: EQ gate, equivalence gate

The output of an Exclusive-NOR gate is TRUE if the two inputs are the same, the output is FALSE if the inputs are different.

XNOR gates have only two inputs and one output.

The Exclusive-NOR gate is also known as EQ (EQuivalence) gate.

It is written as: P = A XNOR B   P = A EQ B

$$P = \overline{A \oplus B}$$

INPUT (A)	INPUT (B)	OUTPUT (P)
0	0	1
0	1	0
1	0	0
1	1	1

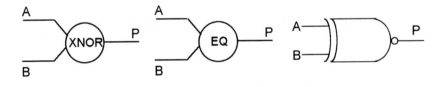

Figure C18.9: XNOR or EQ gate

LOGICAL EQUIVALENCE AND COMBINATION OF GATES

All logic circuits can be constructed in many different ways, using different combinations of gate circuits. In particular all logic circuits can be constructed using only NAND gates, or only NOR gates. Choosing the easiest, or cheapest, to make can influence the manufacture of computer circuits. The following examples are only a small set.

Equivalence for NOT logic

A NOT gate can be made by connecting together both inputs of a NAND gate:

INPUT (A)	A NAND A	NOT A
0	1	1
1	0	0

$$P = \overline{A.A} = \overline{A}$$

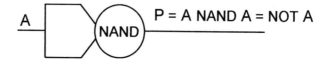

$$P = A \text{ NAND } A = \text{NOT } A$$

Figure C18.10: *A NAND A = NOT A*

A NOT gate can also be made by connecting together both inputs of a NOR gate:

INPUT (A)	A NOR A	NOT A
0	1	1
1	0	0

$$P = \overline{A + A} = \overline{A}$$

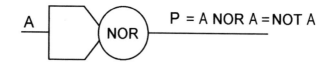

$$P = A \text{ NOR } A = \text{NOT } A$$

Figure C18.11: *A NOR A = NOT A*

Equivalence for AND logic

A AND B is equivalent to NOT (A NAND B):

INPUT (A)	INPUT (B)	A NAND B	NOT (A NAND B)	A AND B
0	0	1	0	0
0	1	1	0	0
1	0	1	0	0
1	1	0	1	1

$$P = A.B = \overline{\overline{A.B}}$$

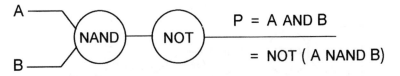

$$P = A \text{ AND } B$$
$$= \text{NOT (A NAND B)}$$

Figure C18.12: A AND B = NOT (A NAND B)

Equivalence for NOR logic

A NOR B is equivalent to (NOT A) AND (NOT B):

INPUT (A)	INPUT (B)	NOT A	NOT B	(NOT A) AND (NOT B)	A NOR B
1	1	0	0	0	0
1	0	0	1	0	0
0	1	1	0	0	0
0	0	1	1	1	1

$$P = \overline{A + B} = \overline{A}.\overline{B}$$

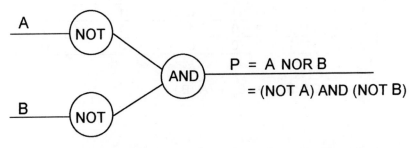

$$P = A \text{ NOR B}$$
$$= (\text{NOT A}) \text{ AND } (\text{NOT B})$$

Figure C18.13: A NOR B = (NOT A) AND (NOT B)

Equivalence for XOR logic

1) A XOR B is equivalent to (A OR B) AND NOT (A AND B):

A	B	A OR B	A AND B	NOT (A AND B)	(A OR B) AND NOT (A AND B)	A XOR B
1	1	1	1	0	0	0
1	0	1	0	1	1	1
0	1	1	0	1	1	1
0	0	0	0	1	0	0

$$P = A \text{ XOR } B = (A + B) \cdot \overline{(A \cdot B)}$$

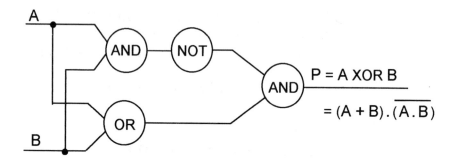

Figure C18.14: A XOR B = (A OR B) AND NOT (A AND B)

2) A XOR B is equivalent to (A AND NOT B) OR (B AND NOT A):

A	B	NOT A	NOT B	A AND NOT B	B AND NOT A	(A AND NOT B) OR (B AND NOT A)	A XOR B
1	1	0	0	0	0	0	0
1	0	0	1	1	0	1	1
0	1	1	0	0	1	1	1
0	0	1	1	0	0	0	0

$$P = A \text{ XOR } B = (A \cdot \overline{B}) + (\overline{A} \cdot B)$$

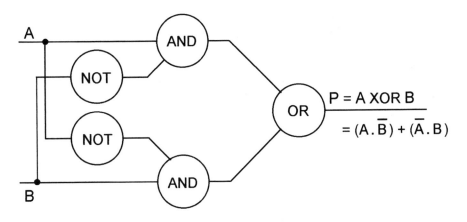

Figure C18.15: A XOR B = (A AND NOT B) OR (NOT A AND B)

3)   A XOR B can be constructed entirely from NAND gates

A	B	A NAND B (Q)	A NAND Q (R)	Q NAND B (S)	R NAND S (P)	A XOR B
1	1	0	1	1	0	0
1	0	1	0	1	1	1
0	1	1	1	0	1	1
0	0	1	1	1	0	0

$$P = A \text{ XOR } B = \overline{R.S} = \overline{\overline{A.Q}.\overline{Q.B}} = \overline{\overline{A.\overline{A.B}}.\overline{\overline{A.B}.B}}$$

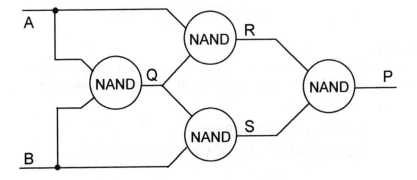

Figure C18.16: XOR circuit constructed from NAND gates

EXAMPLES OF STANDARD LOGIC NETWORKS

Half adder

The half adder can add two bits together to produce a sum output (SUM) and a carry output (Cout). See also *adder*, page 288.

These are defined as:

$$SUM = A \; XOR \; B$$

$$Cout = A \; AND \; B$$

bit A	bit B	Cout	SUM
1	1	1	0
1	0	0	1
0	1	0	1
0	0	0	0

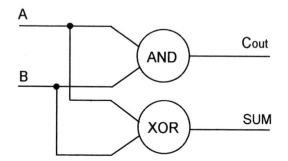

Figure C18.17: Half adder

Full adder

The full adder can add together two bits and a carry input (Cin) to produce a sum output (SUM) and a carry output (Cout). See also *adder*, page 288.

These are defined as:

$$SUM = (A \; XOR \; B) \; XOR \; Cin$$

$$Cout = (A \; AND \; B) \; OR \; (A \; AND \; Cin) \; OR \; (B \; AND \; Cin)$$

A	B	Cin	Cout	SUM
1	1	1	1	1
1	1	0	1	0
1	0	1	1	0
1	0	0	0	1
0	1	1	1	0
0	1	0	0	1
0	0	1	0	1
0	0	0	0	0

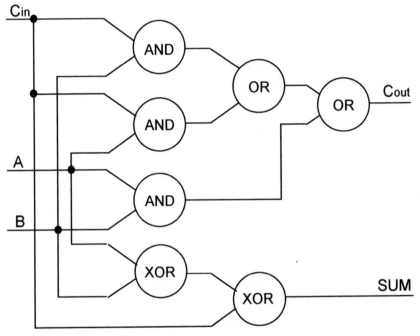

(a) constructed from individual gates

More helpfully, a full adder can be seen as a combination of two half adders.

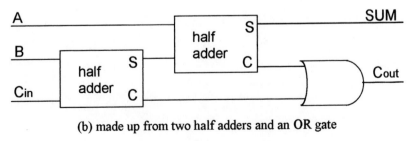

(b) made up from two half adders and an OR gate

Figure C18.18: *Full adder*

Decoder

A decoder circuit is used to select one of several inputs. Address lines are used to indicate the source to be selected. n address lines can handle 2^n sources (e.g. 2 address lines for 4 sources, 3 address lines for 8 sources).

$$P = \bar{A}.\bar{B}.S_0 + \bar{A}.B.S_1 + A.\bar{B}.S_2 + A.B.S_3$$

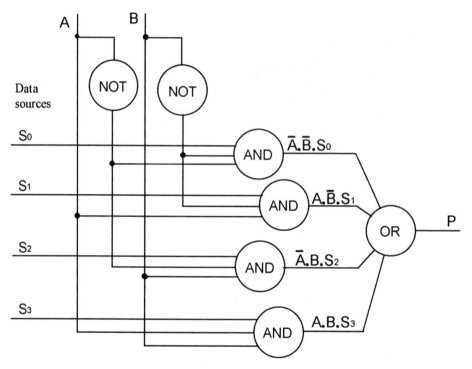

Figure C18.19: Decoder logic circuit

Address switching

A single source can be switched to one of several destinations by a logic network using address lines to indicate the destination.

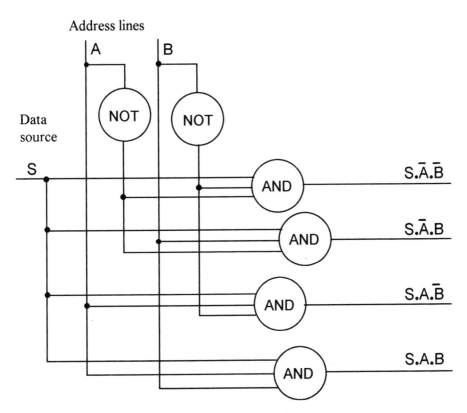

Figure C18.20: Address logic circuit

Part D
Appendices

One characteristic of modern life, and particularly any form of technological activity, is the use of abbreviations, acronyms and other 'jargon' by those who are involved in any specialised activity. This use of words, terms and acronyms when writing for or talking to others involved in the same activity can be a way of economically passing information between like minded people, but on the other hand it can also be a barrier to understanding for those who do not know the meanings of the strange new words. Computer users have always made great use of a vocabulary containing many abbreviations and acronyms. Over time this vocabulary has changed as new ideas are developed and old ones are no longer appropriate.

 No list would ever be complete or up-to-date, but in section D1 there is an extensive list of acronyms and abbreviations whose use is either commonplace throughout most computing activities or is specific to a particular aspect of computing. The list is alphabetic and includes many terms which are treated in the main body of the Glossary, for these terms the appropriate page references are given. For terms which have no page reference, the only information provided is the expansion of the acronym and, for some, an indication (in brackets) of the context in which they may be met.

D1　Acronyms and Abbreviations

Where a page number is given, it indicates where additional information can be found. Brackets are used to indicate the context in which the acronym or abbreviation may be met.

A-to-D	analog-to-digital	*163*
A/D	analog-to-digital	*163*
ACC	accumulator	*288*
ACIA	asynchronous communications interface adapter	
ACK	acknowledgement (ASCII character)	*310*
ACM	Association for Computing Machinery	
ADC	analog-to-digital converter	*163*
ADC/MPS	analog-to-digital/microprocessor system	
ADFS	advanced disk filing system	
ADSR	attack, decay, sustain, release (sound)	*64*
AFIPS	American Federation of Information Processing Societies	
AFS	Andrews' File System	*157*
AI	artificial intelligence	*76*
ALGOL	ALGOrithmic Language	*250*
ALU	arithmetic logic unit	*288*
AM	amplitude modulation (communications)	*308*
ANSI	American National Standards Institute	*252*
APL	A Programming Language	*250*
APT	automatically programmed tools (machine tool language)	
AQL	acceptable quality level	
ARP	address resolution protocol	*45*
ARPAnet	Advanced Research Projects Agency Network	*36*
ARQ	automatic repeat request	
ARU	audio response unit	
ASCII	American Standard Code for Information Interchange	*252*
ASIC	application specific circuit	
ASR	automatic send-receive	
AT	advanced technology (bus)	*295*
ATM	asynchronous transfer mode	
ATM	automatic teller machine	*51*
AUP	acceptable use policy	*103*
BA	bus available	
BABT	British Approvals Board for Telecommunications	
BASIC	Beginners All-purpose Symbolic Instruction Code	*250*
BBC	British Broadcasting Corporation	
BBS	bulletin board system	*50*
BCC	block check character	
BCD	binary coded decimal	*268*
BCS	British Computer Society	
BDOS	basic disk operating system	
BEAB	British Electrical Appliances Board	
BEL	bell (buzzer) (ASCII character)	
BiMOS	bipolar-MOS	
BIND	Berkeley internet domain software	
BIOS	basic input output system	*274*

bit	binary digit	*265*
BNF	Bachus-Naur form	*249*
bpi	bits per inch	*128*
BPP	bits per pixel	
bps	bits per second	*164*
BS	back space (ASCII character)	
BSI	British Standards Institution	
CAD	computer aided design	*26*
CAD	computer aided drafting	
CAD/CAM	computer aided design and manufacture	*53*
CAI	computer assisted instruction	
CAL	computer assisted learning	*74*
CAM	computer aided manufacture	*53*
CAN	cancel (ASCII character)	
CASE	computer aided software engineering	
CBT	computer based training	*74*
CCA	Central Computing Agency	
CCD	charge coupled device	
CCITT	Committée Consultatif International Téléphonique et Télégraphique	*43*
CCP	console command processor	
CCR	condition code register	
CD	compact disc	
CD-I	compact disc interactive	
CD-ROM	compact disc read-only memory	*130*
CDI	collector diffusion isolator	
CEG	Computer Education Group	
CEPIS	Confederation of European Professional Informatics Societies	
CGA	colour graphics adapter	*136*
CIR	current instruction register	
CISC	complex instruction set computer	*282*
CIX	commercial internet exchange	*106*
CMI	computer managed instruction	*74*
CML	computer managed learning	*74*
CMOS	complementary MOS	*128*
CMS	colour management system	*145*
CMYK	cyan, magenta, yellow, key (black)	*144*
CNC	computer numeric control	*54*
COBOL	COmmon Business Oriented Language	*250*
COM	computer output on microfilm	*117*
COMAL	COMmon Algorithmic Language	
CP gate	comparator-gate (=XOR)	
CP/M	control program for microcomputers	
CPM	control program monitor	
CPE	central processing element	
cps	characters per second	*164*
CPU	central processing unit	*281*
CR	carriage return (ASCII character)	
CR/LF	carriage return/line feed	
CRC	cyclic redundancy check	
CROM	control ROM	
CRT	cathode ray tube	
CSCD	carrier sense collision detection	
CSCW	computer supported co-operative work	*50*
CSMA/CD	carrier sense multiple access collision detection	*310*
CSV	comma separated variables (file)	*262*

CTRL or Ctrl	control (ASCII character)
CTS	clear to send
CUA	common user access *280*
CUG	closed user group *51*
CWP	communicating word processors
CYMK	cyan, yellow, magenta, key(black) *144*
D-to-A	digital-to-analog *163*
DAC	data acquisition and control
DAC	digital-to-analog converter *163*
DAT	digital audio tape
DBA	database administrator
DBMS	database management system *20*
DBS	direct broadcast by satellite
DCD	data carrier detect (communications)
DCE	data communications equipment
DCS	telephone data carrier system
DD	double density *128*
DDE	direct data entry *3*
DDL	data description language
DDN	Defense Data Network
DEL	delete (ASCII character)
DES	data encryption standard *57*
DFD	data flow diagram *177*
DFS	disk filing system
DIB	data input bus
DIL	dual in line *94*
dil	dual in-line *94*
DIN	Deutsche Industrienorm *300*
DIP	dual in-line package *94, 300*
DLE	data link escape (ASCII character)
DLT	digital linear technology
DMA	direct-memory access *284/5*
DML	data manipulation language *248*
DoD	Department of Defense (US)
DOS	disk operating system *272*
DP	data processing *2*
dpi	dots per inch *144*
DRAM	dynamic random access memory *128*
DSR	data set ready
DSS	decision support system *6*
DSW	device status word
DTE	data terminal equipment
DTL	diode-transistor logic
DTP	desk top publishing *10*
DTR	data terminal ready
E-mail	electronic mail *38*
EA	extended addressing
EAN	European article number *3*
EAROM	electronically alterable read only memory *129*
EB disk	electronic book disk *130*
EBCDIC	extended binary coded decimal interchange code *252/3*
EBR	electron beam recording
ECD	electrochromeric display
ECL	emitter-coupled logic
ECMA	European Computer Manufacturers Association *226*

EDP	electronic data processing	
EDS	exchangeable disk storage	
EEPROM	electrically erasable PROM	*129*
EFT	electronic funds transfer	*51*
EFTPOS	electronic funds transfer at point of sale	*51*
EGA	enhanced graphics adapter	*136*
EIA	Electrical Industries Association (USA)	
EISA	extended industry standard architecture	*295*
EM	end of message (ASCII character)	
EM character	end-of-medium character (ASCII character)	
Email	electronic mail	*38*
EMI	electro-magnetic interference	*310*
ENQ	enquiry (ASCII character)	
EOF	end of file	*259*
EOM	end-of-message	
EOR	exclusive-OR	*318*
EOT	end of transmission (ASCII character)	
EPOS	electronic point-of-sale	
EPROM	erasable programmable read-only memory	*129*
EPS	encapsulated postscript	
EQ	equal	
EQ	equivalence	*319*
ESC	escape (ASCII character)	
ESDI	enhanced systems drive interface	
ETB	end of text block (ASCII character)	
ETX	end of text (= end of last block) (ASCII character)	
FAM	fast access memory	
FAQ	Frequently asked question	*41*
FAST	Federation against software theft	*107*
FAT	file allocation table	*131*
FAX	facsimile	*49*
FD	floppy disk	
FDD	floppy disk drive	
FDDI	fibre distributed data interface	*152/4*
FDM	frequency division multiplexing (communications)	*160*
FET	field effect transistor	
FETMOS	field effect transistor metal-oxide-semiconductor	
FF	form feed (ASCII character)	
FFT	fast fourier transform	
FIFO	first in, first out	*258*
FM	frequency modulation (sound, communications)	*63, 308*
FORTRAN	FORmula TRANslation	*250*
FPA	floating-point accelerator	*286*
FPU	floating-point unit	
FROM	fusible ROM	
FS	file separator (ASCII character)	
FSK	frequency shift keying	
FSM	frequency shift modulation	
ftp	file transfer protocol	*39*
G	giga	*340*
Gb	giga byte	
GDU	graphical display unit	*137*
GIF	graphics interchange format	*44*
GIGO	garbage-in garbage-out	
GND	ground (connection)	

GPIB	general purpose interface bus	
GPR	general purpose register	
GS	group separator (ASCII character)	
GUI	graphical user interface	*80*
HCI	human-computer- interaction/interface	*80*
HD	high density	*128*
HDD	high density disk	*128*
HDTV	high definition television	*311*
HEX	hexadecimal	*269*
HMOS	high-performance metal-oxide-semiconductor	
HRG	high resolution graphics	*134/5*
HT	horizontal tabulation (ASCII character)	
HTML	HyperText mark-up language	*40*
http	HyperText transfer protocol	*40*
Hz	hertz	
I/O	input/output	*115*
IAB	Internet Architecture Board	*43*
IAM	immediate access memory	*121*
IAR	instruction address register	*283*
IAS	immediate access store	*121*
IC	integrated circuit	*298*
ICMP	Internet control message protocol	*45*
ICT	information and communications technology	*6*
ID	identification	*104*
IDE	integrated (or intelligent)device electronics	*297*
IEE	Institute of Electrical Engineers (UK)	
IEEE	Institute of Electronic and Electrical Engineers (USA)	*296*
IFIP	International Federation for Information Processing	
IGFET	insulated gate field effect transistor	
IIL	integrated injection logic	
IKBS	intelligent knowledge based system	*77*
IO	input/output	*115*
IOP	input/output processor	
IORQ	input/output request line	
IP	Internet protocol or Internetworking protocol	*42, 303*
IPL	initial program loader	
IR	index register	
IR	infra red	
IR	instruction register	
IRC	Internet relay chat	*41*
IS	information systems	
ISA	industry standard architecture	*295*
ISAM	index sequential access method	*190*
ISBN	international standard book number	*3*
ISD	international subscriber dialling	
ISDN	integrated services digital network	*306*
ISM	industry structure model	*98*
ISM	information systems manager	*98*
ISN	initial sequence number	*311*
ISO	International Standards Organisation	*304*
ISP	Internet service provider	*42*
ISR	interrupt service routine	
IT	Information Technology	*6*
ITDM	intelligent time-division multiplexing	*160*
ITU	International Telecommunications Union	*43*

JANET	Joint Academic Network	36
JCL	job control language	278/9
JFET	junction field effect transistor	
JPEG	joint photographic expert group	311
JSD	Jackson structured design	170
JSP	Jackson structure programming	170
K	kilo	340
Kb	kilo-bit, kilo-byte	
KBS	knowledge based system	77
LA	linear arithmetic (sound)	63
LAN	local area network	151
LCD	liquid crystal display	138
LED	light emitting diode	138
LEO	Lyons Electronic Office	112
LF	line feed (ASCII character)	
LIFO	last in, first out	257
Lisp	LISt Processing	250
LPT	(line) printer	
LQ	letter quality	144
LRC	longitudinal redundancy check	
LSB	least significant bit	265
LSI	large scale integration	298/9
M	mega	340
m	milli	340
MAR	memory address register	283
Mb	mega byte	
MBR	memory buffer register	283
MCA	micro channel architecture	295
MDA	monochrome display adapter	136
MDR	memory data register	283
MHS	message handling system	
MICR	magnetic ink character recognition	116/7
MIDI	music instrument digital interface	65
MIME	multi-purpose internet mail extender	40
MIPS	million instructions per second	287
MIS	management information system	6
MMI	man-machine interface/interaction	80
MMU	memory management unit	284
MNP	Microcom network protocol	306
modem	modulator/demodulator	160
MOS	machine operating system	
MOS	metal-oxide-semiconductor	128
MOSFET	metal-oxide-semiconductor field effect transistor	
MPEG	motion picture expert group	311
MPS	microprocessor system	
MPU	microprocessor unit	
MPX	multiplex	
MREQ	memory request	
ms	millisecond	
MS-DOS	Microsoft DOS	272
MSB	most significant bit	265
MSD	most significant digit	
MSI	medium scale integration	298/9
MTBF	mean time between failures	
MTF	mean-time to failure	

MTU	maximum transmission unit	*303*
MUG	multi-user game	*43*
MUX	multiplexor	*160*
n	nano	*340*
NAK	negative acknowledgement (ASCII character)	
NAND	Not AND	*318*
NEQ	Not Equivalent	*318*
NFS	network filing system	*157*
NLQ	near letter quality	*144*
NMI	non-maskable interrupt	
NMOS	n-channel metal-oxide-semiconductor	
NOR	Not OR	*317*
ns	nanosecond	
NSFNET	National Science Foundation Network	*36*
NTSC	National Television Standards Committee (USA)	
NUL	null (do nothing)	
OCR	optical character recognition	*116/7*
OEM	original equipment manufacturer	*117*
OLE	object linking and embedding	*171*
OLR	off line reader	*42*
OMR	optical mark reader	*116*
OOD	object-oriented design	*171*
OOL	object-oriented language	*171*
OOP	object-oriented program(ming)	*171*
OS	operating system	*272*
OSI	open systems interchange	*304*
OV	overflow	*193*
p	pico	*340*
PABX	private automatic branch exchange	*160*
PAL	phase alternating line	*138*
PBX	private branch exchange	*160*
PC	personal computer (IBM-PC compatible)	*110*
PC	program counter	
PC-DOS	personal computer disk operating system	*272*
PCB	printed circuit board	
PCI	peripheral component interconnect	
PCI	programmable communications interface	*295*
PCM	pulse-code modulation	*308*
PCMCIA	personal computer memory card international association	*296*
PD	phase distortion (sound)	*63*
PDA	personal digital assistant	*110*
PDM	pulse duration modulation	
PIA	peripheral interface adapter	
PID	personal identification device	*104*
PILOT	Programmed Inquiry, Learning Or Teaching (language)	
PIN	personal identification number	*104*
PING	packet internet groper	*47*
PIO	parallel input/output	
PIXEL	picture element	*135*
PL/1	Programming Language 1	*250*
PLA	programmable logic array	*300*
PLC	programmable logic circuit	
PMOS	p-channel metal-oxide-semiconductor	
PNG	portable network graphics	*44*
PoP	point of presence	*46*

POP3	Post Office protocol 3	*45*
POS	point of sale	*156*
ppm	pages per minute	
PPP	point to point protocol	*45*
PRN	printer	
PROLOG	PROgramming in LOGic	*248, 250*
PROM	programmable read-only memory	*129*
PRR	pulse repetition rate	
PRT	program reference table	
PSN	packet switching network	
PSS	packet switching system	*303*
PSTN	public switched telephone network	*311*
PSU	power supply unit	
PSU	program storage unit	
PSW	program/processor status word	
PTO	public telephone operator	*311*
QBE	query by example	*247*
QD	quad density (disks)	
QIC	quarter-inch cartridge	
QWERTY	conventional typewriter keyboard	
R/W	read/write	
RAID	redundant array of independent (or inexpensive) disks	*123*
RAM	random access memory	*128*
RD	read	
RDBMS	relational database management system	
REM	remark(s)	
REN	ring equivalent number	
RF	radio frequency	
RFC	request for comment	
RFI	radio frequency interference	*310*
RGB	red green blue	*138*
RI	ring in	
RISC	reduced instruction set computer	*282*
RJE	remote job entry	*279*
ROM	read-only memory	*129*
RPG	report program generator	*248, 250*
RS	record separator (ASCII character)	
RSA	Rivest, Shamir, Adleman (algorithm)	*58*
RTF	revisable or rich text format(file)	*262*
RTL	resistor-transistor logic	
RTS	request to send	
SAA	systems applications architecture	*280*
SAR	store address register	
SBC	single board computer	
SCR	sequence control register	*283*
SCSI	small computer systems interface	*296*
SDR	store data register	
SHF	super high frequency	
SI	shift in (ASCII character)	
SIC	silicon integrated circuit	
SID	standard interchangeable data (file)	*262*
SIMM	single in-line memory module	
SIMS	Schools Information Management System	
Simula	SIMULAtion	*250*
SIO	serial input/output (controller)	

SLIP	serial line Internet protocol	*45*
SLSI	super large scale integration	
SMPTE	Society of Motion Picture and TV Engineers	*70*
SMTP	simple mail transport protocol	*45*
SNA	network architecture	*280*
SNOBOL	StriNg Oriented SymBolic Language	*250*
SO	shift out (ASCII character)	
SOH	start of header (ASCII character)	
SOS	silicon on sapphire	
SOT	start of text (ASCII character)	
SP	stack pointer	
SQA	software quality assurance	
SQL	structured query language	*247*
SSADM	structured systems analysis and design method	*173*
SSI	small scale integration	*298/9*
STD	subscriber trunk dialling	
STX	start of text (ASCII character)	
SUB	substitute (ASCII character)	
SVGA	super video graphics array	*136*
SWR	status word register	
SYN	synchronisation character (ASCII character)	
sysop	system operator	*50*
TCP	transmission control protocol	*306*
TCP/IP	transmission control protocol/internet protocol	*45*
TDM	time division multiplexing (communications)	*160/1*
TEMP	temporary	
TLA	three letter acronym	*40*
TP	teleprocessing	*172*
TP	transaction processing	
TP	twisted pair	*162*
TPA	transient program area	
TPI	tracks per inch	
TRL	transistor-resistor logic	
TSV	tab separated variables (file)	*262*
TTL	transistor-transistor logic	
UART	universal asynchronous receiver/transmitter	
UDP/IP	user datagram protocol/Internet protocol	*45*
UHF	ultra high frequency	
UJT	unijunction transistor	
ULA	uncommitted logic array	*300*
UPC	universal product code	*3*
UPS	uninterruptable power supply	
URL	uniform resource locator	*41*
US	unit separator (ASCII character)	
USART	universal synchronous/asynchronous receiver/transmitter	
USRT	universal synchronous receiver/transmitter	
UTP	unshielded twisted pair	*162*
UUCP	UNIX to UNIX copy protocol	*45*
UV	ultra violet	
VAN	value added network	*158*
VANS	value added network service	*158*
VDG	video display generator	
VDT	video display terminal	
VDU	visual display unit	
VESA	Video Electronics Standards Association	*295*

VGA	video graphics array	*136*
VHF	very high frequency	
VLSI	very large scale integration	*298/9*
VM	virtual memory	*132, 285*
VMOS	vertical-current-flow metal-oxide semiconductor	
VR	virtual reality	*33*
VRAM	volatile read only memory	*137*
VRML	virtual reality mark-up language	*45*
VRR	vertical refresh rate	*137*
VSAT	very small aperture terminal	*311*
VT	vertical tabulation (ASCII character)	
WAIS	wide area information server	*44*
WAN	wide area network	*151*
WIMP	windows icons mouse pointer	*80*
WORM	write once, read many	*130*
WP	word processing	*9*
WR	write	
WS	working store	
WWW	World Wide Web	*37*
WYSIWYG	what you see is what you get	*13*
XGA	extended graphics array	*136*
XNOR	exclusive-NOR	*319*
XOR	exclusive-OR	*318*
ZIF	zero insertion force	*300*
4GL	fourth generation language	*246*

D2 Units

Symbol	Prefix	Meaning	Decimal	Power of ten
T	tera	one million million	1 000 000 000 000	10^{12}
G	giga	one thousand million	1 000 000 000	10^{9}
M	mega	one million	1 000 000	10^{6}
K	kilo	one thousand	1 000	10^{3}
		one	1	10
m	milli	one thousandth (1/1 000)	0. 001	$10^{-3} = 1/10^{3}$
μ	micro	one millionth (1/1 000 000)	0. 000 001	$10^{-6} = 1/10^{6}$
n	nano	one thousand-millionth (1/1 000 000 000)	0. 000 000 001	$10^{-9} = 1/10^{9}$
p	pico	one million-millionth (1/1 000 000 000 000)	0.000 000 000 001	$10^{-12} = 1/10^{12}$

In computer storage terms, the symbols K, M, G and T have particular values related to the powers of 2, not to the powers of 10:

K is $2^{10} = 1\,024$, thus 8K bytes of store is $8 \times 2^{10} = 8\,192$ bytes

M is $2^{20} = 1\,048\,576$, thus 4Mbytes (4Mb) is $4 \times 2^{20} = 4\,194\,304$ bytes

G is $2^{30} = 1\,073\,741\,824$, thus 60 Giga-bytes (60 Gb) is $60 \times 2^{30} =$
$$64\,424\,509\,440 \text{ bytes}$$

T is $2^{40} = 1\,099\,511\,627\,776$, thus 2 Tera-bytes (2 Tb) is $2 \times 2^{40} =$
$$2\,199\,023\,255\,552 \text{ bytes}$$

Tables and Figures

Index